man vs. toddler

By Matt Coyne and available from Wildfire

Dummy: The Comedy and Chaos of Real-Life Parenting
Man vs. Toddler: The Trials and Triumphs of Toddlerdom

man vs. toddler

The trials and triumphs of toddlerdom

Matt Coyne

WILDFIRE

First published in 2019
by WILDFIRE
An imprint of HEADLINE PUBLISHING GROUP

1

Cataloguing in Publication Data is available from the British Library

Hardback ISBN 978 1 4722 4506 9
Trade Paperback ISBN 978 1 4722 5393 4

All images courtesy of Matt Coyne

Typeset in 10.5/16.75 pt Avenir LT Std by Jouve (UK), Milton Keynes

Printed and bound in Great Britain by Clays Ltd, Elcograf S.p.A.

MIX
Paper from
responsible sources
FSC® C104740

Headline's policy is to use papers that are natural, renewable and recyclable
products and made from wood grown in well-managed forests and other
controlled sources. The logging and manufacturing processes are expected
to conform to the environmental regulations of the country of origin.

HEADLINE PUBLISHING GROUP
An Hachette UK Company
Carmelite House
50 Victoria Embankment
London EC4Y 0DZ

www.headline.co.uk
www.hachette.co.uk

For Charlie and Lyns

Contents

Preface

As a parent, perhaps the biggest adjustment you will ever have to make is this:

To a baby you are omnipotent, you are all-giving, all-powerful, all-knowing, all-benevolent.

YOU. ARE. GOD.

To a toddler . . . you're staff.

Introduction

Introduction

So, the first book did really well. Which is great. But it's probably best not to get too carried away. Yes, it was a bestseller but so is heroin, the first Color Me Badd album and Vagisil.

The really good thing about that book being successful, though, is that I got asked to write another one . . . and so here we are.

Of course, everyone knows that sequels are usually shit. For every *Godfather Part II* there is a *Speed 2: Cruise Control* or a *Piranha 3DD*. So with this in mind, I would encourage you not to see this book as a sequel but as a continuation. Part two of an epic and ongoing heroic saga, if you will, rather like *Lord of the Rings* but with fewer wizards and no one getting fucked up by an orc.

Dummy covered the first year of Charlie's life and my first year as a parent. And whilst doing promotion for that book I would occasionally be approached by parents of older children. Often cutting quite a haunted figure, they would explain that they had read *Dummy* and, whilst they enjoyed it, they believed the book to be fundamentally flawed. They explained that parenting a newborn is actually the easy bit and that I was a fool to think that the first year was in any way the hardest or the most chaotic. After all, we still had **the toddler years** to come.

We'd laugh and chat for a while and the conversation would move on. But then when the time came for us to part, they would fall quiet, take me by the arms, fix me with a hard stare and with mystery and dark menace they would utter three simple words:

Just.

You.

Wait.

They would then throw an arm of their cloak across their face, throw a smoke bomb at their own feet and disappear backwards into the fog.

'Mm. That's weird,' I thought.

It goes without saying that I never took these warnings seriously and not just because I'm an idiot. Experienced parents are like the Princess Cassandra of Greek mythology. Cassandra had the 'breath of Apollo on her' and was cursed to be able to see into the future but never be believed about what she saw. It's the same with the parents who go before us. We choose to ignore them and their hard-won experience and opt to live in blissful denial of what is to come. New mums and dads are nothing if not ostriches.

So disbelieve these Cassandras I did. And not just that, I scoffed. After all, 'How the fuck could looking after a toddler be harder than looking after a baby?' I reasoned. Toddlers sleep, don't they? Some of them even feed themselves. Often they can walk, so you don't have to carry them around everywhere like a fucking pet log. The really good ones don't shit their pants and even dress themselves. Apparently, some of them even talk. 'It'll be nice to have a new, younger person's perspective around the house,' I imagined.

Yes, it all sounded rather civilised.

Except it isn't.

In reality, looking after a toddler is about as civilised as living in a bin and surviving by drinking your own piss. It turns out that toddlers are, in fact, *destroyers* of civilised life.

From the Romans to the Aztecs, the greatest of civilisations have been brought to their knees by sudden change and your personal civilisation is no different. From hygiene to time-keeping, all the trappings of an ordered life are brought crashing to ignominy by sharing your life with a small child.

And it is the suddenness with which your baby becomes a toddler that catches you off guard. It seems instantaneous. It is as though one day you wake up and that simple, calm, placid, burbling bundle of dependence has gone and in its place someone has left a box on your doorstep. You take that box into your living room, unwrap it with care and excitement only to find that inside is a short, drunk arsehole . . . who now lives with you.

The comparison between a toddler and that mate you had at college who was a complete dick when they were drunk is a fair one.

Both are destructive, rude, crazy and prone to peaks and troughs of wild emotion. They are quick to anger and slow to back down from a scrap. They think themselves invincible, invulnerable to danger, whether it's from road traffic or falls from a height. They both slur their few words, fall over all the time and don't always have exemplary bowel control. They pass out in random places. They have rubbish coordination. No impulse control. And little sense of shame. They hurt themselves all the time. They remove their trousers for no good reason. Their decision-making skills are shit. And when the mood takes them . . . they really, really want to fight you.

In truth, you could drop the average toddler into a kebab house in Newcastle at closing-time on a Saturday night and they would fit right in. The only thing that would give them away would be their height and their Gruffalo jimjams.

The main problem with a toddler being just like a terrible pisshead, is that the parent is forced to fulfil the role of 'sober friend'. Which is, of course, the most thankless task in the world. You must pick them up when they fall over, make sure they eat and replace their drink when they drop it (again). Keep them safe when they want to climb scaffolding or take their clothes off in inappropriate places. You must stop them from starting a fight in the soft play (because another kid has nicked a particular plastic ball), defusing the situation by stepping between the two hotheads with a: 'Leave it, Keith, he's not worth it, mate.' You must take them home when they don't want to go home and, whether they like it or not, get them to bed, safe and sound.

In essence, it is your job to get your kid through the wild city-centre of childhood and into the taxi of adulthood in one piece, without them being hurt or causing significant criminal damage.

So toddlers are like drunks and a parent is the designated driver. But here is where the comparison falls apart. This is not just one Friday night, this is our daily existence. From common assault to lewd behaviour, toddlers can commit seven arrestable offences before breakfast. Their destructive impulses and lack of respect and shame is not fuelled by drink but by the essence of what and who

6

they are. And dealing with that every day can feel relentless and tough.

But there is another side to our drunk arsehole mate . . . is there not? And it is here where we find the toddler too.

They can make you laugh until your jaw and stomach hurt. They can be crazy in a way that makes you marvel at the imagination. They don't dance like no one is watching, they dance like **everyone** is watching and they just don't give a fuck. They sing too. Not even words, sometimes not even a tune, but they sing anyway, just for the sake of singing.

They stumble. They fall. They repeat. Because, so what?

They tell tall tales and are not just open to new experiences, they demand them. Yes they fight, but that's because they are capable of a passion that as adults we seldom muster and they feel that way about almost everything. They embrace foolishness and wear it like a happy, bright coat. But they can also be kind and sensitive and desperate to let you know how much you mean to them.

And in this mess and in this madness, they do something that is at the heart of what it means to be human.

They create stories

*

Oh, one other thing.

If you are the parent of a newborn, a pre-toddler, reading this with scepticism; if you are in those first few months of parenthood and finding it impossible to imagine how it gets more insane, more chaotic, more life-changing; if you are, like I was, naively looking to the future as though this parenting stuff must surely get easier . . . I have only one thing to say:

Just.

You.

Wait.

1
What is a Toddler?

I was chatting to someone the other day and alongside her was her little boy, fast asleep in his pushchair. I asked how old he was and she answered 'eighteen months' and then began to wonder out loud if that meant he was now a toddler or whether he was still a baby.

I looked at the woman. I noticed that her shoes were on the correct feet and her fingernails weren't bitten down to the knuckles. I noticed that her hair didn't have sugar puffs or gob in it. She seemed sane, lucid and had the calm air of a person who was finding parenting to be something that came easily, naturally and as its own reward.

I pointed to her little boy.

'That there is a baby.'

What is a Toddler?

The lifecycle of a child is one of nature's great wonders and the transition from baby to toddler is a remarkable thing. Comparable in many ways to that of the caterpillar and the butterfly.

The caterpillar, just like the human baby, is a simple creature; unsophisticated and driven by instinct. But then suddenly it is transformed into something else. A thing unrecognisable, capable of much more than its previous incarnation. Interesting, busy, complex, capable of tapping your heart with its beauty. Able to fly.

The newborn is just such a miracle waiting to happen. Like that caterpillar, a baby is the simplest of things. A creature driven only by instinct, until one day that infant child undergoes a metamorphosis and transforms into something else, something more: a slightly taller child that walks, talks, smashes the place up and shits in a small plastic bucket in the middle of your living room.

A toddler.

But what is a toddler? At what point does a baby become a toddler? And why can they be such dicks about everything? These might seem like simple questions. But they are not questions to be taken lightly. There is great responsibility that comes with writing a book on parenting. It's important that you approach these things with diligence, that your research is extensive and fact-checked, that the whole thing is approached with intellectual rigour.

[*fires up Google*]

So, after a solid sixteen minutes of research on the internet (only half of which was spent watching this video of a guy playing the

20th Century Fox theme tune on an arse-flute: https://www.youtube.com/watch?v=QZ96KL2p-YM), here's what I discovered:

1. It's possible to play a flute using just your arsehole
2. Not everyone agrees about what a toddler actually is

It should be simple. The word 'toddler' comes from the verb 'to toddle', which means to walk, 'but to be quite shit at it'. Okay, that seems straightforward enough: a baby, then, becomes a toddler when they start walking, when they stop humping the floor and start strolling about the gaff, winking and giving you the finger guns. Well, not exactly.

We stumble, once more, into the ever-recurring problem with professional parenting opinion: experts disagree about even this. Whilst some argue that a baby becomes a toddler as soon as they stand up and take a step, others contend that it is when they reach the age of two or begin to talk. Still others insist it is when they begin to display emotion, express likes and dislikes, or start losing their shit and headbutting you in the teeth because their socks aren't their favourite shade of 'lellow'.

Whatever the case, it seems defining a toddler is not that straightforward and knowing exactly when your baby has become one is unclear. So, how **do** you know if your caterpillar has become a butterfly? How do you know if you are now the owner of an actual fully-fledged toddler?

Well, here are five clear indicators:

Indicators that your baby is now a toddler No. 1: You start to give their age in years

A good way to tell if your baby has become a toddler is the way you respond to questions about how old they are.

Parents of babies give the age of their little one in weeks and months, like they are a cheese or they're doing a stretch in prison. But there comes a time when you can no longer be arsed to keep track of how long they've been on the planet with quite such accuracy. And so parents of toddlers, without really noticing they're doing it, start ageing their children in years (or, if you're mad keen, half-years). This is one of the differences between babies and toddlers that is to be welcomed and embraced as soon as possible.

Compare these two examples:

Example 1:	Example 2:
'How old is he?' *'Well . . . he was twenty-seven months, three weeks and four days last Tuesday.'*	*'How old is he?'* *'Two, Janet. He's two.'*

As you can see, example 2 is far easier to work out and remember than example 1. And making your life as simple as you can should be a toddler-parent's guiding principle. (The last thing you need is old ladies stopping you in the post office and throwing maths questions at you.)

There are other reasons why it makes sense to move to this simpler ageing system. For a start – and I can't stress this enough – no one cares. It's true. No one cares how old your kid is. Certainly not with that kind of precision anyway. Asking the age of your little one is a polite question not a genuine enquiry. It's like when someone asks 'How are you?' they mean generally speaking. They don't want to hear about your persistent thrush, or that you're fine but your brother Malcolm has got an appointment at the hospital to go and have the 'camera up'.

The response 'He/she is two' is fine.

Also, if your kid is older than two and you're still giving their age in months and weeks, stop it. You sound like fucking Rain Man. And beyond the age of two, knowing the exact amount of time elapsed since your child was born makes the rest of us look bad.

Besides all this, at some point you **have** to stop with the 'weeks and months thing' anyway, otherwise:

'Hey, Barbara, your eldest has just gone off to college, hasn't he, how old is he now?'

'Oh, he's 234 months, 4 weeks and 3 days. But, it seems like only yesterday that he was 39 months and 17 weeks.'

'Okeydokey, Barbara. Anyway, nice to see you. Give my best to Malcolm. I'm going to have to get on because you're boring my tits off.'

So there you go. If you're a normal parent and you notice that you have stopped giving your child's age like you're a supercomputer calculating pi, then congratulations, that's a pretty good first sign that they have achieved toddlerhood.

Indicators that your baby is now a toddler No. 2: Your house is barely standing

There's this comet that passes Earth every now and again called 109P. It's better known as the Swift–Tuttle comet. Scientists keep an eye on it because it is a planet-destroyer and each time it passes it has a 0.0002 per cent chance of striking Earth. It's twenty-seven miles across, larger than the one that killed the dinosaurs. Even a near miss would cause untold destruction as a dust cloud would cover the Earth. Animals would die off, plants wouldn't grow and civilisation would be decimated, as in the devastation every corner of the Earth would be left utterly uninhabitable for humans.

And I'm confident that if this were to happen, the only area of the planet that would not look any different is our living room. A space that still hasn't recovered from the events of two weeks ago when Charlie's nannan gave him a full tube of smarties, a can of coke and a foam sword.

Take a look at your house right now. If you're at home and read-ing these pages, glance up. Does it look like the show home you envisioned when you moved in? Does it look like it should be gracing the pages of a lifestyle magazine? Is it a sophisticated, min-imalist, tidy and ordered sanctuary?

Or does it appear to be a disgrace. Like a herd of wildebeest have been gangbanging in a field of landmines?

If this sounds more like what you see when you look up from these words, then the chances are you now share your living space with a toddler. Obviously, a house with a baby in it has its own mini-brand of anarchy and disorder. But if babies are a hand grenade, a toddler is a warhead. Their destructive force is biblical by comparison.

Like most parents, we'd kind of got used to the mess and clutter that comes with having a newborn. A baby needs lots of stuff. Also, the attention they demand means that you don't have time to carry out the day-to-day upkeep that the average home needs, and so standards lower to cheerful slum conditions. But, the thing about babies is that they don't actively smash the place up just for a laugh. It's one of a baby's finest qualities, they just don't have the inclin-ation, motivation or upper-body strength to fuck shit up like toddlers do. I love that about babies.

Babies create mess without intent. But for toddlers it is their purpose. It is their calling. They have guiding principles about mess, an unwritten constitution, a manifesto of sorts: it is their life's work to destroy. To make any living space look like a city under siege. They are rioters, looters, anarchists and vandals, and your attempts to police their behaviour are pathetic because . . . 'fuck da po-lice'.

It is as though they are only comfortable in a space that looks recently burgled. And so they fashion chaos like an interior designer who has had a psychotic break. They crayon vague cocks on the walls and paint the TV with Sudocrem and Nutella. And do not tell me this is not deliberate. This is a picture of Charlie's chalkboard.

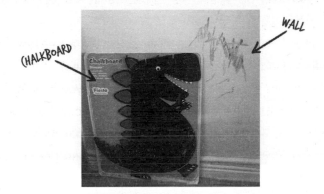

(Seriously . . . what is wrong with this kid? The chalkboard is right there. You can't miss it. It's shaped like a bloody dinosaur. It's Right. Fucking. There.)

When they are not expressing their artistic freedom, toddlers are expressing their artistic temperament. When the mood takes them, they can wreck a room in a matter of minutes. Emptying drawers, cupboards, bookshelves, recycling bins, laundry baskets and anything else they can find to deconstruct. Spilling the contents of their multiple toy boxes until every inch of the floor has disappeared and you are up to your ankles in plasticky crap. And they season this destruction with a sprinkling of forgotten drawings, half-eaten biscuits, discarded clothes, leaking sippee cups and mashed-up banana. Until your home doesn't look just untidy, it looks as though a giant bastard has picked it up, turned it upside down, shaken it and then gone striding over the horizon giving you the giant finger.

Toddlers are relentless in this pursuit of disorder. While you're putting jigsaws away, they're emptying a tonne of Stickle Bricks on to the floor, while you're straightening an armchair they're making a den out of a settee. Hoover the carpet, put the vacuum cleaner away, and you will no doubt return to the unmistakeable crunch of Rice Krispies being mashed under tiny feet.

So, tidying up whilst they are awake and playing is an exercise in futility. It's like trying to paint a fence whilst a horse pisses against it, there is just no point. Obviously, it is best to wait until your child is asleep, occupied elsewhere or out with your partner at the park. But the fight for a tidy house is one that can never be won. And there is nothing more soul-mangling than finally getting a room tidy, only for a toddler to wake up or return home and wander into that room as though it is nothing more than a blank canvas for their destructive artistry.

Know this: if you have ever spent hours tidying a room only for a child to enter, pick up a box of Lego, or a game with 740,000 component pieces, and cold-dead stare into your eyes as they dump the whole thing on the floor . . . You will know, in that very instant, that you are in the presence of evil. A demon in tiny human form sent from the very arsehole-end of Hell to lay waste to your sanity.

You also know that no matter how many times you tell your child to pick their mess up, no matter how many times you sing-song the words 'come on, tidy-up time now', no matter how many times you insist that on **this** occasion you will not do it for them, under any circumstances – you are a liar. You **will** do it for them. This is not because you are weak but because you are out of your depth. You are attempting to do battle with nature. For your child, 'tidy-up time' is an assault on who they are.

It's not just that they don't care about the mess, they revel in it. They embrace the chaos, they enjoy the chaos, they live for the chaos and they stride through it like Lt Colonel Kilgore in *Apocalypse Now* just loving the smell of napalm in the morning.

Take solace in the fact that you are not alone. Yes, there are the usual celebrity magazine shoots and the Insta-bullshitters who swear by 'storage solutions' and look like they live in Ikea. But these homes are rare. There are not many that survive being taken apart by the presence of children like a house of cards in a busy tornado. From what I understand, most households with kids in residence resemble battlefields pretty much all the time.

Ours certainly does.

A letter from this morning's frontline:

2nd February, 2018

As I write this I am staring at the field of battle. 'Tis a scorched earth. The chaos has raged since 5am but the enemy has fallen silent . . . for now. (After falling asleep watching Despicable Me 3.*) But what was once a living room is now a torn landscape, littered with the remains of plastic dinosaurs, Duplo bricks, chunky jigsaw pieces and a horrifyingly dismembered Lego Olaf. Rice cakes and Pom-Bear crisps crack under foot like the bones of the fallen. And the sofa is a forgotten fort, a single broken breadstick pokes out of the ruins like an abandoned bayonet . . . or a forgotten pole for a flag that was lost in its surrender.*

And don't get me started on the state of the fucking car.

Indicators that your baby is now a toddler No. 3: You can't remember the last time you had a shit without an audience

Aaaah. It's so adorable when your little one wants to be with you all the time, isn't it? No. No it isn't. Especially when you can't just go and have a shit without having a three-foot-tall observer standing in front of you and asking you repeatedly 'what ya doing?' whilst running a small toy tractor across your knees.

There are two things that every human being feels uncomfortable doing whilst being watched. One is obviously eating either a banana or a Cadbury's Creme Egg. But the other is being observed whilst going to the bathroom. It is a measure of a civilised society that our toilet habits remain private, and yet a lack of privacy becomes part of your daily life as the parent of a toddler.

For the most part, babies are barnacles. When they are awake they are attached to you like an extra limb. But toddlers let go. They are alive with the idea of independence. They detach themselves from you and go off and do their own thing, explore their own interests. Don't get me wrong, they don't sod off down town or anything, but they will happily play independently for a while, or watch TV on their own for a bit. A toddler is just less limpet-like than a baby. Apart from when it comes to the simple act of you going to the toilet, when, it seems, they can't stand to be away from your side.

I have yet to find an answer to this intrusive problem. The easiest solution is to not let your toddler into the bathroom. Lock the door. Simple. But that is really no solution at all. Because, as annoying as it can be, going to the toilet with this audience is marginally better than trying to go as your child sits on the other side of the bathroom door, kicking and screaming howls of abandonment like you have just dumped them in a box at the side of the A42. (Or much, much worse trying to go when they **stop** howling. Nothing chills a parent's blood quite like a child in another room who has suddenly gone a bit quiet.)

Another solution is to try and sneak off to the toilet without them noticing. Which is a virtual impossibility. Animals have all kinds of extra-sensory abilities. Some can feel vibrations in the air, others can detect the smallest changes in the electromagnetic energy of their surroundings. These skills allow them to sense everything from the coming of the tides to the approaching rain. And toddlers develop their own almost telepathic abilities for when an adult has nipped to the bog.

A parent can be as quiet as they like – as they attempt to sneak away for that five minutes of bathroom alone time – but few have the required stealth to succeed. Wherever your child is in the house they will stop whatever they are doing, tilt their head to one side, sniff the air, know exactly where to find you, and be in attendance before your pants hit the tiled floor.

It seems that this strange ability is a vital one for all toddlers to master. Because, for some reason, they think that a parent going to the toilet is an event they must attend, something not to be missed. In that moment, it is the greatest show on Earth.

I genuinely do not know what toddlers think a parent is doing in that small room which demands this interest. I do not know what they believe they are missing as they shriek outside the door, or kick the living shit out of it like narcs who can hear you flushing bags of smack.

In fact, if there are any toddlers reading this, I have a message:

IMPORTANT MESSAGE . . . FOR ALL TODDLERS . . . FROM ALL PARENTS . . . EVERYWHERE:

When we go to the toilet and close the door behind us, you are not missing anything. We are not splitting the atom in

there, we are not turning lead into fucking gold. We are Just. Having. A. Shit. So please, you are our greatest achievement, our testament to humanity. We love you with the glare and heat of a thousand suns but . . . fuck off for five minutes eh?

Indicators that your baby is now a toddler No. 4: You are poor

People always say that there is nothing that can really prepare you for being a parent and that's probably true. But there is a simple and fun way to recreate the economic impact of having kids: simply empty your bank account. Take all that cash, place it in a wheelie bin and then set the whole thing on fire whilst dancing round the flames quietly weeping.

Children are expensive. And maybe never more so than when they are toddlers. Just take a look at this scientific chart that I just made up:

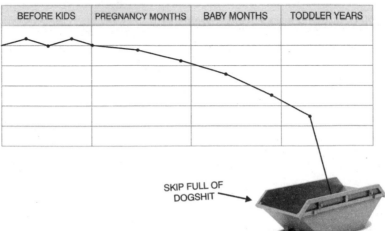

PARENTAL FINANCES

BEFORE KIDS	PREGNANCY MONTHS	BABY MONTHS	TODDLER YEARS

SKIP FULL OF DOGSHIT →

So another great way to tell that your baby has become a toddler is that you are now poor. Tramp poor. Hovering near the discount fridge in Tesco, waiting for the young man to put an orange '30% off' sticker on a chicken, poor. Broke.

According to the latest research it costs approximately a quarter of a million pounds to get a child from birth to adulthood. That's £250,000 to get a human being from out of a person and all the way to university. Oh, and if they want to go to university you can bundle another £40,000 on top of that. To put that in perspective that's the same as a supercar or the average-priced house (or if you live in London, a small wooden crate with a bucket and a pillow in it).

And whilst babies might be expensive, make no mistake, by comparison toddlers are a wood chipper for your finances. They are industrial machines that chew through everything you earn with efficiency. Until one day letters from the bank are as welcome as newspaper-wrapped, flaming dog shit on the doorstep. And credit-card statements become the most uncomfortable viewing since *The Farm*, a 2004 Channel 5 reality TV show in which, lest we forget, someone wanked off a pig.

So a newborn might be a drain on the bank balance but when they become a toddler that drain becomes a sinkhole. They are suddenly needy for all this crap they never really required before, extravagances like childcare and proper shoes. And a lot of this stuff is unexpectedly expensive because it lasts all of two minutes.

In fact, shoes are a really good example. Babies don't really need them, toddlers do. And the cost of shoes alone is enough to make your wallet self-harm. Twenty quid might seem reasonable for a pair, but not if by the time they've tried them on and you've taken them to the till your kid has gone up a size. Shoes can fit perfectly, but a week later your child is bursting out of them like they are the Hulk and someone's just called them a 'green prick'.

As little kids my parents bought us shoes that were too big for us and it was always with the assurance that we would 'grow into them'. I now understand why. Yes, I started my first day of school looking like I'd mugged a clown. Yes, I made a flapping noise when I walked. And yes, the other kids called me 'Bingo' and asked me where I'd parked my tiny car and whether I was going to entertain them by pouring custard down my trousers. But I now get it. Shoes are expensive, and if you can make them last more than a month it makes sense.

It's not just the financial demands of a toddler's feet that are alarming. It's their entire wardrobe of trousers, jumpers, coats, gloves and hats that they continue to outgrow with the alarming speed that they did as a baby. Now, though, they are not just outgrowing this stuff, they are also testing it to destruction in mud and in puddles, on rocks and in trees and leaving random items behind on park benches and soft-play coat hooks. (I've been in soft-play centres as they close for the day and the piles of clothes that toddlers leave behind make it look like the entire place has been raptured.)

What about food? No longer are they tiny birds surviving on very little. No longer will formula or breast milk suffice. Now they consume three square meals a day, plus snacks. Or, in reality, snacks and three square plates of food that your child looks at for ten minutes, like you've served up chimp shit, and then you scrape into the bin.

Ninety per cent of food is wasted. Seventy per cent of activities and trips are rendered pointless because of a meltdown or because your toddler has fallen asleep just as you've arrived. We blow hundreds of pounds on toys that remain entertaining for about as long as Honey G. (If you're wondering who Honey G is, that's kind of my point.) And this is all before you start to factor in the cost of pre-school childcare. The invoices for which have you wondering whether it's best to pay by cheque, bank transfer or kidney.

Of course, added to all this is the **real** financial game changer: unlike babies, toddlers 'want' things. Actually, that's not quite true . . . they want **everything**. They want toys they see, ice creams they see, CBeebies magazines with a plastic tiara stuck to the front of it. They see it, they want it. They want sweeties. They want chocolate. They want the Earth on a fucking stick . . . No, not that stick, the other stick! And it is simple supply and demand. They demand it and you supply it and, for them, money is no object.

In fact, now I come to think of it, £250,000 is starting to sound like an underestimate. I've put at least half that in the Thomas the Tank Engine coin-operated ride-on outside my local Co-op. We can't call in to get a pint of milk without that money-grabbing shit-house shouting 'all aboard' as we walk past and Charlie consequently demanding 'pennies'.

I am not someone who is in any way frugal or tight-fisted, but Thomas doesn't cost 'pennies'. Thomas costs a pound. For that pound he goes twelve inches forwards, and then he goes twelve inches backwards for a grand total of sixty seconds. That's it. I worked it out, and it's the equivalent of sixty quid an hour. No wonder Thomas is grinning. Pro rata this smiley twat earns five times more than me and he barely has to fucking move.

But I put the money in. For two reasons. Charlie likes it and I prefer him when he's cheerful. And if I don't, I'll be dragging him inconsolable around the supermarket by one arm for the next fifteen minutes. Overacting his devastation, like he's Brad Pitt and he's just discovered Gwyneth Paltrow's head in a box.

Perhaps this is at the root of why the parents of toddlers are poor. Aside from all the other expenses that come with parenting, a large part of our budget goes on blackmail. On buying our children's compliance and purchasing stuff to bribe them with.

There's no shame in this. I'm aware that every time I put a pound into this ride-on train that I am conceding ground, but so what? 'Giving in' may seem weak, but in that moment a pound seems like a reasonable price to pay to avoid the hassle. And in handing over a hundred pennies we can usually then enjoy a relatively calm wander around the shop and leave happy and content.

Until we pass Thomas on the way out.

'All aboard!'

For fuck's sake.

It's no wonder we're broke.

Die, Thomas, die.

Indicators that your baby is now a toddler No. 5: You look fucked

Whilst on a fur-trapping expedition, a fella called Hugh Glass was attacked and mauled by a grizzly bear. He was somehow able to kill the giant bear but then he passed out. His group left him, thinking he would never survive the wounds or the 200-mile journey to the nearest town. Glass regained consciousness only to find himself abandoned, without weapons or equipment. He was disorientated, lost and on the verge of death. He was suffering from a broken leg, the cuts on his back were exposing bare ribs, and all his wounds were infected.

So, he cleaned his wounds with maggots, fought off hungry wolves, made a makeshift boat and six weeks later made it back to civilisation, crawling a large portion of the way.

Now, obviously I'm not comparing what Hugh Glass endured to the experience of being a parent of a small child. Of course I'm not . . . I mean, who the fuck's got time to make a boat?

But, whatever Hugh looked like when he finally stumbled out of that forest and back into civilisation is pretty much what I look like right now. I look fucked. And there's a pretty good chance you do too. Because it is as we enter the toddler years that the effects of being a parent start to really take their toll on your appearance.

From the moment your little one is born it feels like the ageing process is accelerated. As though the second they arrive you celebrate by drinking from the wrong Grail. As a new parent, at first you are tired, then you are exhausted. But then as your baby is transformed into a toddler you enter what I like to call the 'Hugh Glass' stage of parenting.

It's not just in the mirror that you observe these changes in your appearance. I first noticed the changes in mine when gauging the reactions of friends who I hadn't seen for a while. Obviously, friends are too polite to mention that you look like a wreck. (Unless your friends are complete dicks, like my mate Glyn who I bumped into yesterday and who told me that I looked like 'stacked shit'.) But before we had Charlie, people would genuinely comment about how young I looked for my age. Now those comments have dried up and more recently when I bump into old friends the reaction is a fleeting facial expression. An expression seen more usually on the face of a lady in a horror film, when she opens up a walk-in freezer and a corpse falls out.

It's not hard to understand these effects. At the toddler stage, the lack of sleep we experience as the parent of a baby is compounded by the lack of five minutes to relax, sit down and do something fun like breathe in and out. The obsession with your child's health comes at the expense of your own and the closest thing you get to a nutritious meal is a grab bag of Frazzles and a Yop. The undeniable stress of a newborn is replaced by new stresses both large and small. Large ones: such as keeping them out of danger and alive (despite the fact that they are on an hour-by-hour mission to kill themselves). And relentless smaller stresses: like when

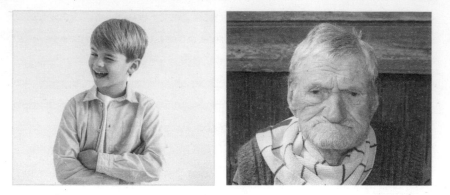

*Here is a picture of me before having Charlie in 2015.
The other was taken this morning. If you look closely at the photograph on the right, you can spot some of the telltale effects of
being a parent.*

you are in a rush and your kid demands to fuck with your day for no reason at all. Hugh Glass's survival was credited to his astonishing will to live. But I guarantee his will to live would not have survived the twenty-five minutes I spent this morning, standing in our door-way, as Charlie insisted he could zip up his own coat.

To make matters worse, throughout this entire time you still have **the** cold. I wrote about the parenting 'perma-cold' in the last book. And as a parent to a toddler it continues to cling to you like a second child. There has never been a moment since Charlie was born that me and/or Lyns haven't been nursing a fun low-level illness. Whether in the hacking cough stage or the sore-throat, dripping-nose stage, the cold virus moved into our house when Charlie was born, put its feet up on the settee and hasn't pissed off since. This is one of the other reasons that when you look in the mirror you expect to see the Grim Reaper behind one shoulder giving you the thumbs up.

There is no great mystery to this but I read a news article a few months ago about a parenting institute in the US that had commissioned research into why parents of young children are so susceptible to colds and flu. The research was to take three months at a cost of 45,000 dollars.

As far as I know they have yet to release their findings. But if any of the researchers are reading this, I can save you the best part of 50,000 dollars and tell you in five seconds for a tenner.

- Ongoing sleep deprivation
- Stress
- Terrible diet
- And being in the permanent company of an unhygienic, snot-drenched, tiny creature repeatedly coughing and sneezing into your fucking eyeballs every forty seconds

You're welcome, I'll send an invoice.

So, whether it's caused by stress, low-level illness, diet or the fact that children are energy vampires feasting on your life force until little remains but dust and bones . . . congratulations, your death-like appearance can be an indicator that you are now the owner of a toddler.

So, after all that, what is a toddler?

Okay, your house looks like Kabul, **you** look like something Burke and Hare dug up, and you are broke and exhausted. But you have begun to feel a bit like a parent and on the whole feel happy that you now share your life with your own small weirdo.

But the real change, the real difference between a baby and a toddler is not in any of these things. The biggest distinction is that toddlers have character and charm and infuriating personality.

Babies are incredible. They are life-changing and beautiful. And they will always be that first version of our children that we will love and love with a magnificent simplicity. They're also really boring. There, I said it. Babies are boring. They just are. No one tells you about the monotony and the routine of taking care of them. And as the parent of a newborn you just don't notice how dull they can be. You are too full of adrenaline and hypnotised by fear and the fact that you are responsible for their existence. You are captured by the novelty of the whole thing.

Also, we let babies off for being boring because they look cute and their heads smell really good. But what do they do? Not a lot. When it comes to babies, stuff goes in, stuff comes out. They are basically a two-foot-long Tamagotchi.

Not so toddlers. You can accuse a toddler of many, many things, being disruptive, crazy, emotional, wiping their nob on the curtains. But you cannot accuse them of being boring. Ever.

As parents to a baby we imprint characteristics on them that aren't there. The way that humans see patterns and faces in wallpaper, we convince ourselves that we can see evidence of a personality that hasn't yet begun to form.

But in a toddler, that personality cannot be denied any more than a lion in your front garden. It is real. It is alive. It roars and it bites. And it is a marvel.

Everything is interesting about toddlers. Everything fascinating. They are a creature that can create a world under a duvet, and a universe in an empty cardboard box. They can go from devastation to elation at the production of a biscuit from a pocket. They are unpredictable and at times completely insane. And yet, that is part of their charm because their capacity to surprise is constant and ongoing.

Charlie can be extremely sensitive and caring. He will place his hand on your face when you're upset and tell you not to worry. 'It'll be okay.' Other times he is as sensitive as a monkey on a tyre swing flinging his shit at a wall. And you never know which version you're going to get. With toddlers, one moment they are an orchid, the next they are a firework.

And they have opinions. Real opinions. Not necessarily about interest rates or bloody Brexit but real opinions nonetheless. Charlie's favourite pyjamas have dinosaurs on them and other pyjamas are entirely unacceptable. During the day I could dress him in a Lidl carrier bag and a KFC bucket with an eye-slit scissored out of it, and he wouldn't give a shit. At night time, though, he wouldn't be caught dead going to bed in anything other than his dino 'jamas.

Telling Charlie that his favourite night attire is in the wash can infuriate him but it's not just that. He's the same way about his baked beans touching his fish fingers. He's just as adamant about the spoon for his cereal being the one with the orange handle and not the green one. Or at least he is today; tomorrow it will be something different, or the exact opposite, but either way he will be just as passionate.

I envy that about toddlers, their passion. As adults, we LOL without laughing out loud and feign fury about everything from the existence of God to litter on the streets, but we are rarely as passionate about anything as a toddler can get about absolutely nothing.

And whilst this force of personality can be maddening and frustrating it is also a thing that changes the way that you feel about them. Our love for them becomes different, not so reliant on instinct, and stronger for it. I love Charlie differently to the way that I did when he entered the world screaming and resembling an angry boiled ham. Since that first moment I knew that I would smash planets together to make him happy. But now I feel that way not because of **what** he is. Now I feel that way because of **who** he is.

So I think that is the main difference between a baby and a toddler: personality. It changes everything. A toddler is nuts. Completely fucking nuts. And each has their own peculiar version of bat-shit that makes them unique.

And this goes to the very heart of the question. The question that we began with:

What is a toddler?

Simple. Toddlers are you and me. Us. Humans stripped of all the bullshit. In our most raw, passionate, fascinating, dumb, perfect, mad-as-tits form.

And aren't we awesome?

2

The Basics – Walking and Talking

'These boots are made for walking
And that's just what they'll do.
One of these days these boots are gonna walk all over you.'

– Nancy Sinatra

The Basics – Walking and Talking

One of the most likeable and irritating things about toddlers is their complete lack of self-doubt. Their belief that they can do absolutely anything has yet to be eroded by life. And so they go through a stage when they refuse all of your attempts to help them, and demand: 'I can do it.'

They say these words with utter conviction as though you are insulting them by your lack of faith.

'Don't patronise me. I don't need your help. I can do it. I am more than capable of tying my own shoe laces/opening this drink/zipping up my own coat/changing a tyre/resolving the crisis in the Middle East. I am capable of doing anything! I am the controller of my own destiny. I am my own God! You are just in my way, you tall dickhead.'

Of course, this is nonsense. Toddlers believe that they are capable of anything but they can't get a straw into a Capri Sun without fucking it up in colossal fashion. So, it's safe to say, they are rather overconfident when it comes to their own abilities.

To make matters worse, when something goes wrong it is the parent's fault. When Charlie insists that he can open his own yoghurt, I try to dissuade him. But he is utterly adamant that he can do it. And when he tears off the lid and coats himself, the walls and the dog in Munch Bunch fromage frais it is me he looks at accusingly. What were you thinking letting me open my own yoghurt, old man? I'm only two, you fucking idiot.

So, your number one role as a parent is to teach your son or daughter the ways of the human. You are Mr Miyagi to their Daniel.

Obi Wan to their Luke. Master Shifu to their Kung Fu Panda. You are the greatest teacher they will ever know. And it starts with the basics. Walking, Talking and Crapping. Because what is a human, if not a machine for all three?

We'll come to crapping later.

But for now . . .

Walking

One of the reasons I didn't include the ability to walk in the last chapter (as an indicator that you are now the proud owner of a toddler) is because all kids learn to walk at a different rate and for most of them it is a very gradual learning curve. It is not a skill that is mastered overnight. On the whole, babies don't just pop up from crawling one day, demand a pair of Reeboks and piss off around the block. It's a process.

Kids take ages to find their feet, and I don't mean metaphorically I mean literally **find** their feet. It seems to come as a surprise to them that they are right there at the end of their legs. Other animals fall out of their mum, land on their feet and sod off, with little more than a stumble and a backwards glance, but not our lot. To begin with our offspring are decidedly crap at getting around on their own. They have to be taught. But let's not be too harsh, humankind took millions of years to get off their belly and upright, and toddlers manage it in a matter of months. Besides, walking is really hard.

We covered crawling in *Dummy*, which if you recall had five stages, from 'The Plank' to the 'Inverted Turtle' to the 'Zombie Drag'. And, according to paediatricians, there are an additional three steps that then take your child from crawling to walking and eventually on to disco.

1. **Pulling Up**

After your child has been crawling for a while they start to show signs that they are keen on attaining a new outlook. Understandably, they get bored of being stuck in a prone belly position. They get sick of constantly looking at feet and the shocking state of the carpet and so one day they make the momentous decision to shift their perspective from 'foot-level' to 'balls-level'.

So, the first sign that they are ready to take those all-important first steps is when they start to pull themselves upright using furniture. The reason why they do this is because it is a child's arm muscles that develop first. And they are powerful muscles. Apparently, a lot of babies can lift their own body weight using just one arm. (That's how strong they are, they can do one-arm chin-ups. Add a boom-box blasting 'Eye of the Tiger' and you've got the beginnings of a pretty sweet eighties training montage.)

Unfortunately, despite this impressive ability, babies hauling themselves up in this way is not an entirely graceful endeavour, due to the fact that their legs don't really join in. Charlie's attempts to do this were fairly typical. He spent weeks pulling himself up and clinging on to the furniture, with all the grace of a drowning man trying to get aboard a life raft after his legs have been blown off. In these circumstances parents are encouraged to leave their little one to their own devices and not help them. And so for weeks your child spends much of their day hanging off of the sofa like Jack at the end of the film *Titanic*, clinging to a floating door as Rose refuses to budge up.

2. Cruising

Once your little one starts to pull themselves upright in this way, they start to do something called 'cruising'.

I wouldn't google 'cruising' if I were you. Apparently the word has three meanings: one to do with this stage of development in walking; one to do with holidaying on a boat; and one, apparently, to do with hanging around public toilets on the off-chance of a hand-shandy.

I think I'm going to stop using Google as my primary research tool. This last definition threw up way too many image search results. Most notably a photo of a large man in a motorway services near Wakefield, wearing only his socks. A man I'm almost certain works behind the counter in our local butcher's.

Anyway, in terms of walking, cruising is the technique toddlers use to develop their stepping ability. Rather than just clinging to the furniture, they now start to lurch from one piece to another, strengthening their leg muscles without the risk of falling. (I'm not actually sure why they call it cruising but during this phase they do look like someone who is shit-faced and on a cruise ship in choppy waters, so maybe it's that.)

3. First Steps

And then one day (cue the music from *2001: A Space Odyssey*) . . . daah . . . daaaah . . . daaaaah . . . da'daaaaaaaah. We have a single independent step.

And the crowd goes absolutely wild!

It's no wonder. When you think about it, it is an astonishing feat. In a matter of months your baby has been born, taken control of their own limbs, coordinated those flailing arms and legs and adjusted their eyes and ears to their own personal horizon. They have compensated for the fact that they find themselves hurtling through space on a planetary ball that is spinning at 460 metres per second. And, in doing so, defeated one of the most formidable forces in the known universe: gravity. All to take a first step into a singular future.

It is little surprise that when that first step comes we applaud and cheer. When Charlie first took a step we were ecstatic. We treated it as a thing to behold. It was like that moment in the Bible when Jesus cured a lame man and said to him, 'Take up thy bed, and walk'. To us, Charlie's first step was just as miraculous and I understood in that moment why it is such a big deal.

We celebrated it not because it was a milestone or a tick-box on a form. Not because websites and books said that it was evidence of the development of Charlie's 'gross motor skills'. But because humans are nothing unless they are propelled in some way, and the best of us have places to go. This nod towards independence felt like an announcement: 'Look out, world, our boy is coming', and we couldn't have been more proud.

And Charlie, seeing our excitement and joy, responded too: he got distracted, panicked and with a wide-eyed expression that said 'what the fuck!?', he face-planted into the kitchen door.

(In fairness, this probably also happened to the fella in the Bible.)

Independence

You have brains in your head.
You have feet in your shoes.
You can steer yourself any direction you choose.
You're on your own. And you know what you know.
And YOU are the guy who'll decide where to go.

'Oh, the Places You'll Go' – Dr Seuss

In a thousand things I've forgotten about the past couple of years, I **do** remember that first step with amazing clarity. Charlie releasing his grip on Lyndsay's index finger and then stumbling forward. First one, then two, then three steps. He didn't walk until he was eighteen months and whilst we tried not to worry that he was 'late', we couldn't help but peer over at the other kids in the park swaggering around the place, like little Liam Gallaghers, as cocky as you like. And so when Charlie's moment came we were obviously delighted.

. . . Then over the next few days we began to wonder why the fuck we had ever wanted this in the first place.

What were we thinking? It soon became clear that this was not a time for celebrations. Instead, it was a time to imitate the action of the tiger, stiffen the sinews, summon up the blood, move everything we owned above five feet, put those shitty little plastic safety catches on all the drawers and cupboards. And do something about the limitless number of sharp corners and edges that apparently have always existed in our house. (I had been under the impression that our home was a soft, squishy, comfortable environment but it soon became apparent that this entire time we'd been living in a deadly cubist painting.)

Everything was harder now.

As soon as your child can walk, the genie is out of the bottle and, as much as you may want to, you can't punch the genie in the face and stuff it back in again.

If, like me, you're a dribbling gonk, with all the foresight of a balloon, you may at some point have entertained the idea that things would be easier once your little one joined the ranks of the walkers.

To me it made sense. Obviously, life would be easier. Not having to carry Charlie around everywhere. Or constantly get him in and out of his pushchair. How could it not be? Far better to have him happily skipping alongside me as I carry out errands. What a pleasant idea.

As it turned out, what I had imagined – a tiny mini-me happily holding my hand as we cheerfully ambled down the high street – was a ridiculous fantasy. The reality is that walking anywhere with a two year old is more like herding a mad chicken.

Toddlers don't pleasantly skip alongside you as you carry out your errands. They don't do that at all. For a start that would mean heading in a specific direction instead of what toddlers actually do, which is piss off in entirely random directions like a possessed Roomba.

They do this for a very simple reason: for them, walking in one direction is boring. So, they zigzag, they go backwards and sideways with little or no concern for traffic or the fact that they might be about to walk off the end of Skegness pier or into a lion's mouth. Their eye snares a butterfly or a bird, or they hear a sound, and they are drawn towards it like a Bisto kid catching a whiff of gravy. The world is theirs to discover and that can mean in **any** direction, for **any** reason at all.

Delays

Toddlers fight hard to achieve their independence and the ability to move under their own steam. It's no wonder they want to stretch their legs and explore, it is an expression of their inquisitive nature. Which is all well and good, until a trip to the shops becomes a four-hour expedition.

Along with the ability to walk, toddlers attain an accompanying skill: the ability to completely fuck up your day. To slow you down and prevent you from getting anything done in an efficient manner. Walking just complicates everything. Even just nipping to the shops.

The problems start before you even leave the house. Because your child is walking, you must now contend with the fact that they need to wear proper shoes. Which, as we have already established, toddlers are more than capable of putting on themselves, thank you very much, you patronising twat.

Actually, in fairness, in Charlie's case this is true. Like most toddlers, he is, strictly speaking, capable of putting on his own foot-wear. In fact, here is a picture of me as we're about to nip out for a loaf of bread, waiting for Charlie to pop his shoes on:

'I can do it, Daddy.'
'I know you can, Sunshine, but by the time you do, Daddy will be dead.'

The battle of the shoes is only a small part of a toddler's mission to sabotage the most simple of activities. Once outside the house, your attempts to get from A to B in anything like a normal or timely manner are screwed even further.

One of the first times I took Charlie to our local newsagents without his pram, Lyndsay phoned me after an hour and a half. She was worried and wondering where we were.

'Lyns, he just won't go in a straight line,' I said. (As though we needed to take him to Kwik Fit to get him adjusted.)

'What do you mean he won't go in a straight line?'

'What do you mean, what do I mean?! He won't go in one direction, and he won't let me pick him up either. I don't know what to do!'

'You've been gone hours, where are you?'

'Erm . . . well, just look out of the window.'

She peered through the blinds with some confusion. We had made it roughly twelve feet from our front door.

On this occasion, the problem wasn't just that Charlie was heading in random directions or walking around in circles outside our house. Even if toddlers start to wander in vaguely the right direction, they do it ball-achingly slowly and they also stop a lot. Because **everything** is interesting. For a while Charlie stopped at anything unusual he found in his path. And by unusual I mean every discarded can, empty crisp packet, every pebble. All were worthy of his inspection. Every piece of crumbling white dog shit or every weed that sprouted through a crack in the pavement would have him crouching, squatting on his heels and examining it like David Attenborough encountering the very rarest of species. Which, in fairness, all these things were. In a very real sense, toddlers are aliens charting an undiscovered planet.

I have one of those running apps on my phone that records your mileage and GPS position and then charts it on a map. I used to switch it on when I'd go walking with Charlie in his baby carrier or in his pushchair. As an experiment, I tried it again recently and I think it demonstrates the issues I'm talking about:

Below are three maps for comparison, each one shows us heading to the local shops.

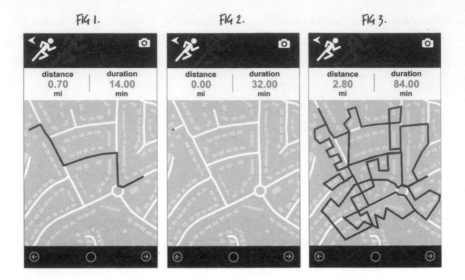

FIG 1. FIG 2. FIG 3.

Fig. 1 As you can see in the map on the left, getting to and from the shops with a non-walking Charlie was straightforward enough. Straight there and straight back in around fifteen minutes.

Fig. 2 The map in the middle shows absolutely no progress or movement at all, due to the fact that as we left the house we discovered that on our doorstep was a dead ladybird.

Fig. 3 This final map shows a morning when my son spotted a cat. Which led to an unscheduled quest as Charlie insisted on pursuing the cat to give it a cuddle. Charlie could not be dissuaded from this course of action until a considerable time later when the cat disappeared into a shed, where it no doubt promptly died of exhaustion. The cause of which was the hour and a half it had just spent being pursued by a crazed, pint-sized maniac demanding 'A CUDDLE!'

In this instance we did make it to the shop just before it closed. But toddlers really do seem to be on a quest to derail your day. They have no sense of time, let alone urgency, and no interest in the need to get from one place to another. Those are adult concerns for adults. And in the world of the two year old, there is not a single adult concern that can compare with a dead ladybird or the opportunity to squeeze a freaked-out cat.

Hazards

For the parent, all this can be incredibly stressful. Especially as your toddler increasingly refuses to be carried and constantly shakes free of your hand-holding to do their own thing. It's not just the face-clawing slowness with which you get anywhere. It's also the stress of keeping them out of harm's way in the process, when they seem utterly determined to kill themselves.

This is hard enough at home but outside the house with a walking child it is a constant battle. It is a persistent challenge to keep them safe; by the side of roads and in car parks, near ponds, nettles, brambles, train tracks and electrified fences. Broken glass, wet paint, cattle grids, cliffs, mine shafts, forest fires, weapons silos and Mordor. If there is something dangerous within walking distance, a toddler will head towards it. Like they've got an appointment with death.

Not only that, the ability to walk has yet another unfortunate side effect. It soon becomes clear they are diverting so much of their energy to putting one foot in front of the other that apparently their ears no longer function.

The very moment Charlie took a step he lost the ability to hear us. When on the move, he ignores everything I say and volume is irrelevant. If he legs it I shout 'Charlie! Charlie!' with increasing volume. And his lack of even the slightest acknowledgement has me wondering whether I have somehow died and am now like a Bruce Willis-style ghost-parent trying to make contact with him from the afterlife.

And this selective deafness is another layer of stress to contend with. Keeping your toddler safe is just a lot harder when they refuse to hear your screaming suggestions that they don't walk into traffic or the blades of a combine harvester.

Born to run

It can be scary to let your toddler explore things on their own but, by their very nature, they refuse to be restricted and confined. And so the only thing you can do is shepherd them around, assessing the dangers that they seem intent on marching towards. This is the reality of that first step that you cheered with such enthusiasm. Mums and dads spend a large amount of their time treating their toddler like a little wind-up toy that is heading towards the edge of a table. You see a hazard, you pick them up, you turn them around and you send them off in the opposite direction . . . until they meet another one. This is your life now.

Eventually you adjust to this new reality. You come to accept that your role is less that of a parent and more of a harassed health-and-safety officer slowly losing their mind. Just as you come to accept that being late wherever you go is the new normal. It doesn't matter where we are going. If Charlie finds a puddle he likes we can be stranded until he gets bored of stomping in it. If he discovers a pigeon it can mean following it in circles until it finally concedes and takes flight. For him, these are vitally important tasks and everything else can wait. Doctors' appointments, job interviews can all go on the back burner . . . This pigeon will not chase itself.

And a parent's role in all this is simple: keep your child safe and try not to get so frustrated that you lie down in traffic yourself.

So there are many milestones that form part of our new life as the parent of a toddler. But none change the game quite like the ability to walk. As adults we use this incredible ability to get to where we need to go, but toddlers use it for a higher purpose. They use it as a means to discover. For them, a walk is not a way to get to work or to the local post office, a walk is a chance for adventure. And a run is a run not because they are trying to get fit, or catch a bus, but because they are intrigued to know what could be around the next corner.

One thing is certain, a child with the newfound ability to walk is new territory for any parent. Up until this point the chaos has been contained. We have been dealing with a controlled explosion. But not any more. Our little one is on the move. It's time to keep up.

Anyway, got to go. I'm writing this bit in Costa and our son has just walked away from our table and started legging it towards the escalator.

'. . . You little shi . . .Chhhaaaarrrrrlllieeeeeee!!'

Talking

I read an article the other day about dolphins being the smartest of all mammals. Apparently, they have a brain that is more structurally complex than humans and they have an 'incredibly sophisticated language'. I'll be honest, I'm not convinced. How sophisticated is your language going to be when all you need to do every day is blow air out of your head and have some fish?

Most intelligent creature on the planet? I suspect this is pro-dolphin bullshit. They can't drive, they never invented the combustion engine, sequenced DNA or landed on the moon. Fuck those fishy-breath, rubbery dicks. (Not really, I like dolphins.)

The reason why humans were able to achieve these incredible feats, though, is because rather than communicating with clicks and

45

screeches, and by head-butting beach balls, humans developed the most astonishing ability to communicate. We evolved to describe our surroundings and therefore took command of it. And, when we had done that, we wrote poems and books and made movies about it. Our ability to communicate through words what we see, hear, feel and imagine is probably the greatest achievement of any species that has ever existed.

And we all start out with 'poo-poo' and 'it's mine'.

First Words

I've written about Charlie's momentous first word before. There is still some debate as to whether his first word **was** actually 'daddy'. I've rechecked the video evidence and it may well have been 'baddy', 'flappy' or 'Dappy'. Although why he would've chosen to mention the lead singer of N'Dubz as his first word makes this last one unlikely. (I mean, they haven't had a hit since 2010: 'We Dance On' feat. Bodyrox).

So, on balance of probability, to my mind at least, Charlie's first word was indeed 'daddy'. And, in some ways, this first utterance – that we could understand at least – was as momentous as his first step. Maybe even more so. Words can take you where you want to go much more efficiently than legs. Books are a case in point.

The speed at which language develops from burbling to a first word to carrying out a conversation is miraculous. In a matter of months, Charlie went from dribbling to saying the word 'apple'. To standing in our hallway and insisting, 'I don't like this hat, this hat is stupid, this hat smells like dinosaurs and poo'. And then holding his own in an argument with me about whether he could possibly know what dinosaurs smell like.

By the time a baby is one year old they usually know a couple of words, but by the time they are two or three their vocabulary has increased exponentially to around 200. It is remarkable to witness.

Obviously, this is not true for all kids. Children learn at different rates and there are plenty of adults who never attain a vocabulary this impressive, as anybody who has watched the President of the United States give a speech about new'cular weapons will testify.

Kids Say the Funniest (Creepiest, Most Insulting and Profane) Things

Kids really do say the funniest, cutesiest little things. I once caught the end of a conversation being held on a bus into Rotherham when a boy of about ten was arguing with his mum. I have no idea what they were discussing but the boy finished with the line: 'Yeah? Well, so what? Grandma's a bellend.'

It really is so precious when they use their words.

As toddlers, though, it is mispronunciations rather than deliberate expletives that come first. For example, I remember Lyndsay taking Charlie to the cinema when he was around eighteen months. I had no idea what they'd been to see, so it came as something of a relief to discover that this is what he meant when they came home and he kept repeating the word 'cockporn'.

(My confusion was not helped by Charlie's insistence that they'd been to see the 'penis movie'. He meant *The Peanuts Movie*.)

Such misunderstandings are incredibly common. As they learn, toddlers often struggle to make the correct sounds. They also imitate the sounds that they hear and, in the mishearing, their words become other words. Here are my top three favourite words and phrases currently in Charlie's vocabulary:

Dalek Bread (Garlic Bread)
Crack Whores (Crackers)
and, of course, Helicockter

At various stages in the development of Charlie's language skills, a fork has been a 'fuck', elevators have been 'alligators', tentacles 'testicles', and biscuits 'big tits'. Which is all fine in the privacy of your own home but not so great when you're in a crowded café and your two year old is demanding a crack whore . . . preferably with big tits.

Surprisingly, this isn't the most offensive thing that Charlie has ever uttered. Even worse is when your child mangles words until it sounds like they are saying something **deeply** offensive. I'm pretty certain our two year old doesn't have a racist bone in his body but for a couple of months his pronunciation of 'blackcurrant' made us nervous to leave the house.

I've heard other kids tell their parents that they are 'dickless' (ridiculous), and my nephew absolutely loves Thomas the Tank Engine but prefers 'pussy' (Percy). I know at least one three year old who calls the Olympics 'the limp dicks' and another who when he wants his Play-Doh shouts at his dad: 'Pedo! Pedo!' which can cause raised eyebrows when they're enjoying craft hour at the local library.

Toddlerspeak

So, toddlers chew up the English language as they stumble to grasp the basics. But it's not all expletives and offence. Some mispronunciations are charming and smart. I love that any day in the past Charlie refers to as 'lasterday'. There is something quite poetic about it, that it is a day that is gone forever. 'Strangled eggs' (rather than scrambled eggs) is another one that raises a smile. And I have a soft spot for that classic childhood mispronunciation 'skellington'. This is a word that has always been, somehow, better suited to its task than the more correct 'skeleton'. Skellington just seems so much more rattley, with those upright 'l's stacked up in the middle of the word, like ribs.

There are other toddler words and phrases that I've come across that are also better than the originals. An article I read about just this subject had one mum who reported that her son Dexter called fire extinguishers 'fire squishers'. Which is perfect. And a toddler's tendency to name things by the noise they make is brilliant too. Cars become 'beep-beeps' and ambulances 'nee-naws'. (Although famously 'microwave' in Welsh is 'popty-ping' so, in these cases, they may just be speaking Welsh.)

So much of what toddlers say is dismissed as gobbledygook or babble, but toddlers can be fascinatingly inventive with language and it can make them much more interesting conversationalists than most adults. I mean, who doesn't prefer a chat with a human who chases 'flutterflies' and worships 'little baby cheeses'?

Despite your parent/teacher role it is tempting not to correct these small 'errors' that toddlers make as they learn to talk. These stumbles can indeed be charming, funny and at times beautifully serendipitous. But, as your child gets older they may well become less so. It's important to keep in the back of your mind that there are not many things more irritating than an adult who uses the word 'supposably' or the phrase 'damp squid'. This might sound pedantic but my mum's friend Carol pronounces the word duvet: 'jew vay'. She's sixty-five. Fucking 'jew vay'? I was going to correct her but one day she invited my mum out to play 'bagminton' and I just thought there was no hope.*

For Fox Sake

The misunderstandings inherent in learning a language become less of a problem as toddlers become more adept and confident with their words. But this can bring a whole new set of issues.

No longer do they accidentally issue a bad word because it sounds like something else. Now their ears are tuned to swear words and they pick them up and throw them around like toys.

It is strange how teaching a toddler a new word or phrase – that you would like them to learn – can be an arduous task, whereas a swear word can be whispered on the breeze and a toddler will snatch it from the air and immediately enunciate it perfectly.

* My mum's no better. We once went to a relative's funeral in our local church and, as we sat down, the organ music abruptly stopped. At that precise moment she loudly commented that she could really 'smell the incest in here'. I think she meant 'incense' but it was a Catholic church and the guy getting buried was from Pontefract, so who knows?

Me: Say please.

Charlie: . . .

Me: Say please.

Charlie: . . .

Me: What's the magic word?

Charlie: . . .

Me: It's please, can you say please?

Charlie: . . .

Me: Say please.

Charlie: . . .

Me: (under my breath) For fuck's sake.

Charlie: For fuck's sake.

So, if you are not careful, toddlers learn swear words easily. And I've discovered that once they are learned they are unlearned with some difficulty.

I'm not saying that Charlie struts around the place cursing or answering questions like, 'What would you like for lunch?' with a casual, 'Fish fingers and bastard beans, you fucking dickbiscuit.' No, he very occasionally will repeat a bad word that he hears from me. And it is from me, because Lyns rarely swears. It is entirely my fault that he knows words that would stop a nun's heart. But it is **both** our faults that he understands the power of these words. Because it is both of us who often stifle a giggle when he repeats something he shouldn't. I know this is immature of us but I fail to see what the appropriate response is when a two year old leans over to inform you that the cheese sandwich you've just made him is 'shite, Daddy'.

And this is the heart of the problem. Toddlers notice the reaction that swear words provoke, they realise that these are words with power and that's why they repeat them like spells.

So if you don't wish to have a child who turns up to their first day of school with a mouth like a toilet, it falls to you to clean up your own act, to wash your own mouth out with soap and water and stop being quite so foul-mouthed.

I swear quite a lot. I like to think of swear words as 'sentence enhancers' but in truth it's just a habit I've picked up and, like all habits, it is a difficult one to stop. You may remember the swear jar we introduced when Charlie was a baby.

The idea was to curb some of my language well before Charlie was old enough to speak and mimic what I was saying. Suffice it to say the swear jar didn't work. I found it impossible to stop throwing expletives at the TV and filled the jar completely on one particular day just watching *Question Time*, Sheffield Wednesday get stuffed by QPR and an episode of *Location, Location, Location*. (Yes, we know you want a four-bedroomed property in Central London with a garden and a ballroom but you've got forty fucking grand, you dopey twats.)

We clearly needed a different solution. Fortunately there is one.

Back in the eighties and nineties, if they showed a film before nine o'clock that contained a swear word, rather than bleep over the profanity they would substitute it for another word and dub it over the top. 'Get the *shoot* out of my *freaking* house or I will kick your *apples*!' etc.

(Actually, they still do this a lot on US network TV. I saw *Snakes On A Plane* over there recently and it had the king of the 'motherfucker' Samuel L. Jackson issuing the immortal line 'I've had it with these monkey-fighting snakes on this Monday-to-Friday plane.')

This 'shit for sugar' approach of replacing bad words with harmless ones is a method that a lot of parents also use, and almost without thinking I started doing it myself. Here's a few examples of words and phrases I substitute regularly:

Fuck = *Fudge*
Shit = *Sugar*
For Fuck's Sake = *Fox Cake*
Son of a Bitch = *Son of a biscuit*
Motherfucker = *Melon farmer*
Bastard = *Basket*
Bollocks = *Bollards*
Katie Hopkins = *Countryfile*

So, fascinatingly, as we tried to teach Charlie to speak and learn our language, my own language changed too. And it wasn't just this use of soundalike swear words. The way I speak has become more child-like as well.

These days, if I make any kind of mistake, rather than shout 'fuck', I am much more likely to say things like 'oh dear' or 'whoops a daisy', like I'm a little girl tripping over as I collect dandelions. I say 'whoops a daisy' regardless of the circumstances or incident. It has become such second nature that I could slice off a thumb whilst chopping vegetables and I would still 'whoops a daisy' as blood jetted around the kitchen and I lost consciousness. These new turns of phrase have become embedded in my daily language to the point that I even talk in this softened way when Charlie isn't around. I recently had a falling out with an obnoxious taxi driver. It was only after I was out of the taxi and walking home that I realised that calling him a 'silly sausage' lacked the devastating cut-to-the-bone insult I'd intended.

'Whoops a daisy,' I thought.

Honesty

Eventually, your child moves beyond imitating your words and they begin to engage in actual conversation. And as their language skills develop even further, profanities become the least of your worries. Because in conversation what they have to say can bring even greater offence.

> Man vs. Baby – 11th November, 2018
>
> Apparently, it's quite common for men to put on a bit of weight when they become dads and I reckon I have put on a few pounds over the past couple of years. A fact cruelly pointed out to me last week by Charlie when out of the blue he patted me on my stomach and said 'Aah, baby'. Cheeky shit.

So, I thought being body-shamed by a toddler couldn't get much worse until today. I took Charlie swimming and whilst I was getting dressed afterwards he pointed to me and said 'Ooh, little willy' . . . I mean, for fuck's sake, I don't claim to be hung like a minotaur but at least take into account that on days like today those cubicles can actually get quite chilly.

It is a dangerous thing, a person who can speak but has none of the understanding of social niceties or the need for diplomacy. (I swore I wouldn't mention Trump again but you get the idea . . .) As adults we get used to sparing each other's feelings. We tell people that they are 'looking well' when they look terrible and we insist that their new hairstyle suits them when we don't think that at all. It is common decency that makes us wait until they are out of earshot before we say to each other, 'Jesus, did you see that fringe? She looks like fucking Ringo.' Speaking truths behind others' backs may be two-faced, but it is the foundation of civilisation, and it would collapse if we all just went around saying what we actually think.

Toddlers have no such filter. A toddler will sit on your lap, facing you, and point out your spots. Your big nose. The fact that you have hair where you shouldn't. And bully you about a mole. They will point out every blemish with a matter-of-factness that is nothing short of brutal.

'Daddy, you've got a spot on your chin . . .'

'Yeah, I . . .'

'It's big.'

'Yes, I know.'

'Not as big as your nose . . . that's really big.'

'Okay.'

'But not as big as your ears . . . like a elephant.'

'Alright, alright!? Fuck off now . . . Daddy-quasimodo's self-esteem is in the toilet at this point.'

This honesty is not restricted to a child's own parents either. They happily point out friends' and relatives' flaws too. Making sure to mention Auntie Jean's 'prickly moustache' and the fact that our neighbour Mick's head is 'very shiny'. As awkward as this can be, it is apparently quite normal. For example, a guy on twitter @nottompettysgirl shared this interaction between his toddler and his grandmother:

He was cuddling with her and being very sweet (he was about three at the time).

He takes her face in his hands, and brings his face close to hers, then tells her that she's very old, and will die soon.

Then he makes a point of looking at the clock.

Like I said. Brutal.

Even complete strangers are not spared. Most parents have a tale to tell of how their little one has stopped in their tracks in a supermarket to point out how 'very fat' someone is. Or inquired as to why the person they are sat next to at the bus stop smells like mushrooms.

Children are masters of creating situations that make you wish the earth would open up beneath your feet and swallow you whole. I mean, what is the correct response to the question: 'Why is that person so fat?' You can't just reply: 'Oh, I don't know, son. Overeating, lack of exercise, maybe an underactive thyroid?' You just have to pretend that you didn't hear them, pretend that the question has never been asked and exit as quickly as possible.

Leaving those words to swing there silently, like a hanged man.

Weirdness

Sometimes the things that a little one says are not so much offensive as just weird and creepy. Regularly, we pass a cemetery on our walks and Charlie stops at the same point, each and every time, to say that he can see someone standing in the middle of the churchyard. He actually waves at them. 'Hi, Mister!' he shouts at no one. I don't believe in ghosts and all that stuff, and I wouldn't put it past Charlie to be doing it just to weird me out, but we definitely walk a bit faster at that point.

When I mentioned this on 'Man vs. Baby' it was surprising how many parents had their own examples of toddlers saying things that were just plain creepy. Like this from @spacemanjonny who tweeted about babysitting his friend's toddler once:

> . . . and he drew me a picture. It was basically a squiggle so I asked him what it was and he said, 'It's a cat then a vampire.' I said, 'Does the cat turn into a vampire?' and he looked me dead in the eye and said, 'It does if you do science to it.'

And these others too:

> A friend of mine's child told him, 'Daddy, I love you so much that I want to cut your head off and carry it around so I can see your face whenever I want.' @GatorMcGovern

My three-year-old daughter stood next to her new-born brother and looked at him for a while, then turned and looked at me and said, 'Daddy, it's a monster . . . we should bury it.'
@Like_I_was_sayin

So, Charlie sees dead people, swears occasionally and calls people fat in Tesco. By these examples, it could be a hell of a lot worse.

Talking the Talk

The truth is, whether its mispronunciations, profanities, or trampling on social taboos, toddlers just don't care. And there's no good reason why they should.

Sometimes, it is difficult as an adult to grasp why the things that we say and hear upset us so much. So it's no surprise that children are clueless.

And, as embarrassing, as mortifying, as this lack of understanding can be, it is their inability to understand that is actually one of the greatest things about a toddler. The fact that they don't care about all this stuff is one of the many ways in which they are better than us.

Offence is not something a toddler has learned to offer and so they speak unguardedly and innocently in a way that we lose as adults. Our own conversation and language is caged by conformity and the weight of history. And nuance and the possibility of offence falls on our language and tethers it, but not a child's.

When a three year old asks why a person is a different colour to them or points out that a man's chair has wheels, they mean nothing more than precisely that. They don't understand fat and thin as positive or negative. A mirror is something to dance in front of, or pull faces in.

And so, when they sit on your knee and point out every mark that makes your face unique, they are not studying blemishes or imperfections, for them there is no such thing. They are just describing a face that they love.

And we think **they** are the ones who talk nonsense?

3

The Terrible Twos

It should be remembered that the average toddler is kind of a dick when things don't go their way. You may think that your relationship with them is one of doting parent and loving child but between the ages of one and four it is probably better thought of as being like the relationship between Vegas magicians Siegfried and Roy and Mantecore, the pet Siberian tiger that they loved and cared for, and which loved them in return . . . but when they got on its nerves it tried to tear their fucking arms off.

The Terrible Twos

Man vs. Baby – 3rd March, 2018

Charlie is (seemingly like every other kid his age) in the 'smacking phase'. So I read some stuff this morning about teaching a toddler right from wrong. Apparently 'It's all about communication, eye contact, using a *serious* face and telling the child calmly why their behaviour is unacceptable. Communication is key.'
Okeydokey. So:

1. Charlie: [smacks me in the face]
2. Me: 'Okay, so remember what we said, we don't smack other people in the face it's really naughty and bad and we shouldn't do it because it's not very nice and it makes the other person very, very sad.'
3. Charlie: [looks at me like I'm a whiny little bitch and then smacks me in my *serious* face]
4. Repeat.

. . . until Charlie finally gets bored and wanders off to do something vaguely more interesting like squeeze his Frube into my shoes.

This is bullshit.

And I told him so.

But he just smacked me in the face.

I posted this on 'Man vs. Baby' when Charlie was about eighteen months old. He had discovered smacking a couple of weeks before and the more we discouraged it the more he did it. Every unintended slight, everything he disapproved of, he reacted to, using a smack or a bite. This change in behaviour came as something of a shock and like most parents we began to think that it was a problem. What were we doing wrong? What happened to that lovely, compliant kid we brought home from the hospital? And when was he replaced by this violent, unpredictable, shape-shifting house-demon?

Random Acts of Violence

As it turned out we were not alone. Apparently, all toddlers discover violence around about the same time. And they like it. They're good at it.

It became clear from the comments and messages that followed this post that Charlie's behaviour was not unusual. In fact, it was pretty tame.

One of the first responses I got was from a woman who was mortified to report that, just that day, her two-year-old girl had throat-punched a chicken. An admission that began a thread of confessions from other parents. A thread that revealed that kids punch an awful lot of shit. Chickens, ducks . . . I mean, these confessions revealed that toddlers seem to have a real problem with poultry. But one of these kids went at their nan with a cricket bat and I had a chat with one bloke whose son rammed a plastic lightsabre up a Yorkshire terrier's arse.

These kids didn't just sound aggressive they sounded utterly deranged. The advice to get them to stop smacking is to calmly talk about it while making eye contact with your child. But reading this stuff made me never want to make eye contact with a toddler again.

One of these little buggers took on a goose. A goose!? I'm nearly six feet tall and I wouldn't take on one of those hissing, wingy bastards if I had a handgun and a fucking shovel.

I started to think two things:

1. We are lucky to have such a well-behaved toddler
2. These parents must be exaggerating

Of course, this was a conclusion reached using my trademark dimness. We weren't lucky to have a well-behaved toddler at all. Because, whilst officially a toddler, Charlie was only eighteen months old at the time, so he was still semi-baby. And these parents weren't exaggerating their experiences. Because by the time that children become **actual** toddlers, they resemble tiny little storms. And make no mistake . . . they bring the thunder.

Ladies and gentlemen, we have arrived at 'The Terrible Twos'.

☠ *Et bonum est dominus miserere animabus nostris.* ☠

. . . And may the good Lord have mercy on our souls.

The Terrible Twos

The 'terrible twos' are a real thing. One of those parenting truths that are so real, in fact, that they are part of the landscape of things we all know, even before we become parents.

But it is only when you become a mum or a dad that you truly come to appreciate that the age of two is a kind of portal. A mystical gateway. An age at which a child sheds their amenable and happy baby skin, undergoes a transformation and emerges blinking into the light as a little shit.

(Of course, no one talks about the 'arsehole threes' or the 'fascist fours'. But let's not get ahead of ourselves. The 'terrible twos' are enough of a shock to the system.)

And they **are** changed. This creature, who has always accepted your attempts to take care of them, to clothe them, to feed them, to ensure that they get the rest they need, suddenly decides that they are their own person. And that they are a person that doesn't like socks, or food, or your stupid face. And, whether you have their best interests at heart or not . . . they are not going to take your shit any more.

The timing of it is awful. The terrible twos are a mutiny on a boat that is already barely afloat. But experts argue that this milestone is a vital stage of any child's development. The terrible twos are not just an arbitrary age, they are the point at which a child begins to understand their individuality, begins to recognise that their wants and needs can differ from yours, and apparently this is okay. In fact, Dr Rebecca Chicot in *The Calm and Happy Toddler* goes further and says that it is more than Okay. This mutiny, these terrible twos are something that as parents we should celebrate!

Celebrate? Okay, doc, but I know at least one goose and a Yorkshire terrier called Max – with a lightsabre lodged up his arsehole – who would disagree.

The Tantrum

The cornerstone of the terrible twos is of course The Tantrum. And tantrums are some serious stuff. It's why they are also referred to as:

- '*Meltdowns*' (as in the devastating overheating in a nuclear reactor)

- *'Hissy fits'* (from the Japanese *'hish'i'*, which means 'desperate')
- and also *'being a nob'* (from the parlance of playgrounds in the 1980s when someone was acting like a nob)

It's easy, when you first become a parent, to assume that you know what a tantrum is. In its simplest form it is a display of temper involving crying and anger-snot. But they can actually have many different moving parts. A toddler has a variety of weapons in their tantrum arsenal and they play these weapons like cards:

The Collapse

One of the most annoying and frustrating elements of a tantrum is 'the collapse'.

From a distance it appears as if they have been hit by a sniper. A crack-shot who has targeted your child's spinal column, leaving them completely unable to stand. It is as though in an instant all of their bones have been removed, causing them to fall incapable to the floor. The toddler does not regain the ability to stand up until their demands are met. Consequently, you are forced to pick them up, kicking and screaming, or drag them along the floor like an angry mop.

Note: You will notice that the collapse is only ever deployed outside the home, ordinarily in a supermarket or shopping centre, to deliver optimum embarrassment and maximum exposure to the fact that you are a useless dickhead.

Screaming . . .

. . . Until it feels as though your ears are about to prolapse. Fortunately, Charlie's not really a screamer. But I've seen other kids rattle the Earth's core with their screeching and the decibel level can be pretty disturbing. It is a fact that toddlers' screams are pitched at between 3500–5000 Hz, which scientifically speaking is the precise frequency that makes humans want to bash their head against a door until they feel the sweet release of unconsciousness or death. It's also a little-known piece of trivia, but Edvard Munch's most famous painting 'The Scream' is not actually inspired by existential dread but by a three-year-old kid Munch saw in The Bluewater shopping centre going ballistic because they'd dropped their ice cream on an escalator.

Shouting

As I said, Charlie isn't one for screaming but he does do something worse: he shouts. Which doesn't sound all that bad. But the things he shouts are quite specific. Here's an example: Imagine you want to leave the park but your child is reluctant to do so. So you pick him up and whilst he's kicking and crying he is shouting at the top of his voice over and over again: 'Help me! Help me!' or 'He's grabbing me!' Or, a personal favourite, 'I want my daddy! I want myyy daaaaaddddy!' despite the fact that his daddy is the one carrying him under one arm.

Charlie shouts this stuff all the time, whenever he doesn't wish to be picked up, in fact. And the effectiveness of this tactic can be measured in the number of times I've found myself walk-running to my car before I get rugby tackled by concerned citizens who are naturally worried that I'm engaged in a fairly brazen abduction.

Many times I've had someone give me worried glances or asked if everything was okay, when what that person is actually asking is: 'Are you kidnapping that child?' (To be honest, I wish they'd just ask me outright if Charlie belonged to me . . . Usually by that point I'm inclined to say 'no', hand him over and drive off at speed.)

Hitting

Everything a child does at this age has an edge of aggression about it. Even simple tasks. (Try asking a toddler to brush your hair. After half an hour it will feel like you've been attacked by an owl, and your hair will still look shit.) So you get accustomed to being knocked around as a parent even when your child isn't particularly pissed off at anything.

But when they do get annoyed or frustrated, hitting and smacking is really common. From a toddler's point of view sometimes adults just need a slap.

The first time Charlie smacked me came as something of a shock. We were in The Lego Store in our local shopping centre and I had just insisted that we leave for the fortieth time. Charlie was obviously reluctant (as he was earnestly working on one of his Lego masterpieces at the time, which if I recall was just a tall stack of bricks with a Lego cow at the top that had a windmill for an arse). On the forty-first time Charlie refused to leave, I picked him up . . . and he went crazy. He reacted like I was insane for wanting to leave this incredible place. And to make his point he slapped me across the face as though I was utterly hysterical and he needed to bring me back to reality.

In all honesty, my reaction was one of pure embarrassment. I got down to Charlie's level and explained how wrong it was, how disappointed I felt. I then put the Lego kit we were going to buy back on the shelf and carted him out of the store over one shoulder, certain that I had made my point.

'He's grabbing me. He's grabbing me. Where's my daddddy?!' the little shit insisted.

I don't think you should be too dismayed if your toddler is going through this smacking phase. It's disconcerting, but it's understandable that they do. It's a natural instinct for all humans to lash out, especially ones that are new to the rules of civilisation. As adults we develop impulse control. We have to. Otherwise we would wander around dishing out slappage wherever we went too. Someone pushes in front of you in a queue? Slap. Someone uses the word 'holibobs'? Slap. Michael Gove? Slap. Clearly this is madness. The world could not function if this were the way that we behaved – not least because the queue permanently in front of Michael Gove's face would be several miles long.

I worked at Burton Menswear in the early nineties and I had a manager who once described me as a 'waste of space' because I'd folded some pants incorrectly. I've never wanted to smack someone so much in my entire life. I didn't. I employed impulse control. Placed in the same position of frustration as I was, a child would have lashed out at my boss physically. But as a civilised mature adult, I took a more sophisticated approach and instead just made up a rumour about him having a medically tiny cock and balls.

So this is where (most) adults and children differ. Toddlers don't bother with all that impulse-control stuff. You step out of line and they react and lash out. Like ice hockey players, the gloves come off and they throw down. For them, smacking is a more than acceptable tool in their tantrum kit.

Biting

Vampires, werewolves, cannibals, zombies . . . for humans, biting is the stuff of nightmares. There's just something we find deeply disturbing about it. Over the years, professional footballers have head-butted, karate-kicked and stamped on each other. In one infamous incident Vinnie Jones attempted to tear off Paul Gascoigne's bollocks with his bare hands. But when Liverpool striker Louis Suárez bit a defender, mid-game, the whole world was appalled. The reaction was the same when Mike Tyson sank his teeth into Evander Holyfield during a boxing match. This was two men who were there for the sole purpose of beating the living bejesus out of each other, for cash, and yet one bites the other and everyone goes mad.

Collectively we just find biting to be inhuman and animalistic. And toddlers are biters.

For a while, when Charlie got into a biting mood, mid-tantrum, he'd bite anything: himself, the windowsill, a door. He was like a dog with distemper. And for a short time everything in our house had bite marks in it. But mainly he liked to bite me. A lot. I have the little moons of teeth scars to prove it. Fortunately, Charlie's 'biting phase' didn't last long but at its worst I didn't know whether to muzzle him or offer him a side plate of fava beans and a nice Chianti.

Kicking

It's clear that toddlers will use whatever is at their disposal when it comes to tantrumming. And just like any good cage fighter, toddlers are pretty handy with their legs and feet too. Kicking you in the shins when they're annoyed or waiting until you lie down and giving you a quick boot to the head. But picking a child up when they don't wish to be picked up? That is when kicking can become a powerful weapon. Especially for a man. Nature has designed the toddler to be the perfect size to (whether it be by punch, kick, pile-drive or headbutt) cause as much damage to the male organs as possible.

And holding a toddler in your arms – whilst they are mid-tantrum – provides the perfect angle of attack for the feet to the bollock-area.

A flurry of kicks to the genitals can have a chastening effect on the most determined of dads.

Actually, I can think of at least one occasion when the consequences of this tactic were even greater than just a bruised nut:

A couple of months ago I was on my way in to London for quite an important meeting and Charlie and Lyns walked with me to the train station. Charlie was wearing his wellies and along the way he began to trudge through every muddy puddle he could find.

After a while I realised I was going to miss my train if we didn't speed up. And understanding that hurrying up is not something that toddlers do, I scooped Charlie into my arms to carry him, and he reacted as expected. After a bit of back arching and a light round of shouting, Charlie proceeded to welly-kick my balls like he was doing testicle keepy-uppies. Demanding that I put him down.

Eventually, I made it for the train, waved goodbye to my family and tried to ignore the dull pain. It was then that I noticed that one or two people, as I boarded, were taking an interest in my groin area (not something that happens often). So I looked down. It seemed that their attention was drawn to the fact that I had a large flurried patch of mud centred entirely around my nuts.

It looked as though I'd been felt up by a horny farmer.

I immediately made my way to the toilets and was scrubbing vigorously at the offending area with wet wipes when, with my back to the packed carriage, the door swooshed open. To reveal a scene which, let's face it, did nothing to dispel my growing reputation for being the train pervert.

Arriving in London I realised that, whilst I no longer had a muddy area around my privates, I did have an obvious wet patch. Which I managed to cover with my bag until I got to the office building for the meeting.

After checking in at reception, I excused myself to go to the bathroom again, where I found a hand-dryer. Which, using my initiative, I figured would be perfect for drying myself off. The day was saved. Unfortunately, it was one of those Dyson ones that you lower your hands into, so I had to sort of teabag the thing for it to work.

It was at this point that someone entered the bathroom, gave me an understandably strange look, enjoyed an uncomfortable piss and then left without saying a word.

But I got dry and crisis was in theory averted.

Obviously, it goes without saying that the gentleman who gave me the horrified glance in the toilets turned out to be the TV executive chap I was meeting. And let me tell you, it's amazing how badly a meeting can go when the person you are there to see believes that they just witnessed you bumming a hand-dryer.

I suppose the point I'm making is that 'kicking', as part of a tantrum, can have dire and unanticipated consequences.

Weaponry

Whilst unarmed combat is tough enough, a tantrum can be doubly difficult when your toddler is armed. Here is a list of things that I have been clubbed with just this week: a breadstick, a hoover attachment, a fitness DVD entitled *Beverley Callard's Body Blaster* (it was in our holiday rental cottage . . . 'a selection of DVDs', my arse), a garlic ciabatta and an Iron Man torch.

For a toddler, whatever is to hand is a potential weapon. And the damage that can be done is frightening. I am forever glad that toddlers don't have the wherewithal or the hand-eye coordination to use proper weaponry. If you can draw blood using *Beverley Callard's Body Blaster* imagine what these little sods could do if they worked out how to use a crossbow or nunchucks.

Actually, it is throwing weapons that are some of the deadliest. Toddlers love to throw stuff when they're annoyed. Ninjas used to use shuriken stars and throwing knives called 'kunai', but toddlers can achieve a precision strike to the face using anything from a shoe to a pork pie.

Nipping

Well, nipping can just fuck off.

Shame

One of the strongest tactics toddlers use as part of a tantrum is not physical at all, and employs the age-old battle strategy of using your own weakness against you. And when it comes to the tantrum, your greatest weakness is this: your capacity for embarrassment.

It's worth noting that there is a significant difference between the toddler tantrums that occur inside and those that occur out-side the home. Charlie will only shout 'Help me, help me' when we are in public. And, as I've mentioned, toddlers very rarely employ a full 'collapse' when they do not have a public audience. Kids are cunning; they know that these tactics don't work when you're at home because you can just ignore them: *Roll around on the ground as much as you like, sunshine, all you're doing is cleaning the floor.*

But toddlers notice, very early on, that in public things are a bit different. That with an audience your voice changes when you're making a demand of them. That your point is not made quite so forcefully when other people are around. They observe that outside the home you speak through your teeth a lot more, and with rather more of a sing-song in your voice.

'Hey, sweetheart! Be a little treasure and try not to throttle that duck to death, there's a good girl.'

With a predator's instinct, toddlers notice this change in your voice and demeanour and they sense a weakness. They understand that you have an Achilles heel that they do not. You have shame. You care about what other people think. Worse than that, crazily you care about what **strangers** think. And so in public they target this weakness to get what they want.

Anybody who has dealt with a two year old in public knows that scrutiny from others is one of the hardest things about dealing with a full-blown meltdown. It is as though in those moments your inepti-tude as a parent is laid bare for all to see. Your terrible secret (that you haven't got the faintest idea what you're doing) is exposed. The glances that people make in your direction become hard stares and eye-rolls in your mind. Often irrational thoughts creep in about the assumptions that those glancers are making. Maybe they think we are

74

raising a monster, maybe they think we're idiots. When Charlie was tantrum 'smacking' we even started to worry that people might assume he was imitating us and that there was some sort of violence in our home (other than the occasional 'Dutch-oven').

In reality, I think these attitudes are surprisingly rare, particularly amongst other mums and dads. Parents often feel like they are being judged when their little one is kicking off at the park, but those glances from other parents are usually glances of recognition, sympathy and relief that it's your kid's turn to be an arse and not theirs. And anybody else looking over with genuine disapproval or annoyance has all the empathy of an upturned bucket and shouldn't be allowed outside. Fuck them. Even if they don't have kids themselves, there's a pretty good chance they were one once.

Toddlers are, of course, unconcerned with the politics of all this; they just sense that you are uncomfortable and use that discomfort to their advantage. They put on a show. It's why we call them 'drama queens', and talk about tantrums as a 'performance'. That's exactly what they are, dramatic productions for an audience. And toddlers are not stupid. The simple truth of the matter is it works. Kids are more likely to get what they want if they can make you look like a dick in public.

That's a fact.

Guilt-tripping

Finally, we come to the greatest weapon in the tantrum arsenal. Guilt. When all other tactics have been tried and eliminated. When you have withstood the best that your child has to offer. When you have endured the screaming, the collapses, the ball kicks, the titty grabs, the eye pokes, the concussion. When you have stood with fortitude against the tantrum onslaught, your child still has a nuclear option at their disposal: guilt.

A toddler's ability to make you feel guilty, like this whole episode has been your fault, is a form of magic. A kind of Jedi mind trick. Their cries turn to racked sobs, their eyes become wider and they look into your very soul and show disappointment with what they find there. Your inability to understand their upset becomes a grand betrayal. And the devil on your left shoulder kicks the dandruff from its feet and begins to whisper in your ear. 'How could you? How could you, you heartless beast?' And slowly you start to feel bad that it came to this. That you have failed at your most basic of parenting functions: to love.

And so you do the only thing that is reasonable in the circumstances. You scrape the toast into the bin and make some more, but cut it into squares this time instead of triangles . . . because triangles was yesterday, you fucking idiot.

Levels of Tantrum

Any combination of these tactics can be used to create a display of temper. But not all tantrums are created equal.

According to an article on babycentre.org, as parents it is easy to lose perspective. To start to feel as though each tantrum is as bad as the last. Apparently, we gauge outside tantrums as worse than ones that take place inside, even though the behaviour may be exactly the same. We have a tendency to think that our own child's tantrums are worse than every other kid's. When that probably isn't true either. We also think that tantrums are made worse by certain TV programmes, by nursery or by diet, when again that may not be accurate.

For example, some recent research suggests that sugar has

absolutely no effect on the behaviour of children. According to these behavioural scientists, parents just think it does. Mums and dads simply become more sensitive to bad behaviour when their child has had a Freddo or a glug of Tizer.

(For the record, I think this research is bullshit and if any of the lead scientists want to test their theories by babysitting for us one night after Charlie has been to a party and is off his tits after eating his own bodyweight in cake icing, they'd be more than welcome).

So, according to the article it is useful for parents to keep tantrums in perspective. And to make that easier, they suggest thinking of displays of toddler anger as graded in intensity from 1–5. It goes something like this:

1 = Whining

2 = Whining, crying, throwing

3 = Screaming, stiffening or falling to the floor

4 = Biting, kicking, scratching

5 = Uncontrolled rage

6 = Save yourself. Run. Run while you still can

and

7 =

Okay, I added no. 6 and 7 myself. But there are those rare occasions when grades 1–5 just don't really suffice. Thankfully, with Charlie we have only experienced a '7' event once. This was because Charlie was a bit unwell, tired and hungry, and his favourite cuddly toy had just fallen into the toilet.

Admittedly, I am occasionally prone to exaggeration but just to give you an idea of the intensity of this tantrum: the Cascadia Earthquake of 1700 was so phenomenally powerful in magnitude that it actually changed the rotation of the Earth and the duration of the day was consequently shortened by 1.8 seconds. Well, if anybody was wondering why night time came half an hour early on 18 December 2017, I can tell you. It was because Charlie had a cold, skipped his afternoon nap and then accidentally dropped Justin Beaver in our downstairs shitter.

Level 6 and 7 events are actually pretty rare for most of us. But 1–5 can be daily and tough enough. So, what brings on a whinge and what creates a detonation?

Understanding the Causes of a Tantrum

The first thing to understand about what triggers a tantrum is that toddlers are diametrically opposed to everything you want them to do. Take a look at this Venn diagram showing two distinct circles and where 'the things you want a toddler to do' and 'the things a toddler wants to do' overlap:

You will have noticed that the circle with 'the things you want a toddler to do' is not actually visible. Not only does it not overlap, it doesn't actually make it on to the page. Because that is how far toddlers are from giving a fuck about what you want them to do.

So what causes bad behaviour and what can trigger a tantrum?

On the following page is a comprehensive list:

Literally.

Fucking.

Anything.

From requiring them to put on socks to the fact that you have given them a banana when they specifically asked for a banana. Toddlers go mad about everything and, more specifically, nothing.

Many of the reasons why they kick off are just downright baffling. Charlie has tantrummed because I couldn't repair the biscuit that he himself had just bitten in half. He has tantrummed because I wouldn't let him grab a goat by the testicles. And he has had a meltdown on at least one occasion because his 'feet won't come off'. I call these the 'what the fuck?' tantrums and I came across plenty more examples online.

My son screamed incessantly, 'I don't want to go! I don't want to go! You can't make me go!' for a whole hour. We weren't going anywhere and no one had even mentioned the possibility of going somewhere . . . He's fucking crazy. – Max R

My daughter once went mad because I took her dirty nappy off and put it in the bin. The only way that she could be consoled was by taking it back out of the bin and burying it in the back garden. We had a small ceremony as she said a very tearful: 'Bye bye poo poo, I love you.' – Sarah D

And these were not the only examples. There were many more tales of this sort of tantrum from followers of Man vs. Baby. Epic meltdowns . . .

Because:

- 'I wouldn't let him eat my tampons'
- 'He couldn't see his eyes'
- 'I finished having a shower before he finished his shit (apparently we were racing)'
- 'I wouldn't stop the car and let him get out and "live in the trees"'
- 'He lost his eyebrows'
- 'I wouldn't lock her in the boot'
- 'I wouldn't let him put his finger in seagull shit'
- 'Her pet cat wouldn't sing "Starships" by Nicki Minaj'
- 'His middle name is David'
- 'His reflection in the fireplace wouldn't share his orange'
- 'Andy from Andy's Prehistoric Adventures wasn't coming for Christmas'
- 'I wouldn't let her get in the oven'
- 'She has teeth'
- 'I said "good morning"'
- 'I wouldn't let her eat a battery'
- 'His milk was too loud'
- 'We couldn't put her wee back inside her'
- 'She wanted to touch a chicken (we don't own chickens, and don't know anybody that does)'
- 'I wouldn't let him honk my boobs whilst food shopping'
- 'I wouldn't let him stick his finger in his oblivious brother's arsehole'

- *'Whilst visiting a church I wouldn't let him literally dance on people's graves'*
- *'We don't own binoculars'*
- *'I refused to take the bones out of her legs'*
- *'The sun kept following us'*
- *'She wasn't allowed to press spoons into her baby brother's eye sockets'*

When I said 'literally fucking anything' I was not kidding.

To complicate matters, from one day to the next, toddlers are entirely inconsistent about the things that piss them off. And the things that infuriate one toddler don't even register as a problem with another.

They each have individual desires that evolve all the time. Their moods are affected by a thousand variables: tiredness, hunger, the moon, the tides, fracking, Sagittarius entering Gemini rising. Who knows?

Even the most obvious causes of a tantrum are complicated. Take tiredness, for example. There is no doubt that this is a major trigger for a toddler meltdown. But tiredness can be because they have skipped a nap, slept for too long, slept for not long enough or slept when they didn't need to sleep. They can even be 'overtired'. A mind-bending situation when they are **too tired** to go to sleep.

To see the madness in all this, let's recap: they can be furious because they are too tired, not tired, overtired and slept when they weren't tired. Oh, and, by the way, they're usually really pissed off when they've just woken up.

It's the same with mealtimes. Toddlers kick off because they are not hungry, too hungry or past hungry. And the actual food placed in front of them can cause a problem just as easily: not too hot and not too cold; they demand that it be 'just right'. They are like Goldilocks, if Goldilocks were a complete arse who also demanded her porridge be in the red bowl and not the bloody *Monsters Inc.* one.

Their likes and dislikes when it comes to the actual food are also bizarrely random. One day pasta is Charlie's favourite thing. The next day he reacts to it as though he finds himself in the jungle, me and his mum are Ant and Dec and we've just served up a portion of possum anus.

That's without the ongoing battle to get him to ingest a vegetable. There are days when nothing can provoke a tantrum quite like the suggestion that our child eats a carrot. Days when he will happily lick floors and walls, and unidentifiable bits of glob retrieved from beneath his car seat, but baulk with horror at the idea of ingesting anything resembling a vitamin.

So when it comes to understanding the causes of tantrums we soon learn that most of the time it's just not worth figuring out. It is impossible to pin down the ever-changing opinions, ideas and random musings of a two to three year old. There is rarely a single reason why they are losing their minds and the variables too many. Trying to understand is to attempt to give order to chaos.

But then there is another type of tantrum that is easier to understand. The mummy and daddy of all tantrums: the tantrum brought on by the word 'NO'.

NO

The number-one trigger for a toddler tantrum is not tiredness or hunger or even over-stimulation. These things may contribute, but the primary cause of a toddler meltdown? The perfect way to turn your day from a cheerful amble to a complete bin fire?

The word 'NO'.

In toddler terms it is the most offensive word you can possibly think of. There is no adult equivalent. (The closest thing I can imagine is – maybe over Sunday lunch – calling your grandma a c**t). Toddlers really, really do not like this word and they respond viscerally, as though to hear it is the injustice of the ages. A savage blow to the heart.

Scientifically speaking, apparently, being told 'no' releases cortisol in a child's tiny brain, a hormone that neuropsychologist Dr Michael Portegol calls 'toddler juice'. It increases blood pressure, speeds up breathing rates, leads to confused or unclear thinking and triggers the fight-or-flight response. In neuropsychological terms . . . they completely lose their tiny shit.

Maybe we shouldn't be too surprised that 'no' triggers such a powerful response. It may seem like an innocuous couple of letters, but 'no' is a word responsible for every single war human beings have ever fought. It has laid waste to vast civilisations and destroyed gods. And, make no mistake, the word has just as powerful an impact when telling a two year old that they can't have another 'nobbly-bobbly'.

In a way, of course, this reaction is entirely our own fault. Since the very first moment our children open their eyes they are given everything they could possibly need, instantly. Whether that is food, affection or warmth. And they achieve this by doing nothing more than scream in our gormless, dopey faces.

Seemingly overnight, this approach no longer works. Now when they want something it can be refused. It can be questioned. No wonder they're annoyed. From their point of view it is us who have revolted. Us who have suddenly changed the rules. It's little wonder they react like an angry king.

Little wonder too that they act out their frustrations in the way that they do. Two year olds don't have the language necessary to negotiate or communicate their frustration with this new world in which things can be refused.

Upon hearing the word 'no' they can't just take their mum aside for a moment to say, 'I'm sorry, Carol, I simply disagree with your reasoning on this occasion,' and chat through the options. And so they do something else . . . they cry and scream, claw, kick and wrestle, or hit you in the face with a *Finding Nemo* moneybox.

Tactical Tantrums

So there are many reasons why toddlers act out. Some tantrums are baffling. Others are fired by over-excitement, tiredness or by frustration at their own limitations. In so many ways, they just can't help it.

But that is not the whole story . . .

Be in no doubt, tantrums can also be tactical. They can be deliberate shows of temper to get you to change **your** behaviour. To get you to change your mind. To get you to change an adamant 'no' to a reluctant 'yes'.

Who hasn't caught their child looking out of the corner of their eye to see if you are softening your position whilst they're supposedly inconsolably upset? Who hasn't caught their kid checking to see if their tears are having the desired melting effect on your resolve? And let's face it, the speed at which a toddler can go from completely devastated to delighted as you concede to their demands? That is suspicious as fuck.

Charlie can be seemingly distraught as you refuse to let him watch just 'one more' episode of *Blaze and The Monster Machines*, but the very moment you say, 'Okay, fine, just one more' the tears dry, the shouting stops, the curtain is brought down on the drama, he all but takes a bow, and he settles down to watch 'one more' episode as though all is well with the world. On these occasions, instantaneously, the moment he gets his own way, there is total contentment on his face and maybe the slightest up-curl of his mouth that lets me know what he is actually thinking: *Ha, you dumb shit, fell for it again, eh?*

And it is in that quiet, contented smile that we perhaps see the truth of these terrible twos. That, at this age, kids do begin to kick off for all kinds of reasons, but more often than not they do so because they are testing boundaries, probing for weakness and examining your resolve. These early tantrums are the first skirmish in a battle of wills, and make no mistake, it is a battle your child intends to win. The terrible twos are first and foremost an insurrection, an uprising, a revolt. A rebellion.

What is a parent to do?

Crushing the Rebellion

So, as Dr Chicott said, the terrible twos are a normal and natural testing of boundaries. Moreover, the terrible twos are a thing to be cheered and celebrated!

Your kid deliberately spills an entire box of cereal on to the living-room floor, pulls on their wellies and carefully stamps the lot into the carpet, all whilst maintaining that eye contact with you that says, 'Eat shit, fuck-face'? You should cheer, set off a couple of party poppers, hooray!

Expert: Always try to remember that it is perfectly natural as your child begins to explor—

Parent: Oh, fuck off, and help me clean up these Cheerios.

Okay, let's forget celebrating the terrible twos. How do we stop this mutiny, this revolt, this rebellion? There is surely only one way. It seems obvious. We must be tough. We need to crush these individual freedoms and take back control. Never giving an inch, we must enforce the rule of law and quell this uprising. We must become a dictator. Our very survival depends upon it.

There is only one problem.

We have no power. No real way of enforcing our laws, no way of crushing rebellions. It turns out that, as a parent, you are not the head of a dictatorship at all, you are just a lowly subject. The real dictator is three feet tall and fucking up a display of beans in Sainsbury's because they want a lolly.

Toddlers change **your** behaviour, not the other way round. Think about it, who is limiting whose freedoms? Who is managing whose behaviour? Who is the megalomaniac enforcing their own will, their own laws in your home?

Look at your life, look at your clothes, look at what you have become. You fool. The very idea that you could dictate to **them**? When **you** are the poor soul crushed beneath tyranny. We are not dictators. Our children are.

And faced with the endless demands of this all-powerful regime, you do not stand a chance.

Your best hope is to join the resistance . . .

[*whispers*]
Come with me . . .

4

The Resistance

The Resistance

Communique from HQ . . .

Transcript of last communication picked up from resistance parent. Codename: *Squirrel*

Comrades, how long must we remain under these conditions. How long must we be crushed beneath the tiny boots of tyranny. How long must we be cowed. We are stronger, we are taller, we have wisdom and experience in our favour . . . It is time to rise, to take back our lives, take back our freedoms and say no more. It is time to say: 'I am parent' and break free of the shackles and . . . Oh, hang on . . . I think our youngest just woke up . . . won't be a minute . . . (inaudible) . . . No, it's bedtime now, sweetheart. No . . . yes . . . no . . . but you've just had a drink . . . no, I don't know where it is . . . it's not . . . look, where's Mummy . . . ? Don't get your crayons out . . . don't pour that on to the . . . How can you need a wee wee?! You've just . . . please . . . No! You can't watch Nella the bloody Princess Knight . . . it's half ten . . . Alright, alright, just stop screaming . . . (inaudible) For fuck's sake! Sandra!! Sandraaaa?!

And that's the last we heard from codename: *Squirrel.*

Many members of the resistance have fallen. We must stay strong, find ways to prevent the takeover of our lives and fight back by any means necessary. Here is your manual. Read it. Memorise it. Destroy it. This message will be covered in felt tip, bean juice and snot in 5 . . . 4 . . . 3 . . . 2 . . . Ugh. For fuck's sake.

1. Know your history

2. Be consistent...ish

3. Pick your battles

4. Engaging the enemy:
Distract, ignore, remove

5. Smacking?

6. ~~Negotiating~~ Giving in

KNOW YOUR HISTORY

Modern life is scary. Everybody says so. We live in a time of unpreced-ented technological advances, superbugs and nuclear threat. A time when, according to the host of *InfoWars*, Alex Jones, the government are 'putting chemicals in the water that turn the frickin' frogs gay'.

And many experts like to suggest that it is modern living that is the cause of naughty behaviour amongst toddlers. That somehow it is a new phenomenon and is caused by modern diet, too much TV, overstimulation, YouTube, sugary drinks or lack of attention from the busy modern parent. In reality, toddlers have probably always been the same. Half a million years ago Neanderthal kids were no doubt smashing up their caves just as efficiently as today's are destroying the modern semi-detached in Leeds. It's just that, back then, the things that annoyed toddlers were different; they were not allowed to go near the fire or play with their favourite rock. Instead of shouting, 'Be careful near the swings, sweetheart' par-ents were shouting: 'Get down off that bloody woolly mammoth, Dylan, I will not tell you again', etc.

So, as parents, we are supposed to worry about modern living and all the various ways in which it is poisoning our young. But one of the reasons we know that the terrible twos aren't a modern-day curse – fuelled by telly and fizzy drinks – is because we have a record of people trying to solve the problem years ago, before the advent of telly, iPads and Irn Bru.

Traditional Remedies

Before Dr Spock released *Baby and Child Care* in 1946, experts used to have various bat-shit ideas about causes and prevention of 'bad behaviour' in babies and toddlers. These theories were usually based on withholding affection or giving your kid a quick back-hander. But there were other more bizarre solutions too.

One guy suggested that the problem was simple: that women were crap at being parents and that children should be raised exclusively by their fathers. Physician William Cadogan said:

> In my Opinion, this Business has been too long fatally left to the Management of Women, who cannot be supposed to have proper Knowledge to fit them for such a Task.

It's an interesting opinion. And I do wonder how well this went down with Bill's wife. I like to imagine that on reading it she grabbed her coat and told him she was off out to Margarita night at TGI Fridays. Oh, and the baby's just done a massive shit. 'And by the way, I'm not a hundred per cent sure the little'un's yours, I've been banging your brother Phil for years.'

Others suggested that the problem was in the biology of the toddler themselves and preferred to correct behaviour using medicine like 'Stickney and Poor's Pure Paregoric Syrup', a simple but effective remedy that had 46 per cent alcohol and one and three-sixteenth grains of opium. Yum.

In fairness, this was probably a phenomenal cure for tantrums. As my old grandma used to say, nothing dampens the terrible twos like good old paint thinner and a spot of heroin.

These 'solutions' were passing fads that soon fell out of fashion, but one idea that persisted was the importance of withholding affection. This was a theory overwhelmingly embraced until well into the 20th century. The principle was simple: whatever you do, don't be too nice to your kids.

Being a dick to your child was accepted wisdom, the only sure-fire way of preventing and correcting ill discipline. All the experts thought so. If, back then, there had been the equivalent of a *Supernanny* show, each episode would have been about five seconds long and simply involved a robust-looking lady banging on your door, coming into your house, giving your kid a quick clout and then just fucking off.

The parenting gurus of yesteryear had no time for mollycoddling, timeouts, drying tears and being vaguely decent. They discouraged parents from even picking up their little one when they cried.

In 1928, John B. Watson in *Psychological Care of Infant and Child* wrote,

> *Never hug and kiss them, never let them sit in your lap. Bouncing babies on your knee will 'spoil' them. If you must, kiss them once on the forehead when they say good night. Shake hands with them in the morning. Give them a pat on the head if they have made an extraordinary good job of a difficult task.*

Steady on, softie.

Why do I get the impression that John B. Watson wasn't exactly a hands-on kind of a dad? He was apparently one of the foremost experts on child behaviour during this period and he sounds like he has never met a child in his life. Although, I do like the idea of toddlers and adults engaging with this kind of precise etiquette.

Good morning, Son. [Delivers firm handshake.]

Good morning, Father. Mm . . . Apologies, Father, I appear to have shat my pantaloons.

Watson wasn't the only intellectual that suggested being distant from your offspring and frowned upon being nice to your kid. In a 1911 book, one expert insisted that holding a baby for the sake of it 'would produce a little tyrant'. A paediatrician writing in *Bringing up Babies* agreed: 'If we teach our offspring to expect everything to be provided on demand, we must admit the possibility that we are sowing the seeds of socialism.' This frothy-mouthed chap called Sackett went on to compare overindulgent parents to Hitler and Stalin. Which is a little harsh given that an overindulgent parent might be guilty of giving a nipper too many chocolate buttons, whereas Hitler and Stalin were guilty of wanky moustaches and the genocide of about 40 million people.

It is easy to mock these ideas, to imprint our modern thinking and understanding on to old theory. But it is with the greatest of respect for these esteemed academics that we must now accept that the likes of Cadogan, Watson and Sackett were a bunch of fucking idiots, literally just making stuff up. (And if you think that is a bit harsh you should read their theories about why babies should be left out in the garden, be eating bacon and eggs at eight weeks and be weaned on to coffee at six months.)

The very idea that starving children of affection is a good way of preventing bad behaviour we now know to be monumentally stupid. One of the dumbest fucking ideas in history in fact (at least until some idiot changed the recipe for Roast Beef Monster Munch in 1996). The most heinous of crimes committed by humans are incomplete without backstories of how the perpetrator failed to be loved as a child. All starving children of affection does is create a sad kid and a badly adjusted adult. In fact, two of Watson's own children committed suicide, which most modern-day observers ascribe to the fact that their dad was a massive arsehole. So that tells you a lot about his 'be a dick to your kids' theories.

It goes without saying that we have moved on in recent times. Thankfully, instead of this bunch of idiots just making stuff up, we now have a completely new bunch of idiots just making stuff up.

Yes, it is time to take down from your bookshelf all those books (that you never read) about pregnancy and looking after a baby, and replace them with a load of other books (that you will never read) about toddler behaviour.

Hear the call . . . of the Naughty Step.

BE CONSISTENT . . . ish

Thankfully, I can't find a single modern-day parenting expert that says withholding affection is a good thing and it is generally agreed that being horrible to your child is not a good idea. But you can still find experts and non-experts willing to peddle the notion that raising a child is like breaking a horse. That, when it comes to discipline and tantrums, **all** battles are worth fighting and that you must **never** give an inch with a toddler. It's all about 'consistency'.

Experts in discipline love this word. It's as though they believe that consistency in a house with a child in it is actually a thing.

*'It's essential to be patient and **consistent**' – Supernanny Jo Frost*

*'You can help minimize the occurrence of tantrums by keeping things **consistent**' – care.com*

*'The best way to deal with tantrums is a **consistent** approach' – nannyjob.co.uk*

Yes, it's all about the three Cs: consistency, consistency, consistency. I'll be honest, that's not the 'C' I'm thinking of when I hear yet another expert banging on about consistency.

If by some miracle there is a child-discipline expert reading this book, can I just make the point on behalf of all parents everywhere: we understand what you are saying, we really do, but . . . you do know that kids are mad-as-tits, don't you?

Consistency just does not sit well with toddlers. Not in real life. As we've already seen, their desires, wants and needs can be too chaotic, their moods affected by too many variables. To apply consistency to something so random is impossible. And to suggest that tantrumming has a simple solution is stupid and makes parents feel like they are doing something wrong or just not making the required effort to ensure that their kid behaves.

Don't get me wrong, I understand the thinking, we all do. But even if you do somehow manage to turn your house into a realm of the smoothest consistency, how do you account for the influence of nursery, other kids, or when they spend time with grandparents (who back when they were just your parents denied you everything, but now treat your kids like they are a Little Lord fucking Fauntleroy, whose every wish is their command). What about when the clocks go back? You've just mastered consistency with something like bedtime and those arseholes in charge of time bugger it all up again: 'Hey, lads, let's add an hour on to the day or take one away, it'll be a right laugh.'

Seriously, stop fucking around with the clocks you piss-taking shit-houses.

I digress, but in these demands that we must be consistent, there is barely a mention of the many factors that are out of a parent's control. And no mention at all of the days when you just can't be bothered. Yes – shock horror – there are days when you just can't be arsed. When you are exhausted. When you are just too tired to argue with a pissed-off hobbit, for hours on end, about everything and nothing. There are days when consistency can go piss up a rope.

Professionals just don't seem to allow for these factors. For example, co-author of *Mommy Guilt*, Aviva Pflock says: 'As tempting as it is to sometimes bend the rules, you'll be doing yourself – and your kids – a disservice.'

Well, despite the fact that Aviva Pflock has a cool-as-fuck sci-fi name, I can't help but think that a home in which the rules aren't a bit bendy sounds unrealistic and maybe even a bit miserable.

It's easy to say that conceding to a toddler's demands – even once – is to make a rod for your own back. And that to give in to a crying or upset toddler is to let them 'win'. But all kids are different, fighting every contest sounds exhausting; and if you fight every battle all you would do is find yourself on a permanent war-footing.

Besides, this idea of allowing your toddler to 'win' is moot. Who 'wins' and who loses is not up for debate. As we've already established, your children single-handedly destroy your social life, wreck your finances, slowly kill you with stress and anxiety and then when you die they get your house. So . . . spoiler alert:

They Win.

Pick Your Battles

So, comrade, once you accept that you are not the sort of uber-parent who never gives in, the kind of Terminator parent who never bends the rules, you will find yourself alongside the rest of us. The muddlers. The INconsistent. And when you come to accept that this is the way that normal people parent, then it comes down to this: picking your battles.

pick one's battle(s) To choose not to participate in minor, unimportant, or overly difficult arguments, contests, or confrontations, saving one's strength instead for those that will be of greater importance or where one has a greater chance of success.

Picking your battles is not a coward's way out. It's just sensible. In fact, picking your battles is part of the tactics of any conflict. It says so in my favourite parenting manual from the 5th century BC: Sun Tzu's *The Art of War*:

'He will win who knows when to fight and when not to fight.'

Well duh, Captain Obvious.

So, whether you are a Zhou dynasty Chinese warlord or a parent, the basics for deciding whether to fight a battle or not are the same: how much can I be arsed? What is the expected level of enemy resistance? And above all: how important is it?

How important is it? (out of 10)

9–10: Health and Safety

In terms of whether a battle is worth fighting, it is Health and Safety that will always rank highest. If your child is placing themselves or others in danger, it doesn't matter how much they kick off. You can't avoid this fight.

If your toddler wants to scale a fence at the zoo to lick a tiger, that's probably a 10. Likewise with climbing in the oven, drinking Windolene or doing that thing with a carving knife where you place your hand on a table and stab in between your fingers as quick as you can.

As much as a child might want to do all these things (and they **do** want to do all these things), they can't. These things are non-negotiable. These are battles that must be fought regardless of the resistance and blowback you can expect.

A pretty good rule of thumb is to calculate whether the action they wish to undertake will result in someone being dead, by things like electrocution or fire. If so, these scenarios are a solid 9 or 10.

8–9: Eating and Drinking

On a level below Health and Safety are battles over eating and drinking. Refusing to eat is a big deal. It's one of those things that if you don't do, you have a tendency to not remain alive. Same with drinking. Unquestionably, this stuff has to rank quite highly. But you can survive a fair while without food or water so the occasional refusal is probably okay and not necessarily always a battle worth having.

A more persistent problem with food is that over a longer term you might find that your child only wants to eat things with the nutritional value of a chair leg. A daily diet of Wotsits and Tunnock's teacakes may avoid a tantrum but it is delaying the inevitable: sooner or later you will have to fight this battle. Don't come crying to me when your child is toothless, the size of a bungalow and their blood type is Fanta. So the battle to get your child to ingest the occasional vitamin is not one that can be avoided all the time, hence the importance rating 8–9.

7–8: Bedtime

Bedtime is the Battle Royale that all parents of toddlers face. Every night. Like a looming storm waiting for you to sail into it. And it is a battle that almost always must be fought. Because sleep is really important. It is good for cognitive reasoning and . . . blah blah. The truth is, its importance lies in the fact that if you don't get them to sleep, your kids are ALWAYS THERE.

Whilst we love our children beyond earthly measure, this does not mean that there doesn't come a point during the average day when we would just like them to sod off for a bit.

The time that parents get to themselves begins at the moment their kids fall asleep. Fighting the battle to get them to go to bed is not just about fighting for *their* health and wellbeing, it is about fighting for your own. Fighting for your sanity and the opportunity to have an hour or two each day when you are not wiping arses or answering impossible questions like 'Why is my head?' Their bedtime is a wisp of time when you can watch *Strictly* or scroll through Instagram. Preferably whilst destroying a bottle of wine in celebration that you made it, yet again, between the hours of 6am and 8pm without anybody dying or getting hurt. THAT is what bedtime means and Christ is it worth fighting for.

6–7: Wanting Stuff

Obviously toddlers want a lot of stuff. Choosing whether to battle over your toddler wanting something, is entirely dependent upon what it is that they want. Hence the average score. If they want another chocolate biscuit, maybe it's okay to not put up too much of a fight over it. If they want a seventh chocolate biscuit, then battle. There is one caveat: if they want a kazoo, a whistle or a recorder, fight them. Dear God, fight them. Fight them with your last breath until you are nothing more than bones and sinew. In fact, this is a fucking 11.

5–6: Coming and Going

Sometimes you need to go somewhere or leave somewhere. And toddlers are usually keen on doing neither. If you would like to leave the house, a toddler will usually behave in a way that leaves you in no doubt that you can sod off. Likewise, if you have been enjoying an afternoon in the park for what seems like hours, and need to leave to go back home, your child will react like you are crazy for even suggesting it. What, leave this place?! Leave behind a wanky six-foot plastic slide, two rusty swings and a roundabout that smells suspiciously like a wino's balls. Are you mad? Not a chance. This is nirvana, the greatest place on Earth, you just have to accept that we live here now.

Getting a child to leave the park or soft play when they are enjoying themselves can be like trying to remove a stubborn protestor. If they could they would handcuff themselves to the netting around the ball pool and demand justice for the Wacky Warehouse One! 'It's soooo unfair!' But actually it's not unfair, its reasonable. And if you want to go anywhere or do anything other than sit in the house or take up residence in Wacky Warehouse then this is a battle often worth fighting.

3–4: Manners

Kids have got shitty manners. They're not very polite. You can tell by the way they sometimes just stand there staring into space, deep-picking their own arse. It is important to instil the basics of 'please' and 'thank you'. But just how important? Because they can be pretty stubborn about this sort of thing. I remember once reading about St Vincent who refused to denounce God. He was stretched on the rack and his flesh torn with iron hooks. Then his wounds were rubbed with salt and he was burned alive upon a red-hot gridiron. Finally, he was cast into prison and laid on a floor scattered with broken pottery and **still** he refused to utter the words 'I don't believe in God'. This is the kind of commitment and stubbornness you can expect from a toddler when you would like them to say 'please'.

(And don't let them convince you that they don't know how to say please and thank you. Don't let them fool you into thinking that they've forgotten how to say it, or that it is beyond their language skills. I can repeat the word 'please' to Charlie a million times and he still refuses to say it back to me. But I accidentally said the word 'fucksticks' this morning and it's now his word of the month.)

It's actually even harder to get a 'thank you'. Because that is a demand for manners after the fact. After they have already got what they wanted you can forget it. There is nothing more infuriating than giving a child an ice cream or chocolate and demanding a thank you afterwards. They just sod off. They know what all great negotiators know, that you've handed over your one bargaining chip and you're not getting shit.

So manners are important but fighting battles over manners all the time can test the patience of a high saint. Therefore, unless you're royalty, they rank pretty low on the importance scale.

2–3: Clothing

I rank clothing pretty low too. Obviously they've got to be dressed in something, especially if its sub-zero temperatures and you're going outside. But that probably comes under Health and Safety. What they wear? Who gives a shit really.

Clothing and dressing, though, can be an attritional battlefield. Toddlers each have a unique sense of style. They often have their favourite socks and vest and shoes, and can react with a super-model's fury at the idea that they would wear some of the crap that you pick out for them.

Sometimes they want to wear wellies and sometimes they want to wear shoes. Sometimes they want socks and sometimes getting them to wear socks is like trying to put them in leg irons. Sometimes they just want to wander around arse-naked. Other times they want to go to the supermarket dressed in scuba gear, Incredible Hulk smash hands and an Elsa (from *Frozen*) wig. In fact, most days, given the choice, Charlie would wander around in outfits that make him look insane. His choices are bizarre and he will tantrum with fury at any attempts to get him to dress in a way that is close to normal.

I envy those people able to colour coordinate their children's clothes, especially on days when Charlie is dressed like someone who is high on meth and has just fallen into one of those charity clothing bins you get at the tip. But most of the time? Screw it. Unless it's something really formal like a family funeral, in which case maybe insist that they lose the diamante cowboy hat. For the most part, fashion sensibilities are just not a battle worth picking. Go ahead and dress like dicks. See if we care.

0–2: Tidy-up Time

Yeah, good luck picking this battle. As we've already covered, toddlers make a mess. It is their signature and it is a signature written in random toys, toast with peanut butter face-down and Lego as far as the eye can see. And if they don't want to tidy up their mess, demanding that they do will just make them kick off and trash the place more, giving you more stuff to clean up yourself. I've tried everything to get Charlie to tidy up after himself, from making a game of it to singing the Mary Poppins tidy-up song. A song I sing with gusto whilst I am down on all fours picking up all Charlie's crap as he leans against the wall looking at me like I'm a sad old man.

Sometimes Charlie will tidy up but when he can't be bothered I have to decide whether to argue. I could fight this battle all the time, I could insist that he tidies up until he's screaming and I have the blood pressure of Gordon Ramsay exposed to gamma rays. But fighting for an hour to get a toddler to put away their toys, when you know full well you will be the one picking it all up anyway, it's usually just not worth it.

ENGAGING THE ENEMY: Distract, ignore, remove

So you have picked your battle and decided that it is a fight worth fighting. On this occasion you have chosen the path of the righteous man/woman – and a kick-off is consequently in full swing. But how do we deal with it? After all, it is not like dealing with wrongdoing in adults. Threats rarely work and you can't just apply terrible punishments, like fines, imprisonment or a punch to the nads.

According to everything I've read on this, the techniques for dealing with bad behaviour in toddlers break down into a few simple options.

The Distraction Theory

Sleight of hand is the oldest tool in the magician's book. They use the art of distraction to pull your gaze elsewhere, to draw your attention away from their secrets. They also use it to distract you from the fact that card tricks are phenomenally boring and that magicians tend to be creepy and spend years learning all this stuff just to pick up women. Magicians are kings of the virgin weirdos.

You only need to read that last sentence to see that humans are very easily distracted. Who hasn't been in the middle of a really important task, quickly googled something and then found themselves an hour later lost in some pointless Buzzfeed article about the 'Top 10 ways your penis looks like a potato'.

Our attention spans are limited but with toddlers this can be used to your advantage. Gina Ford swears by the power of distraction. She argues that misdirection is a great way to disrupt the thoughts of a toddler and stop them in their tantrumming tracks. This actually seems like a pretty good idea. Gina goes on to suggest always keeping 'a small selection of balloons, party hats and poppers at hand and bring them out when you see [your child] is about to throw a wobbly'.

. . . Okay, wait, you lost me there for a minute, Gina.

I get the distraction thing, but is this not a bit confusing for the child? One moment they're complaining about not liking peas, and then suddenly, halfway through that complaint, the person they're talking to pulls on a party hat and starts titting about like they're celebrating a birthday party and they are the only total fucking lunatic invited.

But I suppose that is the point. To shake the child away from their annoyance and make them focus on something else. Even if that focus is on their mum or dad having an apparent nervous breakdown.

I came across another advocate of distraction who suggested making 'monkey noises, crazy faces, just use whatever works for your child'. And that does make sense. I've tried these kinds of techniques on Charlie and it does sometimes work. He's not interested in monkey noises and crazy faces, but he can often be distracted by bubbles or my impression of a drunk T-Rex. So it is important to remember when trying to distract them that all kids are unique and distracted by different things.

It was a friend of mine, Mark, who told me about Gina Ford's suggestion to use party gimmicks to interrupt a temper tantrum. It was working for him and his twin boys. Over time, though, it stopped being effective and now the only thing that distracts them is a made-up song and dance routine he does.

It is basically a bizarre performance piece in which he bounds around like a gorilla whilst repeating the lyrics 'I like big boobies, I like big boobies' in a thick cockney accent.

It's infantile, it's shocking to witness and in public it is utterly mortifying. But it works. It does distract his children. No matter how annoyed they are, it makes them laugh. He can take them from furious to happy in five seconds. It's a disturbing miracle.

The first time I saw this in action it occurred to me that Mark should try the same tactics to distract some of his angry customers in the same way, since he works in the complaints department of John Lewis.

Customer: Hi there, I'd like to complain about these pillow-cases, I'm really not very happy about th—

Mark: [*Slowly makes monkey face*]

Customer: Erm . . .

Mark: [*Lets off party poppers and fires silly string into customers face*]

Customer: Er . . . yeah . . . as I was saying, these pillow-cases . . .

Mark: [*Dances in a circle behind the counter chanting in the voice of Danny facking Dyer*] I like big boobies, I like big boobies!

Customer: Okay . . . I think I'd like to speak to a supervisor, please . . .

So it may not work in the customer-service department of John Lewis but distraction can definitely work with your toddler. Especially if you are willing to make a tit of yourself or distract them with something good, like TV or chocolate or the occasional interpretive dance. Toddlers have an attention span that can be measured in mouse blinks and they soon forget why they're pissed off. So take advantage of this; misdirect, distract and trick them. It can be magic.

Ignoring Theory

Hang on. 'Ignoring Theory'? Is this allowed? I didn't know this was allowed?! What? You can just ignore them? This is a revelation. This is the kind of parenting advice I can really get behind.

Actually, the thinking behind the ignoring theory is pretty good. A major part of the reason why a toddler kicks off in the first place is that they crave attention. And apparently even negative attention is better than none at all. So to respond in any way is to add fuel to your tiny arsonist's fire.

> 'Turn your back if you can, and don't get angry or emotional – from your child's perspective, negative attention is better than none . . . the less you acknowledge a hissy fit, the faster it will fade. In cases where parents kept quiet, their kids' screams subsided in less than a minute on average.' – Parenting Magazine

So your child kicks off? Put your feet up, crack open a can of Fosters, stick on the telly and wait for the whole thing to blow over. Lovely. And in less than a minute? Bloody hell. The more I read about this the more it sounds great. High fives all round!

Okay, everybody calm down. False alarm. Turns out this is complete bollocks.

For a start, a tantrum is rarely just a child screeching. Some kids like to tantrum by kicking, biting or smacking and all the things we've already covered, and that can be hard to take no notice of. In these instances, ignoring them is like playing dead around a bear but getting mauled anyway.

Throwing stuff too. I can't just ignore it when part of Charlie's tantrum routine involves throwing whatever he is eating at his nan-nan: 'Just ignore it, Mum,' as she wipes mashed potato out of her eyes and is struck by another fish finger.

And it's all well and good ignoring them if you're at home. Let them scream away, we can wait until the tantrum subsides, sod the neighbours. But what about when you're out in public and in the middle of B&Q? You can't just stand there, leaning against a shelf playing Fruit Ninja on your phone, while your kid is rolling around in the plumbing aisle. You'd look like a total arsehole.

There are other instances that make a mockery of this technique too. What about when you're in a rush to get out of the door or get in the car? What about when you're trying to put them to bed? Ignoring them in these circumstances defeats the purpose. My son kicks off when I want him to put his shoes on. The suggestion that I try ignoring him is nuts. What are you talking about? That's exactly what he wants . . . that way he doesn't have to wear bloody shoes.

No, ignoring is a terrible idea. There is just a fundamental flaw in the logic of this whole approach. Like suspicious rashes or a clown standing in your front garden in the rain, naked from the waist down, the simple reality is there are certain things in life that cannot be ignored. Toddlers are just such a beast. In fact, they are specifically designed **not** to be ignored. It's kind of their thing.

Removal Theory

The idea of removing your child from the environment that is making them angry is a really popular one. If they're annoyed in a restaurant, take them outside. If they are furious in the park, remove them. Take that stimulus away. And transfer them to a place where they will be forced to think about what they've done.

Naughty steps, naughty chair, the naughty mat. We imagine these places as a kind of toddler jail. Places where a child will look into their very heart and confront their wrongdoings. Perhaps chalk up the minutes that they are incarcerated on the walls, and rattle their Tommee Tippee cups along the bars as they sing an old blues song about how their 'woman did 'em wrong'.

The problem is, these places are not actually toddler jail: there are no locks, there are no bars, and herein lies the issue.

I was at my friend's house a while ago. She has a little boy who is six months older than Charlie and we'd taken to getting together on Friday mornings so the two boys could burn off some energy together. Her little man had been in the throes of the terrible twos for longer than ours and the way that he behaved was like a glimpse into our future.

Her boy is awesome but best described as boisterous. In the same way that a rampaging elephant pissed up on fermented fruit and charging through downtown Delhi – in a big fuck-off tank – is boisterous. He is a wrecking ball. But he's a wrecking ball with a smile, and you can't help but like him. That said, when he loses his temper it is like he has taken a swig of a terrible potion. A pall is cast over the day, the sun is blocked out by his menace, the gods cover their eyes and he flips the fuck out.

Like most parents dealing with the height of the terrible twos, Sara read all kinds of theories about how to prevent tantrums and bad behaviour. On this particular day, I knocked on the door and noticed that it was peculiarly quiet and, as she made us a cup of tea, Sara explained that she'd cracked it. She had been reading about 'removal techniques' and the previous day had introduced the 'naughty step'.

And it had been a revelation. Her two year old had lashed out just before we arrived and she had placed him on the bottom step of their stairs, insisting that he not move whilst he thought about what he'd done. I was amazed that it could be this simple. It seemed like a kind of wizardry. And I peered round the corner into their hallway to see the offender contemplating his wrongdoing.

And he wasn't there.

Following a brief panic we discovered that after thinking about his wrongdoings for a minute Max had thought 'fuck this for a game of soldiers', excused himself from the naughty step and climbed through the cat flap in the back door. We found him a few minutes later at the end of their driveway licking dog piss off a lamp post.

Max got bored. He entertained the idea of the naughty step for as long as it was interesting to him and then he moved on to other things.

So another simple solution is run over by the train of reality.

And this is the problem with all these simple solutions. Kids' behaviour is a puzzle that has confounded parents since the beginning of time. And, as with all tough puzzles, simple solutions are rarely simple and never solutions. It's ridiculous that we should be so arrogant as to think that we are the first generation to be smart enough to come up with some grand remedy. A silver bullet.

In fact, it's pretty likely that future generations will look back and laugh at us for our naughty steps and timeouts in the same way that we look back and chuckle about the madness of dosing your toddler up with booze and smack syrup.

It is certainly interesting to consider how the future will judge the following approach to naughty behaviour. It is a controversial one that generates furnace-heat debate. But I'm not one to shy away from controversy. Especially on a subject so full of bat-shittery.

[*reaches for tin hat*]

SMACKING

The theories that we discussed at the start of this chapter, we con-
cluded, were outdated bullshit. But there is a historical remedy for
bad behaviour that still survives today. And it's one that should probably have been left behind in the previous century, along with the
last bottle of Stickney and Poor's Pure Paregoric Syrup: smacking. Or
as Americans insist on calling it: 'spanking'. (A word that I detest,
both because it has a touch of the Benny Hill about it and because
it sounds like an amalgamation of the words 'sport' and 'wanking'.)

While we're on the subject of the past, it's true to say that physical punishment has long been an accepted part of dealing with bad
behaviour in children. History is littered with examples of it. Everything from starvation and hard labour in the Victorian era to flogging
in Roman times. And I read somewhere that the Aztecs would force
a disobedient child to inhale chilli-pepper smoke which burned
their eyes, sinuses and mouths. (But the Aztecs worshipped a big
flying snake-bird, so they were kind of mental anyway.)

More recently, throughout the last century, parents continued to
think that it was okay to correct a child's behaviour by hitting them
with everything from slippers to bits of birch tree. Even in schools
this was common. Not any more.

But corporal punishment is not entirely a thing of yesteryear.
There will be parents, maybe even some reading this book, who
smack their children as a way of correcting their behaviour. And
whilst I try not to judge other people's decisions about how they
parent, I do about this.

I can just about understand the logic of a slap on the wrist, the
shock of a sharp smack to tell a child that something is hot or that
they shouldn't step into the road. I'll be honest, it still sounds like
the way you would train an animal rather than a human but I can

follow the reasoning. That said, as a daily part of your response to a tantrum, I think it's bizarre and archaic.

Not everyone agrees. According to one survey, 21 per cent of parents in the UK admit to smacking their children and a massive 81 per cent in the US think that smacking is okay. In fact, in the US, one in four parents start 'spanking' at six months old. A statistic that is incredible. Half a year on the planet and you are expected to know the rules well enough to expect a slap if you step out of line? Six-month-old babies literally don't know which way is up.

I argued the insanity of this on the radio with a guy who was from a 'Christian' parents institution. An organisation that campaigns for a parent's right to smack. He spoke about parents and children the way that a lot of these people do. He derided parents who were soft on discipline, the ones who treated their children like friends. 'Your child is not your friend,' he boomed. I'm not so sure about that. It would be crap to think that being a parent and a pal to Charlie are somehow mutually exclusive . . . he's a good laugh.

This chap went on to insist that smacking wasn't just a good way to discipline your child but that physical correction was absolutely vital as part of the way we should bring up children.

He called it 'loving physical discipline', which sounds a bit like a contradiction, as though you're trying to soften something that is intrinsically bad, like a doctor telling you you've got 'cheerful gonorrhoea'.

But no matter what argument could be made against his position, this advocate for smacking circled back to the same point. God told him it was okay. According to him, the Bible insists that it is not just allowed but fundamentally encouraged.

(When I mentioned that the Bible also said that a disobedient son should be stoned to death in public he told me I was being 'utterly ridiculous'. But there it is in *Deuteronomy*, just after the bit with the talking donkey.)

The strongest advocates for routine smacking do tend to be religious. Sparing the rod and spoiling the child is the word of God and it is spoken loudly. Particularly in the US where there is a religious conveyor belt of books and seminars based entirely on how best to beat your child. Bizarrely popular books like the bestseller *To Train Up a Child* which encourages parents to 'use whatever force is necessary' to 'bring [a rebellious child] to bay' and 'defeat him totally'.

And then there's pastor Roy Lessin's book *Spanking: Why, When, How?* Which, if it was in the adult section would sound kind of fun but is actually a toddler torture manual in which he advocates a flexible switch and whaling away until the child's 'cry of anger' turns into a 'cry of repentance'.

(Apparently Lessin also promotes creationism and believes that humans did not evolve . . . In his case I think he's definitely got a point.)

Whilst these approaches are on the extreme end of the scale they are part of a wider culture of acceptance of smacking across the pond.

There are plenty of US celebrities, like Kelly Clarkson, Pink and Solange Knowles, who are happy to advocate smacking. And one of the top reality stars in the country, Kate Gosselin, was actually pictured in the press smacking her child. Apparently, this was because the five year old wouldn't stop blowing a whistle. (I don't know whether Gosselin's approach was inspired by biblical teaching but she clearly hadn't read the parenting commandments, because in at No. 1 is: Thou shalt not give your five-year-old kid a fucking whistle, you idiot.)

Parents who smack their children in the US tend to insist that God says it's cool, whereas here in the UK you are more likely to hear the common refrain: 'I was smacked as a child and it never did me any harm.' Okay, well, maybe that's true and maybe it isn't. I used to play a game with my brother called 'Rochambeau' in which you take it in turns to kick each other in the nuts. That never did me any harm either. This does not mean that both things are to be encouraged and that they aren't really dumb shit to do.

In fact, multiple surveys and research suggest that corporal punishment is not only ineffective but also causes more harm than good. It makes children afraid of their parents, encourages kids to be more aggressive with their peers and maybe even lowers IQ.

I didn't know all this. Until I was researching about smacking for this chapter I didn't know that it could make children more likely to be antisocial, or introverted, or less curious.

The reason we don't smack Charlie is not because of any scientific research or psychological studies. I don't smack Charlie because I wouldn't know how. I'm happy to say that I wouldn't know how to go from being someone in his life who removes 'ouchies' to being someone who causes them. And in truth, hitting Charlie would hurt me at least as much as it would hurt him. It would make me deeply unhappy to think that I have made it this far through life without raising my hand to another human being, only to begin with one who is a third of my size.

I'm sure there will be many people who read our adventures with our little boy who think we are 'sparing the rod'. They will argue that the perfectly ordinary tantrums I describe are due to a lack of tough parenting and that they can be corrected by the occasional smack.

I don't think that's true. But even if it was, the truth is I'd prefer that he's a pain in the arse than that he's afraid. And maybe I'm a sissy-raising, snowflake libtard. And maybe it will make my son less obedient, less compliant, less cowed.

That's okay, some of the best humans are.

~~NEGOTIATING~~ / GIVING IN

So what are the foolproof remedies for naughtiness? How **do** we prevent tantrums and solve the problem of bad behaviour? Simple. You don't. For a parent, they are weather. Sometimes that weather is good and sometimes that weather is bad. But it's just weather.

You can be as consistent as the tides. You can remove, you can distract and you can ignore. You can smack and you can issue counts to ten that peter out at nine and you can threaten with naughty steps and timeout chairs. None of this stuff works, at least not all the time – for the simple reason that you can't stop a child from being tired, hungry, frustrated, confused, scared or from taking the piss.

And so most of us don't have a remedy or a tactic, or even a plan. We take a flame to the idea of consistency every day. We negotiate, we bribe, we cajole and muddle, and sometimes – maybe even a lot of the time – we give in. And yes, we know that giving in is the very worst thing that we can do. We are told it all the time. It is the one thing everybody seems to agree on, that by conceding to your toddler's demands you are encouraging future, stronger tantrums; you are validating your child's behaviour and you are confirming, to them, that their tactics work. It is precisely the same reasons why Western governments do not negotiate with terrorists.

Except they do.

Negotiating with terrorists

Despite what they say, Western governments actually negotiate with terrorists all the time because terrorists and toddlers have something in common: they can be pretty stubborn.

Refusing to negotiate with terrorists is fine in principle but not so much when they're standing right in front of you with explosives strapped to their chest. And this is a good way to think of the situation you find yourself in when your child says they want something and is threatening to tantrum.

In this situation, toddlers have a particular demand and they also have explosives (their temper). And you, as a parent, are like a cop with a bullhorn who is 'getting too old for this shit', trying to talk them down. Of course, the right thing to say is 'no', to refuse their demands on principle but, make no mistake, if you do . . . KABOOM. They will blow shit up.

Also, like terrorists, toddlers are tough negotiators in this situation. They play hardball. Because they know full well that they have something valuable to sell: their compliance. The truth is that they may be asking for an ice cream or a toy, but that is not what you are buying. What you are buying is their agreement that they won't go mad. That they won't embarrass you in public or make you look like a moron incapable of controlling your feral offspring. And all this comes at a price.

Some days that is a price worth paying, but some days everybody just wants to get out alive, and so we give in, we say 'YES'. We buy the ice cream or the toy and in doing so we train our child to be the best terrorist they can be.

SPOILED BRATS

So sometimes you give in. Even though everything tells us that this is **the worst thing you can do**®. But don't believe for a second that you are alone as a parent in conceding to your little dictator.

And if you are one of those parents who have never given in, then congratulations. You are as rare as a unicorn's balls. They will build statues to your parental brilliance. You have mastered the art of toddler taming. You are a parenting god. You're also a liar.

We all give in. Sometimes. And there will, no doubt, be people reading these words who argue that this is the very core of why toddlers tantrum. For all the reasons we've looked at here, from tiredness to frustration, there will always be those know-it-all wankers who insist that your toddler behaves the way they do because they are . . . spoilt.

There are lots of reasons why toddlers tantrum, but I'd argue that being spoiled is very rarely one of them. And yet there are those who insist that displays of temper equal precisely that.

We were in Ikea just a month ago, standing in the queue and edging forward with our trolley that contained a flat-pack bookcase, when a little girl just behind us began having a level-9 meltdown. She was clearly upset and tired, and like me rather pissed off to find herself in this fucking Swedish divorce maze on a Saturday. Her mum, obviously flustered and embarrassed, eventually conceded to the little girl's demands that she buy some felt-tip pens. And it was at this point that you could almost hear the swivel as the guy standing next to me rolled his eyes and then leaned in to whisper to his wife, 'Spoiled. Spoiled rotten.' Lyns clearly heard it as well as her face darkened and she looked like she was considering sticking our soon-to-be-purchased FJÄLKINGE up his judgey arsehole. 'Cock,' she coughed.

Cock indeed. No middle-aged man wearing stonewashed grandma jeans and a Nickelback T-shirt should be judging anything.

Lyns then made a point of giving the mum a little smile and they shared a joke about the fact that Charlie was at the time being appeased himself by a large donut.

I hate this idea of spoiling. This throwaway, ill-thought opinion. A conclusion based on a snapshot of a mum or dad's day.

I don't know one parent who concedes to every demand that

their child makes. We are all just trying to find a balance between making our children happy and not giving in to every one of the four thousand demands they make during the average day.

Well, actually that's not quite true. Because with a toddler there are no average days. Each day is a succession of highs and lows, and some days are tougher than others. Some days you have the energy for the battle, to walk the hard path. But sometimes the path of least resistance looks leafy and inviting and so you stroll down that one instead, because in that direction lies sanity.

In fairness, I think the attitudes of people like the bald man dressed as Nickelback's mum are pretty rare. But they do exist and they are hard to face. It is the ultimate judgement: the judgement that you have failed so monumentally as a mum or dad that your child is 'spoiled'.

It is a shitty, disgusting word. Spoiled. Milk spoils. Fruit spoils. Children don't.

It's a myth perpetuated to make you feel like the worst kind of parent, the very ruin of your child. Toddlers don't act the way they do because they are rotten or worthless. And kids don't go bad or rotten just because you concede to what they want sometimes.

They act the way that they do because they are toddlers. You may as well ask why a tiger has stripes or an alligator has teeth. It is the nature of the beast. Toddlers act this way because for them the world is new. It doesn't make a whole lot of sense. And as they try to understand it they get scared or unhappy, tired or just annoyed.

And toddlers are justifiably baffled by some of the daft shit we ask them to do. Don't walk on this bit of the path, but do walk on this bit. Enjoy yourself, don't make a mess. Stand up, sit up straight, hurry up, don't run . . . It's little wonder that they get confused. Adult rules make absolutely no sense.

Knowing this, though, does not necessarily make the terrible twos – or threes or fours – any easier to deal with. Nor does it make a child's moods any more understandable. Whether we like it or not, some days parenthood is a strange land, and . . .

. . . here be monsters.

A BAD DAY

Today was a bad day. I am writing this around midnight after finally getting our little boy to sleep after a day marked by tiredness and frustration.

I make no apology for losing my temper, getting annoyed and standing in a supermarket talking to Charlie through my teeth like a mad ventriloquist. I make no apologies at all. A parent's patience is elastic and stretchy but not indestructible. And we shouldn't feel bad about that.

But today was a bad day.

It is ironic that toddlers worry about monsters in their closets and under their beds because there are days like today, days that we all have, when we want to say . . . 'No. You know what? There is no monster under your bed. The monster is sitting on the bed and refusing to sleep. The monster is the one who spent today clawing at my face, kicking me on the shins and screeching in my ears. Now, for the love of God, go to fucking sleep.'

There are definitely days – not too many – when I want to say this. But I never do. Because I know that tomorrow is new by definition and that by morning the monster will be gone with the sun. And when, over the day, it inevitably returns . . . I will try to remember that at the beating heart of every monster is a creature misunderstood.

And besides, this kid's my monster.

And I love the little shit.

5

The Church of Soft Play

In Dante Alighieri's 14th century epic *Inferno* he paints a vivid, horrifying picture of The Nine Circles of Hell. He describes unbearable torture. Nightmarish scenes, each circle worse than the last, as sinners are punished by being torn apart by Cerberus, the three-headed dog, boiled alive in their own blood and fire, or fed upon by harpies. What Dante failed to mention is that there are, in fact, ten circles of hell. The tenth being an exact replica of Cheeky Monkeys, a soft-play warehouse just off junction 41 of the M62, near Leeds.

The Church of Soft Play

If parenthood is a religion, then soft-play centres are our church. They are temples – that demand we take our shoes off before entering – where we can worship at the altar of child safety. But this wasn't always the case.

When I was a kid, growing up in the seventies and eighties, I don't think 'soft play' existed. We had 'totally lethal play' instead. Our playgrounds were all outside and were comprised of rusty swings made from wood, metal and tetanus.

We had enormous twenty-foot slides that were coated in layer upon layer of snot, marmite and misspelt graffiti – that read things like: 'I've seen Bradley Darwent's Mum's fanny'.

On a cold day, the slides would freeze your arse off and on hot days would burn. We had roundabouts with no speed limit and it was a challenge to spin each other faster and faster until g-force was achieved, our eyes bled and we lost consciousness.

We also had seesaws that were a rudimentary form of Russian roulette. If one of you got off too quickly the 'see' would 'saw' abruptly and the spine of the child sitting opposite would be shattered as they were slammed into the ground (you tried to do this to other kids all the time). And we had hanging bars that were fifteen feet in the air with no safety net or soft ground cover, nothing to cushion your fall but concrete, weeds and pale dog shit.

Here's a picture I stumbled across online of the sort of place I'm talking about. If you look closely you can just make out one child falling to their certain death. No doubt cheered on by every other kid in the park.

This wasn't an unusual sight. Every few minutes in one of these local playgrounds you could bear witness to a momentary contest between a child's head and concrete. A contest that the concrete would almost always win. I have a very vivid memory of a boy called Damien Boxall being thrown thirty feet in the air from a swing and slammed against the side of a garage wall. I've never seen anyone laugh so hard in my life. (Until he noticed blood jetting from his head: 'Shit, it's all over my new coat, my mum's gonna kill me,' he said . . . before having another go.)

It wasn't just Damien, there was always some kid staggering around, bleeding like a lawn sprinkler because they'd taken a swing to the face or got the hood of their parka caught in an out-of-control roundabout.

These places were utterly deadly. And looking back now they seem designed to be some sort of sinister population control for council estates. A way of weeding out the really thick kids. It was Darwinian, natural selection at its finest. Or it should have been but for one major problem. These parks didn't naturally select the idiots, they couldn't: all kids are idiots.

To make matters worse, at 7pm every night these areas became the domain of the older youngsters. A place for surly teenagers to sit ironically on swings whilst smoking menthol cigarettes and drinking day-glo alcohol. Consequently, they were always littered with broken glass and tab ends and the residual haunting sadness of goths.

Fundamentally, in every way you can think of these places were about as child-friendly as Rosemary West.

But then, at some point in the nineties, health and safety was invented.

I know that in recent times 'health and safety' has become a tainted phrase, associated with those namby-pamby liberal types who want to stop us from making toast in the bath or driving around whilst pissed. And I've no doubt that the first time someone suggested making play safer for children, *Daily Telegraph* readers rolled their eyes and shouted hysterically that it was 'health and safety gone maaaaad!'

But, let's be fair. At the time you can guarantee that these people were saying the same about asbestos, fags and *Jim'll Fix It*. So, generally speaking, people who say 'health and safety gone maaaaad' can fuck off.

The arrival of health and safety in playgrounds was actually well overdue. Parents were, no doubt, sick to death of spending hours in casualty with their young ones having broken bones cast and gravel removed from their face. Society started to think that there was something to be done about entire generations losing IQ points and teeth by being flung headfirst from swings and seesaws like they were performing in a piss-poor Eastern European circus.

So, it was at this point, in the spirit of making things less deadly for our children, that someone first said . . . no more.

The First Soft Play

Their name is lost to history, that first person who spoke up for Damien Boxall and all the other millions of children engaged in those daily contests between their skulls and tarmac. This visionary demanded better for future generations than to play in these play-grounds of death in the pissing rain. And they sought to change it. They envisioned a different kind of play and decided to create the very first soft play, the very first Parents' Church:

... AND THUS, THEY WENT TO SEE THE ELDERS (THE BANK) TO DISCUSS HOW THEIR VISION MIGHT BE REALISED (TO ASK ABOUT A LOAN). AND THEY SAID UNTO THOSE ELDERS:

'FROM THIS DAY HENCE, WE SHALL CREATE VAST SOFT PLAYGROUNDS. WE SHALL MAKE THEM INDOORS ... AWAY FROM THE RAMPANT NETTLES AND DOG PISS. AND WE SHALL MAKE THEM SAFE, SO THAT OUR CHILDREN MAY KNOW NOT CON-CUSSION NOR BLOODIED NOSE.

'ELDERS, LET OUR BLESSED OFFSPRING SUFFER NO MORE. GIVE FREELY OF YOUR MONIES THAT WE MAY CREATE THIS SOFT PLACE OF REFUGE, THIS HAVEN OF SAFETY. FOR THE FUTURE. FOR THE INNOCENTS. FOR THE INHERITORS OF THIS EARTH ... OUR CHILDREN.'

AND THEY WERE MET WITH SILENCE.

SO THEY SAID: '... WE COULD SELL PANINIS FOR FOUR QUID A POP, WE'LL MAKE A FUCKING KILLING.'

AND THE ELDERS SMILED.

SOFT PLAY WAS BORN.

THOU SHALT SOFT PLAY

I was vaguely aware of the existence of soft plays before becoming a parent. They were the extensions attached to pubs. Rooms that you sat well away from. Occasionally, the double doors would swing open to one of these rooms and a fury of noise would spill out. A cacophonous barrage that sounded like beyond those doors people were being slaughtered.

Usually, along with the noise, some kid with a face covered in alphabetti-spaghetti juice would come barrelling out, stumble up to a random table, grab a handful of chips and take a glug of Fruit Shoot and go charging back through, back into the warzone beyond. And the pub would return to an agreeable, low conversational hum as if nothing had happened.

It is only when you become a parent that you notice that these places are actually everywhere. Hundreds of them, each with a theme: a dinosaur jungle, a treasure island, Noah's Ark, a farmyard. All sold as their own distinct wonderlands. 'Wonderlands' that are all basically the same: warehouses full of brightly coloured padded scaffolding, ball pools, plastic slides, crap hand-painted wall murals of Buzz Lightyear . . . and total fucking mind-bending chaos.

Parents spend a lot of time in these places, and their impact on our health and happiness is to be questioned. Along with the lack of sleep, poor diet and kids' TV, prolonged exposure to soft play is one of the top ten reasons that parent brains unravel and they spend long minutes every day in a fugue state daydreaming about being dead.

They are very rarely fun, and they are never, **ever** a wonderland.

So, why do we do it? Why do we worship at these churches? Why do we wander in voluntarily, take our shoes off and allow ourselves to be swallowed up in these worlds of garish colour and noise? Let's start with the official reasons why we take our kids to these places, and why those reasons are entirely bollocks.

These are the four main reasons why experts say that 'contained safe play' is super-duper awesome (yay!). (I took these reasons from the homepage of my local soft play's website. I've left them in the typeface, Comic Sans, because apparently soft plays only have access to one fucking font.)

1. GREAT FOR SENSORY STIMULATION!
2. A SAFE ENVIRONMENT TO EXPLORE!
3. SOCIALISING FOR PARENTS AND CHILDREN!
4. IT'S FUN!

1. GREAT FOR SENSORY STIMULATION!

Yes, undeniably, soft play stimulates the senses. But so does having a cannon full of hippo shit fired at point-blank range into your face. Sensory stimulation isn't always a good thing.

The first thing that hits you when you walk into the worst soft plays is the smell. If John McCririck released an aftershave it would smell like this. It's kind of a mix of feet and Quavers.

We all know children are disgusting. And hundreds of these creatures going apeshit in a windowless warehouse creates an interesting assault on the sense of smell. With the older ones sweating, and the younger ones pissing and crapping themselves with regularity, it's a heady olfactory cocktail. Add to that the vague notes of Frubes, dad sweat, a hint of milk-vomit and cheese toasties and it's fair to say that the sense of smell is stimulated almost as much as the gag reflex.

The second thing that stimulates the senses is the sound. The sound, which on a quiet weekday morning is a pleasant, ambient hubbub of children's excitement, giggling and the occasional delighted squeal. But on busy Saturdays during half-term, has an effect on the senses somewhat like a chimpanzee bumming your skull.

The noise of soft play on these days is like nothing on Earth. Try it with a hangover. It is the soundtrack to insanity. Hysterical tears, hysterical laughter and persistent screeching is all accompanied by thematic music. For Pirates' Cove it is sea shanties, for Adventure Planet it is futuristic electronica. And for Jungle Jamboree it is monkey noises and the sound of a parrot having its fucking neck wrung.

When cult leader David Koresh barricaded himself and his followers inside a compound in Waco, Texas, the FBI tried to end the siege by assaulting their ears with the most terrible noises; they sought to send them mad. They chose Tibetan chants, bugle blasts and distorted Christmas carols. They had this mixtape on repeat for hours on end. In the end, it didn't work and they abandoned the idea. If only they'd captured the sound generated by a soft play when there is a superhero party in full swing, Koresh would've surrendered within the day – or at least blown his brains out a lot sooner.

Even the sense of taste is not immune to this sensory bombardment, as all these places have a crappy little café manned by someone who seems surprised to find themselves in charge of serving food to members of the public. Often a bored, listless teenager who would struggle to recognise an egg. Or someone who has worked there for long enough that all sense of fun they once had has died, and so they now have a face like a sad drain.

The food is almost always terrible. Don't get me wrong, I'm not expecting Michelin standards. If you're lucky there might be a basic hygiene certificate (the green one with a single star . . . a certificate that you get for washing your hands and not drying them on your cock). But the food is often spectacularly bad. Charlie is not a fussy eater at all but even he turns his nose up at half the fare served in these places. Which is incredible. When this happens I have to fight the urge to ask the person behind the counter: 'How is it possible that you can mess up basic food so badly, that my kid will happily lick every foot-sweat-tasting plastic ball in this place but won't touch your fucking five-quid cheese sandwich?'

2. A SAFE ENVIRONMENT TO EXPLORE!

Okay, so soft play, good or bad, stimulates the senses. But what about this claim that they provide a safe environment to explore? Indoor soft play is undeniably safer than children's playgrounds of the past, but that's not to say that they are without risk altogether. Let's face it, the average play centre is like a dystopian Snakes and Ladders with screaming murderous kids instead of counters. And there's always a risk of injury with children, because they do dim shit all the time and they are incredibly stubborn about being told what to do.

How many times do you have to tell a child that they must not walk back up the slide they've just come down? I explained this to Charlie at least five hundred times and it still took one fat kid coming the other way to plough through him, at thirty miles an hour, to teach him that maybe I had a point.

Added to that is the risk of eating the food in the cafeteria (which can't be underestimated) and the dodgy hygiene levels generally. In the worst soft plays you can almost hear a hum from the ball pool as it quietly incubates chicken pox and conjunctivitis. And as I've said, Charlie won't leave a soft play until he's licked every plastic ball and tasted every slide in there. So in this regard some soft plays are about as safe a place to play as that island where the CIA tested anthrax.

I also have my own reasons for questioning whether they really are 'safe environments to explore' . . . for any of us.

When Charlie was about one and a half, we were in a themed soft play near where we live called JungleTots. As usual, I was following Charlie as he climbed, tumbled and crawled his way around the two or three floors of animal-inspired obstacles. Eventually, we made our way up to the very top floor where we found the entrance to a snakey slide. It was the biggest slide in the place and one that spiralled from the top floor all the way back down to the bottom.

The only issue was a small sign taped to the opening which read: NO ADULTS ALLOWED!

In my defence, there were three reasons why I still went down the slide:

1. Charlie was really little and I had to lift him over every obstacle to get up there. It took ages to reach the top and it would take the same amount of time to get back down . . . this was clearly a shortcut.
2. Charlie wanted to go down the slide. And me insisting that he couldn't (because he was too small to go on his own and I wasn't allowed), well, that would have gone down like a concrete balloon.
3. Fuck it. Right? No A4 laminate is going to tell me what to do.

So, I sat in the mouth of the snake, took Charlie on my lap and off we 'weeeee'd'. And seconds later we arrived at the bottom into the soft landing of a small ball pool. 'Again! Again!' Charlie insisted, as I looked back at the slide and wondered what all the bloody fuss was about.

Yeah, screw you and your rules and regulations. If I want to take my son down a slide I'm going to take my son down a slide. No one tells **this** dad what to –

Shit.

I looked at my surroundings again. It took a moment to realise that the ball pool we had landed in was only about 5 metres square, with four walls of netting . . . and no exit. The only way out was a small circular hole at about ankle height, like a cat-flap. A flap that your average toddler would fit through with ease but a six-foot-tall twelve-stone idiot like me was just not designed for.

I looked around again and there was a moment of sheer panic. I'm stuck. I'm fucking stuck. There was literally no way out.

I'm not someone who deals well with a crisis and so my measured reaction was roughly Denial, Acceptance and then Overreaction: i.e. *There must be another way out. I'm stuck. Oh my God, I'm going to die in here.*

After a few minutes I began to assess our situation as calmly as I could. I couldn't get back up the snake and I couldn't fit through the flap. I thought about signalling to another parent that I was stuck but immediately ruled out the idea. It occurred to me that my own reaction to being asked for help in this situation would be to get my phone out. I would have had the video on YouTube before you could say 'Look at this nobhead'.

I even thought about sending Charlie through the hole to get help. Like Lassie, I could send him to the café counter to bark until they understood that his master was trapped.

Dismissing these ideas, I did the only other thing I could think of: I phoned JungleTots. I took out my phone, googled their telephone number and called it.

From where I was stuck I could hear the phone ringing and see the woman pottering about behind the café counter doing fuck all. Answer the bloody phone. Answer the bloody phone. Answer the bloody phone.

Eventually she did pick up. I attempted to remove all panic from my voice and tried to sound nonchalant:

'Oh, hello there. Sorry to bother you but I'm stuck in your ball pool.'

'What?'

'Yeah, I'm stuck in your ball pool. If you look to your left I'm the chap in the Thundercats T-shirt waving at you . . . Hi.'

She glanced over, unamused.

'Did you come down the slide?'

'. . . Pardon?'

'Did you come down the slide?'

'Erm . . . well . . .'

'There's a sign at the top that quite clearl—'

'Well, you might want to think about getting a bigger sign, love. Do you think I'd have come down the slide if I'd seen a sign? This is absolutely ridiculous.'

'Uh huh.'

To cut a long story short, it will forever be a source of shame – for myself, my family and my descendants – that I had to be cut out of the ground floor ball pool at JungleTots.

As a small crowd gathered, the woman from behind the counter came over with a pair of scissors and cut the cable ties that held a net wall in place. Essentially, they had to remove one of these walls to get me out. As I was being freed I felt like one of those eighty-stone recluses they used to have on Jerry Springer. The ones who have to have a window removed from their house just to get them out and to hospital ('I just wanna live, Jerry!').

And, incidentally, I was not happy to notice somebody filming my rescue on their phone. 'What kind of arsehole would film this?' I remember thinking.

Anyway, that's how I survived. Rescued by a pair of scissors and a mardy-looking woman called Julie.

I fell out of the ball pool and Charlie arched an eyebrow as I thanked her. With relief I started to chuckle.

'Sorry about that, I guess this happens all the time, eh?'

'No,' replied Julie. 'No. It doesn't.'

. . . You could have lied, Julie. A good person would have lied.

3. SOCIALISATION FOR PARENTS AND CHILDREN!

Okay, what about this claim that it's great for socialisation. Firstly, let's quickly dispel the myth that soft play is in any way an appropriate place for parents to socialise with one another. It isn't. It's a nice idea, but you are definitely there only because your children wish to be. Imagine that, before becoming a mum or dad, another adult invites you out socially and suggests that you meet in the middle of the day. Now imagine that the invite is for a place so noisy it feels as though your ears are being sodomised. It's also too bright, serves inedible food and doesn't have a bar. Yeah, thanks for the invitation but I'd rather stay at home and gnaw my own leg off.

Also, I always thought socialising involved some sort of inter-action or at least conversation. The soft-play environment is not exactly conducive to a catch-up and a chat, especially when you're responsible for a toddler. This is a conversation I heard just this morning. I eavesdropped and took it down word for word:

Mum 1: So did you manage to book your holid— JAYDEN! JAYDEN?! GET DOWN NOW!

Mum 2: No, we were going to go to . . . SAMUEL! THAT IS NOT VERY NICE, SAY SORRY TO JAYDEN . . . Majorca but it was booked up.

Mum 1: So you didn't manage to . . . JAYDEN I AM NOT GOING TO TELL YOU AGAIN, GET DOWN NOW! . . . book your holiday at all then?

Mum 2: No, but we think we might . . . SAMUEL! HAVE YOU DONE ANOTHER POO? POO? HAVE YOU DONE A POO? . . . get away later in the year.

Mum 1: Oh, well that's . . . JAYDEN! GET. DOWN. NOW! JAAAYYYDEN!!'

Listening to these conversations is like listening to a badly tuned radio, constantly flipping between Radio 4 and Little Shits FM.

The circumstances just aren't good for socialising amongst adults. I'm not sure why anybody would ever think that they could be. If you want to socialise with other parents it is best to do what normal people do: dump your kids with the grandparents, find a pub and drink until you can't feel your face.

But what about socialisation for children? Well, this begs the question: why on earth would you want your child socialising with other children? On the whole, other kids are bloody awful.

The first soft play I ever went to was the aforementioned tenth circle of hell: Cheeky Monkeys. On the About Us page of their website it emphasises the 'social aspect' for parents and children alike. It goes on to say that the establishment was named Cheeky Monkeys because of the kids 'who love to come along to our 8,000 sq feet of ball pools, slides and trampolines and act like "cheeky monkeys"!'

To be honest, after four hours in there one Saturday afternoon, I'd say that if they were intent on naming the place after their tiny clientele, a more appropriate name would have been something like 'Little Fuckers' or 'Demonic Midget Bitey Twats'.

This place was like *Lord of the Flies* meets *Mad Max Beyond Thunderdome*: a 20-metre-tall padded scaffolding cage in which a hundred kids were re-enacting the Battle of Carthage, apparently after huffing paint thinner. It was terrifying.

Charlie was barely a year old and on arrival I took one look at the towering play area in front of us and wondered what the hell I was about to introduce him to.

I can't let him play in there, I thought. I wouldn't set foot in there myself, certainly not on my own, and definitely not without some sort of weapon – at least a laser or a can of pepper spray. I might as well be throwing him to the bloody lions. In fact it was worse, at least lions don't stand on top of a slide, drop their trousers and wave their dick around shouting, 'I AM A FIREMAAAN' like one kid was doing. No, this place was madness.

Socialisation is all well and good but some of these kids looked fucking demented.

Not all soft plays are this bad. And to a degree it was my own fault for visiting on a Saturday afternoon. (A simpleton rookie's mistake, never to be repeated.) At quieter times they can be quite bearable. But at busy times most of them have the atmosphere of a Mexican prison in which the inmates have shot the guards and gone mental. In either case, though, there are tactics to surviving soft play. And that begins with understanding the threat.

COMBATANTS

The different types of soft-play kid:

THE BERZERKER   THE BALL-POOL   THE ORPHAN   THE WAY-TOO-   THE VIP
                    ARSEHOLE   OLD KID

The Berzerker

Berzerkers can be quite unnerving. I remember the first time I saw one. When he arrived, he appeared to be a placid, calm child. But as his mum was taking his shoes off, he started to undergo a transformation. He cracked his knuckles, necked his purple Fruit Shoot and looked like he was ready to kill. And as she released him into the play area saying, 'Okay now, play nicely, Thomas, behave yourself,' I couldn't help but think that this kid did not look like he wanted to behave himself at all . . . this kid looked like he wanted to bathe in the blood of his enemies.

The Berzerkers are the kids who arrive at soft play and turn instantly into William fucking Wallace. Running into battle with wild-eyed madness in their eyes, ready to smash some heads together. 'FFREEEEEEDOMM!'

Berzerkers have unlimited energy. They ricochet and bounce around the place like pinballs and throw themselves into and off of everything. And when they take a tumble or endure a fall that would kill most of us, they pop straight back up and do it all over again.

They are aggressive in their play. Every other kid is in their way, every adult even more so. They are stuntmen in an action movie that is playing in their own heads.

Of course, all kids are capable of going Berzerker. Soft-play fever can grip the mind of the most placid of children. And the right combination of lawlessness and sugar does things to the mind. One minute a child can be calm and easygoing, the next they are in the melee, charging around, wreaking havoc and wearing human ears as trophies around their neck . . . or is that 'Nam? I think that might be 'Nam . . .

But I'll be honest, I can't help but like the Berzerkers. I've always admired those really confident kids who throw themselves into everything. I like their wild abandon and attitude. They are no nonsense. They don't take any shit. I was never like that when I was younger, my brother was, and he always seemed to be having more fun. And moreover, Berzerkers have something of the human spirit about them. In another time they would've been Viking generals stood at the front of battle, demanding that tonight we shall feast in Valhalla.

Just stay out of their way.

The Way-too-old Kid

Every soft play has a section for babies and young toddlers. These areas tend to be for children up to about three years old. The slides aren't so big, the obstacles not quite so daunting. And it is designed

137

to be an environment where the younger children can play safely without coming into contact with a Berzerker or an obstacle that is beyond their ability.

The only problem with these sections is The Way-too-old Kid. A child who is about six or seven and has chosen this exact spot to practise his WWE wrestling moves. It is difficult to know why he prefers to be in this section, unless his specific aim is to roundhouse kick a baby's head off its shoulders.

There is usually a Way-too-old Kid in the main play area as well. I don't know what age kids grow out of this sort of thing but I've seen young lads tearing around that looked like they were old enough to vote. I know people mature at different rates – I myself was quite an immature teenager – but I know that by the time I was fifteen I was busy trying to buy weed and get off with Sophie Parkinson, not pissing about on slides and building a fort out of oversized foam Lego.

The Ball-pool Arsehole

The kid I hate most in these places is probably the Ball-pool Arsehole, the obnoxious little shit who lays claim to the ball pool and then refuses entry to everybody else, or defends his kingdom by body-slamming the smaller kids or throwing the balls at them.

It's not just the little kids who suffer. I myself have been bullied by a Ball-pool Arsehole in my time as a parent. On the one occasion I asked politely for a BPA not to throw balls at the smaller children, they turned their fire on me.

'Excuse me . . . Do you mind not . . .' Thonk. (A ball hits me in the face.)

'Seriously, you need to . . .' Thonk.

'Listen, you little . . .' Thonk.

It was at this point and under this severe provocation that I threw one back. I'm not proud of it. But I did catch him pretty sweetly on the side of the temple and he went down like a sack of spuds.

It's just a shame he felt the need to go crying, like a little bitch, to his enormous dad. And me and Charlie had to hide in a small pop-up circus tent until they left.

The Orphan

There is always an urchin child in every soft play. A toddler who appears to have been abandoned. With no parent in sight, no one checking on them even, it is easy to think that maybe they actually live there. Maybe they have a small nest underneath one of the slides from which they occasionally come out for food.

Obviously their parent is here somewhere. But there is no real way you would know it. Don't get me wrong, I've no issue with parents turning up, releasing their kids into the play area and putting their feet up. Especially when the kids are a bit older and can fend for themselves. That's fine. I have no problem with a mum or dad relaxing in these places if they can, having a nice cup of tea whilst they catch up on Facebook or whatever. After all, if you've been awake since 5am, not had a shower or two seconds to yourself, the last thing you need is some judgey tit giving you the side-eye just because you're having a minute.

That said, when your child is tiny, has just learned to walk or is asking you to 'look at me, Mummy' just before they swan-dive off of a 20-foot-tall cargo net, here's a thought: have a glance up. Make sure they are not leaping to their certain death or that they are at least going to land somewhere soft. Maybe have a rough idea where they might be from hour to hour, just to be sure that they haven't sneaked out of a fire exit and fucked off to Wetherspoons.

Which brings me to my real problem with The Orphan. These kids attach themselves to me. I admit that when it comes to soft play I'm a bit of a helicopter parent. I'm one of those annoying, over-cautious dads. I follow Charlie through the play maze always seven inches behind him, clearing his path and making sure he's okay.

The problem with being this sort of soft-play parent (the sort of mum or dad who 'joins in') is that the orphan child, starved of attention, latches on to you. They strike up awkward conversations that go like this:

'I'm four.'

'Er . . . okay.'

'My name's Toby, what's your name?'

'Er . . . well, it's Matt but . . .'

'Do you want to build a castle?'

'Er . . . not really . . . we're just going to . . . go on the slide.'

'Okay, I'll come with you.'

And just like that you've adopted a child. Who will follow you wher-ever you go. Now I'm not just looking after one child, I'm apparently responsible for two. What's more, this new kid is a bigger pain in the arse than my own: 'Watch this!' every two minutes.

And there's always an awkward moment when they ask to be helped up or over an obstacle. You see, I don't know what the rules are for picking up other people's children. Especially when you've never even met their parents. So, even when they're stuck and hanging precariously from a cargo net by one foot and shouting 'Help me!' instinct tells me *You're on your own, kid. I want to help but there's no way I'm risking you shouting 'stranger danger'.*

Of course, these kids aren't really orphans. There always comes a moment when you hear a parent bellowing: 'Brandon!!' or whatever, and the kid's mum or dad pokes their head into the play area to say 'ten more minutes' before eventually reclaiming them. To begin with I thought these were just crappy parents. But it is in that instant, as they give me a knowing glance, that I realise they are not crappy parents at all. For the previous hour their child has been perfectly safe and had a great time. Because, like a complete mug, I have been providing free childcare. At zero cost to them I have been their personal manny, and these aren't terrible parents, far from it; they've just got this parenting thing totally sussed.

The VIP

Finally, The VIP. The opposite of The Orphan, the VIPs are the children who have a bodyguard. An over-involved, over-cautious parent who makes sure that their child's path is clear. That when they fall they are caught, that they are helped over each hurdle and that they can come to absolutely no harm. Through no fault of his own, Charlie is a VIP. He is Whitney Houston to my Kevin Costner. I overprotect him in every way. It shames me, but I'm **that** parent.

I tell myself that there are reasons for my caution. I tell myself that he's still quite young and not that steady on his feet or great at climbing. But, in truth, that's probably because I don't allow him to be. He is rarely allowed to tumble or bang his head and this, I've realised, is not necessarily a good thing. In many ways it increases the danger. Because, by removing the pain and consequences of falling, I have made him all the more fearless. He has no experience of what happens when his head hits things at speed and so has no sense of self-preservation either.

This is my fault. And it is one of my biggest failings as a parent.

To be this overcautious dad is in a lot of ways worse than being the parent of a Berzerker, an Orphan or even a Ball-pool Arsehole.

Not allowing Charlie to fail stops him from learning the art of being crap at something. An art that teaches us all to try harder, to overcome. To be better. I'm not saying that I need to start letting him hurt himself, but I also know that I can't protect him forever, and if I keep protecting him too fiercely I will do him more harm than good. Loving him is no excuse for always polishing off the edges of hard experience.

This was a conclusion that I came to after analysing an array of research and peer-reviewed studies about childhood development. Just kidding. I got it from *Finding Nemo*:

Marlin: I promised I'd never let anything happen to him.

Dory: Hmm. That's a funny thing to promise.

Marlin: What?

Dory: Well, you can't never let anything happen to him. Then nothing would ever happen to him.

The cartoon fish has got a point.

4. IT'S FUN!

Which brings us to our fourth and final reason why soft play is super-duper awesome (yay!). It is fun! With a capital F! And a capital U and an N for that matter! Isn't it so much fun? It's just so much fUcKiNg FuN.

I beg to differ.

As a parent, there are moments in life when your heart sinks. When your kid messes up a room that you've just spent an hour tidying, or pisses in your shoes just as you're about to leave the house. And then there are times when your heart doesn't just sink, but plummets, through the bottom of your ribcage, past your bowels and out of your arsehole. This is the story of one of those times.

It was a Friday afternoon and we (me and Charlie) were enjoying the soft-play delights of Captain Jack's Pirate Cove: 'A truly magical kingdom of swashbuckling, treasure and adventure'. A truly magical kingdom that was situated on an industrial estate in Rotherham, in between a shop that sold paraphernalia for smoking dope and a unit that cleans wheelie bins.

Captain Jack's is huge. It is four floors of the usual crap and is supposed to look like a giant treasure island. Complete with hand-painted palm trees on the walls and three or four massive ball pools made to look like tall ships. Uniquely, there is also an impressive 15-foot plastic pirate that stands astride the entrance to one of the pools. (I think it's supposed to resemble Captain Jack Sparrow but, thanks to the skills of the amateur artists in these places it looks like Johnny Depp's half-brother peering into the back of a spoon.) And every time a kid crawls through the legs of this thing it waves its arms and shouts 'Aaargh! Shiver mi timbers!' or 'Avast, mi hearties!'

Adding to the overall effect, hidden speakers are playing a constant stream of sea shanties and 'pirate' music like 'the sailor's hornpipe'. Which, after three hours on a loop, makes you want to beat any pirate to death with his stupid fucking wooden leg.

I have never liked pirates; to me they are just thieves on a boat*. But I never knew how annoying pirates truly were until I spent an

---

* I think I may have Thalassoharpaxophobia, a fear of pirates. I don't like the way they dress, I can't stand the way they ponce about and I don't like the way they talk: 'Aaargh! Jim-Lad. You be after mi treasure.' 'No, I don't "be after" anything, fuck off, you one-legged, parrot-wearing fuck-face.'

afternoon at Captain Jack's. It's the staff I feel most sorry for. Imagine having to listen to two hundred screaming kids all day, every day, acting out *Pirates of the Caribbean* and beating the living shit out of each other with plastic swords. Now imagine that scenario but to the soundtrack of sea shanties. It's no wonder the girl behind the food counter always looks like she's one 'Yo Ho Ho' away from going full 'Sissy Spacek' and burning the whole place to the ground with her mind.

Yes, there is no escape from the relentlessly piratey theme even in Captain Jack's Treasure Island Café. (Poor Sissy Spacek's job is certainly not made any easier by having to work a sandwich toaster and pour cups of tea whilst wearing a tricorn hat and an eye patch.) Even the menu consists of authentic piratey meals like:

The Swashbuckler! (fish fingers, chips and beans)
The Galleon! (chicken nuggets, chips and beans)
and
The Jolly Roger! (sausage, chips and beans)

Also on the menu is 'Salty Seadogs', which turns out to be just chips on their own; 'Pieces of Eight', which are actually just chicken nuggets on their own; and just 'beans' . . . on their own. It's not an extensive menu.

Although they did also offer jacket potatoes, which inexplicably didn't have a seafaring name. Having ordered one, I would suggest 'The Cannonball' given that the thing was rock hard and had been in the oven so long it was more meteorite than food.

As I've said, I don't expect great things from the food in these places so I may be being a little harsh. In fairness, there is actually a certain authenticity to the meals dished up at Captain Jack's, in that, if you ate there regularly enough, there is a pretty good chance you would end up with scurvy and possibly rickets.

So the scene is set for one of my lowest ever points as a parent.

We had been playing in Captain Jack's for about three hours, with me following Charlie the whole time, the way the overcautious do. Anyway, after hours of swimming through ball pools, friction burning my arse on plastic slides and scrambling up and down rope netting, the time came for us to leave. I could stand no more 'Yo Ho Ho'ing myself and besides, Charlie had finally been exhausted. I scooped him up, laid him down in the reclined seat of his stroller and he went instantly to sleep. *Off we go*, I thought.

It was at this point that I realised my car keys were missing.

They had been in my pocket. Now they weren't.

There was a moment of eerie silence as my brain quieted the noise of the hectic surroundings in preparation for the terrible truth, the slowly dawning realisation that at some point in the previous three hours my car keys had fallen out of my pocket and were now lost. Buried like the most precious of treasure in Captain Jack's pissing Pirate Cove.

I looked up at the four floors of ball pools, nets and garish obstacles. A mother, walking past with her three kids, tutted with disgust as I 'fuck, shit, fuck'ed my horror.

I looked down at Charlie in his pushchair. By this point he was well and truly asleep, his hands behind his head, his pirating day was over. Which meant only one thing. I had to go back in . . . on my own.

And so I did.

Okay. Here's something I learned that day. Nothing screams 'paedophile' quite like a forty-three-year-old man in a pirate-based soft play **on his own**. Try it. Try being a middle-aged man swimming around in an under-eight's ball pool and going up and down slides on your own. Other parents were pulling their kids out of there like there was a shark in the water. And I don't blame them. Half the problem is that these places are designed so you can only get between floors by using the slides. I didn't just look like a pervert, I looked like I was having a bloody whale of a time.

To make matters worse, I could hardly be discreet about it because every time I went through Johnny Depp's fucking legs he shouted, 'Aaargh! Avast mi hearties!' and everyone turned around to gawp and check I was still in there. He might as well have been shouting, 'For God's sake, save the kids!'

After half an hour of this complete humiliation (during which I kept saying 'Sodding car keys' as loudly as possible so at least those in earshot wouldn't think me a complete lunatic) there was no sign of them.

For the record, I did find other stuff. Jonathan Ross, in an interview, said that he once found a dirty nappy in a ball pool and, as disgusting as that is, I can believe it. I didn't find a dirty nappy, but I did come across the following:

A slice of ham (a full slice of ham, just there, stuck to a slide). Two Avengers socks and a PAW Patrol shoe. Cash: £2.17 in total. A weird, pale kid. (He was just lying there under the balls in a ball pool, like some sort of house vampire.) I found food too: multiple rice cakes, raisins and what I hoped to God was half a chocolate brownie. I also found a child's felt-tip drawing of what looked like a crying Chewbacca firing a Nerf gun at a dinosaur's arse . . . this artwork was signed 'Noah'.

Oh, and I think I also came across the dignity of the last poor twat who lost his keys in Captain Jack's Pirate Cove. I buried my own dignity alongside and just kept on looking.

But eventually I gave up. It was like searching for a needle in a . . . well, in a shitty pirate-based soft play. I conceded and called Lyns to ask her to leave work and rescue us with a spare set of keys.

She arrived an hour or so later. Shaking her head and clearly wondering, not for the first time, how she now found herself in a twenty-odd-year relationship with a colossal dickhead.

But she was soon sympathetically pissing herself laughing as I described the previous hour of torment. And as we wandered to the car, I looked back one last time at Captain Jack's and thought about the treasure that that wily old pirate had taken from me that day. And I vowed to return to reclaim that treasure (should my lost property form that I'd filled out for 'Trudy' prove successful).

And it was then, as I collapsed the pram to put it in the boot, that the keys fell out of the stroller's hood, exactly where I'd put them for safekeeping six hours before.

. . . Well, shiver mi fucking timbers.

WHY SOFT PLAY?

I started this chapter by saying that soft play was a kind of hell. And I think that's still a fair assessment. So why **do** we spend so much time in them? How **have** they become the parents' church?

I don't know. Maybe you take your little one to soft play because you enjoy the social element. Maybe you've read about the benefits to your child, the way in which it improves cognitive development and fine motor skills and all that stuff. For most of us, though, these are not the noble reasons why we subject ourselves to Jungle Jamboree on wet Saturday afternoons. We do it because these places are magnificent hamster wheels. Places to burn off the energy, the high-octane fuel, that seems to power toddlers.

But there is another reason why we do it. Kids love these places. And we do all kinds of hellish things because our kids want to.

We may think of soft plays as torturous but our little ones disagree. From their point of view they are not hell, they really are pirate ships and jungles and undiscovered dinosaur worlds. How could they be anything else? Reality is for grown-ups.

And watching Charlie zoom down a soft-play slide, the static setting his hair on end, laughing with the thrill of it all . . . one thing is really clear: reality, and being grown-up for that matter, is really overrated.

So, when I am being a cynical dickhead about these places and feel a grown-up's exasperation with being trapped in yet another 'wacky warehouse', I should remember what is written in joy on the face of every excited toddler arriving at every soft play in the world, because it's this:

I am a little thing and little things stir me. You, old timer, find that thrill in big things like love and anger. And there will come a time when I will be like you, when only those big things stir me too. But for now I am stirred by this . . . a room full of plastic balls, and picking up speed on a twisty slide.

Here is my passion, the world will erode it in good time.

So sit down, shut up, eat your fucking panini and hold my shoes.

Because I'm going in.

Fair enough.

6

The Call of the Potty

In many ways, potty-training is a lot like going camping. In the beginning you're excited and enthusiastic, but a couple of days later you've had enough, everything is wet, and you're sick to death of the smell of piss.

The Call of the Potty

Before becoming a parent, there are very few circumstances in which you share personal space with someone whilst they are having a shit.

It's true. Or at least it was for me. Apparently, there are couples out there who go to the bathroom in each other's presence. But I've always found that a bit weird. I'm no expert on relationships and keeping the fire alive, but I think it best to preserve a little mystery. And relationships in which wives will happily enjoy a bath whilst their husband sits on the throne beside them, cheerfully dropping a load, strike me as lacking in a certain romantic frisson.

I'd say the only circumstances where it is acceptable as an adult to be in the same room as someone else having a crap is if you're in prison and sharing a cell.

(Actually, despite the starch-rich diet of the modern jail, this would probably bother me slightly less than the first example. I'm not sure why. Maybe because if I **were** in prison I'd be too preoccupied with not getting shanked for my tobacco to be that fussed about my cellmate 'Jimmy the Hammer' having a dump in full view).*

So it's weird how quickly you actually get accustomed to another human being just sitting there, in your living room, having a crap. But as your toddler starts to use a potty, that is exactly what you have to get used to.

* Actually, potty-training is a bit different from having to observe a cellmate: when serial murderer 'Jimmy the Hammer' finishes a successful shit I suspect you would be less likely to applaud and give him a sticker.

And we **do** get used to it. It becomes perfectly everyday to find yourself sat watching the TV whilst in your line of sight a small person gurns with effort as they evacuate their bowels. In fact, you reach a point when you barely notice, as you peer around them to catch the last bit of *The Chase*.

I think the reason why we mentally adjust to this situation so quickly is because we have no choice. Fundamentally, we know that this is a means to an end. The move to big-boy pants is vital.

IT'S NOT ALL SHIT

By almost every personal account I've ever heard, potty-training is something of a nightmare and not a thing to enter into lightly. But you can't put it off forever and there are huge advantages to having a toilet-trained child:

1. **No more Poonamis, Poosplosions, Poopocalypses or Shitmageddons.** Parents have all kinds of terms for the most heinous travesties of the arse. But with a toilet-trained child, these major events are things of the past. Imagine it: no more dashing to find a toilet with changing facilities because your kid's backside has spontaneously detonated and their nappy is leaking so badly that you can see shit coming out of their collar like a curious brown snake.

   Imagine never again having to face the 'worst-case scenario' nappies. The utterly catastrophic ones. The ones that deserve their own telethon, in which celebrities stride towards the camera earnestly asking for help. The horrors that you take one look at and briefly consider calling the helpline for the Disasters Emergency Committee before rolling up your sleeves and battling the thing, with heroic fervour, like it's a fire on an oil rig.

Everyone has the one they remember. Their King Kong. The Moby Dick to their Captain Ahab. The ones where your child looks like it has been dipped, and you have to somehow find where the child ends and the crap starts. The ones in which their legs are so coated it looks like they are wearing shit trousers. The ones where it is in their armpits, their hair, on the wall . . . everywhere, including forever in your haunted soul.

These are the war stories that we tell each other over a coffee at Tumble Tots, with the haunted eyes of a war veteran, as if they're dispatches from the frontline. 'You weren't there, maaan! You weren't fuckin' there!'

With toilet-training, these cataclysms can be left in the past. Leaving behind only post-traumatic stress, the occasional sweaty nightmare and a lifetime ban from the toilet facilities at Tibshelf Services.

2. **How about no more baby changing rooms?** I covered baby changing rooms pretty extensively in the last book, but to think you may never have to set foot in one again!? Imagine never having to deal with the shelf of death, the pulsating, throbbing nappy bin of doom and the face-melting stench as you press the foot pedal and release the awesome power of forty-two kids' collective shits. Consider that, as an adult, the only time you will have to face such levels of crap and abomination again will be if you are somehow forced to listen to a track from Sting's new album.

3. **In fact, no more of the simple horror of nappies.** Those tiny white parcels of grimness that fill your bins until they groan. Or sit in

tiny bags hanging from nursery door handles like they've been left behind by those weird dog walkers who throw their bags of crap to hang in bushes like Satan's Christmas-tree ornaments.

Indeed, no longer having to deal with those rogue ones that you find in the bottom of your pram or those ones that disappear under a car seat and reveal themselves weeks later on a hot day when your car begins to smell like you've been carting around a tramp's dead body. No more stuffing them into the top of your wheelie bin and compacting them down, until your hand accidentally splits through the lot, coating your arm like you're a vet who has just had their hand up a cow's arsehole.

4. **No more of the *expense* of nappies and wipes.** Supposedly, the average parents spend a total of around £700 per child just on nappies. And that is the least of it. Every parent on the planet knows the conspiracy of the wet wipe. The truth: manufacturers specifically design them so that, when you are forced to use one hand, they will only come out forty at a time. So we are made to buy more and more. If we spend £700 on nappies we must spend £5,000 on wet wipes. It would be cheaper to wipe our children's backsides with fivers.

Ironically, the only humans who **can** get them out one at a time easily are ill-supervised toddlers (like the one overleaf).

5. **But all this is not the most important cost:** finally – and most importantly – nappies (and wipes for that matter) literally cost the earth . . . Cue Michael Jackson's 'Earth Song'.
🎵 AaaaaaahAaaaaaahAaaaaaaaaaahAaaaaaaaaaaaaaaaaaaah 🎵

Nappies are really bad for the environment. Not bad enough for me not to use them because . . . well, because . . . Look, I care about

Man vs Baby
25th June 🌐

I love the kid but this is a real dick move...

the environment but I am also a modern-day wanker. I bet you've been using them too. Yes, you. You've been killing dolphins and trees and making the Earth hotter just like me, you dick. Unless you've been using cloth nappies and washing them, in which case, well done, you're better than the rest of us. (But I bet you bang on about it a lot and probably use tree bark as deodorant.)

This is a serious point though. If you do use cloth nappies you are definitely walking the righteous path. Disposables really aren't a good thing. The average kid gets through nearly 4,000 nappies before they are potty-trained. To give you an idea of how many that is, if you placed these full nappies one on top of the other the pile would be over a kilometre high. That's just one kid. And if you think that's bad, there are 130 million babies born on Earth every year. So if over two years all babies used an average number of disposables it would be 156 million kilometres of nappies. That is the distance to Mars and back and then back again.

I don't know whether this has ever been considered by NASA but forget sophisticated propulsive rocketry for the mission to the red planet, we could just build a bridge of shit there.

Bear in mind, too, that these things don't biodegrade for ages. They are virtually indestructible. How on earth the planet is not already three feet deep in baby dump is completely baffling.

Whether it's finances, the daily grinding horror of changing your toddler or the desire not to cook the earth, as tough as it's purported to be, there are many good reasons to cross the Rubicon, suck it up and start to potty-train. And let's face it, the vast majority of adults are continent so it can't be that hard. Take a look at your adult friends and work colleagues and you'll no doubt notice how few of them regularly piss and shit their own pants. (Yes, there was that time with Denise in Accounts but she did have gastroenteritis and that was four years ago, let the woman be, like she said at the AGM it was a fart that got away from her.) Generally speaking, adults have pretty exemplary bowel control. That's because at some point they have all been through this process of toilet-training. They have all, each and every one of them, spent a portion of their early life sitting on a tiny plastic potty learning how to crap.

So, no pain, no gain. No guts, no glory. Let's fucking do this. It'll be fine.

[*screen fades to black*]

Narrator: But it wasn't fine. It wasn't fine at all.

When to Start

We didn't even consider potty-training Charlie until he was two and a half and we were a little worried that this was quite late. Apparently, though, it's perfectly normal for kids to start to ditch the nappies at any point between twenty-four months and four years old. Of course, some kids train earlier. Much earlier. I read about one nipper in the newspaper who happily sat on the toilet at just six months. I imagine the kid was being held over the bowl and not just sat there reading the *Financial Times* and smoking a pipe. But still, pretty impressive.

That said, being able to use the toilet at six months old does strike me as a bit odd. (At that age Charlie, like most normal kids, was still licking the floor and looking confusedly at his own elbow.)

I'm sure this kid is great, and I'm happy for the parents that they cracked it so early, but I'll be honest: to me it seems a bit unnatural. It reminds me of my mate's cat Maude who happily uses the human toilet rather than a litter tray. It's impressive but fundamentally a bit disturbing to witness. (This is a real thing by the way, google it. Lots of cats are trained to use the toilet. They even flush afterwards.)

It turns out, though, these baby toilet users are becoming increasingly common. Early potty-training is more and more popu-lar, particularly amongst ruthless tiger mums. In fact, there are whole theories dedicated to it. Techniques for parents who are so ultra-competitive they wish to compete to see whose child can shit in a bucket first.

Incidentally, if you're desperate to show off about how talented your child's bowels are, you may be taking this parenting competi-tion thing way too seriously. This stuff is not going to be on the Oxford entrance exam, cool your boots.

Potty Prodigies

As usual, the gurus of this sort of thing like to confuse things with clever-sounding bollockspeak. They call this early toilet-training process 'elimination communication' or 'natural infant hygiene'. But basically it involves introducing a potty at a really early age, at some point between birth and four months, an age at which most children have yet to take control of their own head.

To most of us this sounds like total lunacy. Not only because babies are completely useless but because between birth and four months is a time when, as a parent, we are so zombie-like that we can barely piss straight ourselves. So teaching someone else the finer points of toileting seems like something of an added stress. That said, by doing so you can apparently avoid nappies altogether and get your child completely trained up by the time they are eighteen months. So the benefits are obvious.

It works like this. Rather than put their babies in nappies, parents are encouraged to observe signals and signs called 'elimination patterns'. It means noticing changes in body language or certain noises that your infant makes just before they 'poo' or 'wee'. Through practice, the parent can 'come to instinctively know when their little one is about to "go" and catch them in that moment', sitting them on their tiny throne with plenty of time to spare.

Much of what I've gathered about these early training techniques comes from sites like treehugger.com and naturalchild.org. Proponents of this method seem to be the same sort of folk who favour a white dreadlock, describe themselves as 'spiritual but not religious' and 'travel' rather than go on holiday. I'm not saying they're annoying but . . .

Actually . . . I probably am saying that.

In support of 'natural infant hygiene' they love to point out that in the past we didn't have nappies. And in parts of Asia and Africa such things are unheard of and in these societies most kids are toilet-trained by the time they are one. In these far flung places, mums carry around their un-nappied baby and 'when mom notices a pattern of behaviour, they simply hold the baby away from their body'. The whole thing, they insist, is so much more natural.

Namasté.

It may indeed be more natural, but I suspect that in the same parts of Africa and Asia where this is popular they don't have carpets. And that simply holding your child away from your body when they go to the toilet probably goes down okay in a remote African village but maybe not so well in WHSmiths, where you may be asked to leave the store because you're getting faeces and piss on the discount Mini Eggs.

As for pointing out that in the past we didn't have nappies and that everybody in prehistory was toilet-trained 'naturally', so what? I'm sick of hearing about how things were so much better in the distant past, before we had running water and fire and the fucking wheel. Just because something was ages ago doesn't make it better. In fact, literally **everything** was worse. Disease, diet, life expectancy. There are very few things that our ancestors did better than us and I doubt that their method of toilet-training is any different.

The truth is that Neanderthals were not great parents, nor great nurturers. There is plenty of evidence that sometimes they **ate** their own offspring, for Christ's sake. And far from teaching their kids effective toilet habits, it's highly likely that, back then, the adults were just shitting wherever they felt like as well. It's why everybody was dying at fifteen from dysentery.

I have no doubt that fans of early training are correct, that this whole thing was, at least, a lot less stressful in days of yore. But we have moved on from an age when you could just crap wherever you like and when the height of sophistication was to squat behind a bush before wiping your arse by dragging it along the ground like a golden retriever.

All that said, you can see the appeal of potty-training early, especially if the claims of its success are true. According to treehugger. com, by eighteen months most children who follow these methods are fully toilet-trained. They call it 'graduating' (which makes it sound like they have an awards ceremony where they get to wear a gown and a cap shaped like a whipped turd). But don't feel guilty about not starting at such an early age just because it's fashionable or part of some competitive parenting trend. I've said it before and I'll say it again, in those first few months of parenthood it's enough of an achievement to just keep everybody alive, let alone introduce mad skillz.

The Call of the Potty

Most people don't choose to toilet-train daft-early. For the majority of us there is enough insanity to contend with when a baby first arrives, without adding this literal shit-storm into the mix. But if you choose to wait until your child is a toddler there is no guarantee that it will be any easier, more straightforward or less disgusting. Far from it.

I have heard from parents who tell tales of barefoot-stepping in crap in their own house. I've heard from others who have had no choice but to replace the carpets in most of the rooms of their home after potty-training twins. I've listened to stories of children crapping on the floor, scooping it up and then using it like paint to create demented artwork on the walls (actually, full disclosure, my mother told me this story. It was about me). And the most disturbing thing that I have ever heard was on a radio phone-in on this very subject. A mum who was in the midst of toilet-training her son had this advice: 'When you're cleaning around the house, for God's sake

159

make sure that the little brown thing you're picking up is actually a raisin before you pop it in your mouth.' Wise words.

And so, armed with these forewarnings about how tough, and weirdly disgusting, the whole thing could be, we did what most of us do. We returned, with tails between our legs, to the experts

Toilet-training Made Easy!

In terms of books on potty-training, I have no particular recommendation as they all basically say the same stuff. Just make sure that the book you choose is a sturdy hardback because at some point you will be throwing it across the room, spitting out your tea on to the pages while laughing at how 'simple' they insist all this is, and then eventually setting it on fire.

The first book we picked up was entitled *Potty Training in Just 7 Days!* which turned out to be the most optimistically titled book since *Get a 12 Inch Gold-plated Dick Using Just the Power of Your Mind!*

All of these books seem to have this in common. *Nappies to Pants in 7 Days*, *A Week to Success*, *The 7 Day Plan* – they all reassure you that it will take, at the most, one week to toilet-train. In essence, they insist that in the same amount of time it takes for Craig David to meet a girl, take her for a drink, shag for four days and then chill, your child should be nappy free.

Yeah, right . . . and thanks to the power of thought, I now have a nine-carat penis.

Other books undercut even these claims of a week to success and insist that you can potty-train any child in three days. I've even discovered at least one title that says you can say goodbye to nappies in just twenty-four hours. Which sounds like a terrible plot for Jack Bauer's next outing (they should've stopped at season 3). But it's a real book. *Toilet Training in Less Than a Day* has sold over 2 million copies. Which means nothing if not that parents are desperate and gullible as fuck.

As it turns out, each of these books follow the same basic principles – stuff about being prepared, communicating with your little one, understanding there will be 'misses' and 'catches'. The one thing all these books seem to miss out is understanding and preparing for something else: that – impossibly – the hygiene levels in your house are about to drop even further, to the levels of 'farmyard'.

But with the knowledge acquired and with the optimism and stupidity of people who had never done this before, we embarked on the flushing descent into the swilling bowl of madness that is potty-training.

Be Prepared

The first thing the books tell you to do is make sure – before you even consider whether your child is ready to potty-train – that you, as a parent, are ready. That you have the time, the commitment, the patience and the determination to embark upon this 'journey'. Apparently some parents are reluctant to start the process because they want to cling to the past. They delay because they are not ready to acknowledge that their baby is not a baby any more. And it takes them a while to accept that it is time to say goodbye to nappies and to teach their growing little one to deal with important stuff on their own.

I understand this reluctance. There is something heartbreaking about the speed at which our children grow and it is natural to want to decelerate that process because when the version of them standing before you is gone, it is gone forever. So it is important to be ready, not just practically but emotionally.

Some people realise they are ready when they notice their little one doing or saying something that reveals that they are growing up fast. And those parents respond to that with a melancholy but also a touching pride and an understanding that . . . it is time.

The point at which I realised I was emotionally ready was one afternoon, after changing Charlie, when I spent five minutes trying unsuccessfully to unlock my iPhone using *Touch ID* before I became aware that I'd got shit on my finger.

So if you're emotionally ready to approach potty-training with your toddler, the next step is to be ready practically.

The Potty

Some experts argue that you should just introduce your child to the lavatory immediately, but that seems like quite a leap, so the most popular theories advocate the use of a potty. A stop-gap measure between your child filling their underwear and filling the actual toilet.

You'd be forgiven for thinking that all potties are created equal. Before we looked to start potty-training, I assumed that they were all basically the same design: plastic pots moulded to the shape of a tiny backside. This is, of course, the classic model. But there is actually a dizzying array of receptacles for toddlers to piss and shit in these days.

What a time to be alive.

For a start, do you want one that fits to the toilet, so they get used to sitting on that? Or do you want a standalone potty that can be used in other rooms of the house so you don't have to race to the bathroom? Do you want one that you can take wherever you go, a collapsible porta-potty, ensuring that you can keep up training outside the home?

(These are a good idea, but I can tell you this: nothing lets you know that parenting has changed your life quite like going through a bag security check at a music festival, only to reveal that you are in possession of no drugs, no contraband alcohol, just a *Swashbuckle* magazine, two Dairylea Lunchables and a portable plastic shitter.)

Is your little one a boy or a girl? Boys need more of a high plastic lip at the front because when they sit down to pee there is little point in having a potty beneath them if they are just going to pee over the top of it and on to the floor.

Do you want one with a lid on it? I'd definitely recommend a lid on it. When you're carrying a pot of piss and shit up a flight of stairs you'll be glad of a lid. Plus, you don't really want to look at the contents while you're getting rid of it.

(It's human nature to look occasionally at your own 'doings' but we don't like to see each other's. This is kind of an agreed-upon thing amongst civilised humans. It's the reason why when we do one that just won't flush – especially at someone else's house – we lay a piece of toilet roll on top of it like it's a dead body.)

Or maybe you don't want a lid. Maybe you like to study your child's waste. Disgusting as it is, I've seen a few parents look at the contents of a potty for a weirdly long time. I don't know what they expect to discover or divine. It's shit not fucking tea leaves. Some of them even photograph it. I know because they send me pictures, (see next page).

What about capacity? This is a real selling point for some, like the Bumbo Step 'n' Potty. A mighty receptacle that can hold up to a massive 50kg. Which is a bit disturbing. I'm really not being judgemental, but Christ!? What are you feeding that kid?

(Oh, hang on, I've just reread that. I think it means the weight of

Kelly Woolston ▶ Man vs Baby
29th September

Toilet training is going better than expected!
My child shits love! 😄💩

the child rather than that the Bumbo Step 'n' Potty can hold seven stones of shit.)

How about making the potty fun? On the market today there is a potty for every child's favourite Nickelodeon or Disney character, incorporated into the design to encourage kids to think of going to the toilet as a game, not a chore but a happy pastime. In this pop-culture-driven world your little one can spend their days pissing on Moana and shitting on Lightning McQueen if they should so choose.

And it's not just branded potties, there are other ways in which you can introduce the good times into the toilet times. There are potties that are shaped like a pirate ship. Others shaped like a duck, another a tank (presumably so your child can crap and re-enact Rommel's desert campaign at the same time).

Then there are the potties with faces. Happily anthropomor-phised with cartoon eyes and an enthusiastic smile. These I find just plain odd. I don't see how this would encourage any child to use the bathroom when as a fully grown man I would struggle to 'go' if the toilet was staring back at me as I pissed in its mouth.

More sensibly, there are potties made to look like an actual toilet, complete with fake flushing noises and toilet-roll holder. And then there are others (that incorporate sound less well) that play a little tune when urine hits the bowl. Which seems like a good idea but I'd be a little worried that this would create some sort of Pavlovian conditioning and the kid would find themselves in their late thirties, hearing the first few bars of 'Frere Jacques' and instantaneously pissing their pants.

And speaking of unintended consequences: maybe the oddest and creepiest of the lot are the new state-of-the-art potties which allow you to record a message for your child.

Christ. Imagine all the kids in therapy in twenty years' time lying on the psychiatrist's couch and trying to get to the bottom of why every time they have a shit they can hear their dad's voice.

Amazingly, none of the above are officially the worst potty on the market. That honour is reserved for a potty for a new generation, for the digital age. One that has a holder for an iPad: the iPotty. I can almost hear the editors of treehugger.com nasal-spraying their açai smoothie in horror. And in this case they've probably got a point. Aside from anything else, combining toddlers, toilets and expensive electronic devices does seem to be a dumb-as-balls idea. The toy industry apparently agreed and in 2013 the iPotty became the only potty ever to have won the worst-toy-of-the-year award. These industry experts described it as 'oppressive and destructive' to young children. I'm not sure how much faith I have in the panel for 'the worst toy of the year'. (I checked and they've never had a bad word to say about Alfie Bear, and everyone knows what a little dick **he** is.) But they are right about this. The iPotty is a terrible idea.

In fact, there's yet another reason why it's a bad invention. When I mentioned the iPotty to a friend of mine he made a different point. He told me that it was an incredibly bad notion to encourage kids to use gadgets whilst going to the bathroom, as his doctor suspected that playing Clash of Clans on his phone for hours whilst crapping is exactly what had given him piles.

(Because this is a bit embarrassing, I've been asked by this mate not to include his name: it's Simon Woodhead.)

So choosing a potty, surely the most basic of tasks, is made over-complicated by adding whistles and bells that are supposed to make all this more attractive to the average toddler, something fun and exciting: Yeeah! Come on! Let's empty our bowels! etc.

These are just the ones that I came across in our local shops and on Amazon. I'm sure there are other potties out there. Ones with a built-in karaoke machine so the nipper can unclip a microphone and belt out 'My Way' whilst unloading. I'm sure there are ones that let off confetti cannons and play 'Simply the Best' on the completion of a successful stool and others shaped like the Iron Throne where a two year old can sit and contemplate the downfall of Westeros and 'that bastard' Jon Snow. Every novelty you can think of has been incorporated into this most simple of objects which, let's face it, is **still** just a bucket. When it comes down to it, toddlers don't really give a shit.

At least not easily.

The Signs

Okay, so you're mentally prepared and practically you are more than ready. But what about your little one. Are **they** ready? There are lots of signs to suggest that they themselves are good to go. According to the potty bibles, the main indicators are:

- Hiding to pee or poo
- Interest in the potty
- Telling you that they're about to go
- Interest in other people's toilet habits

Hiding to pee or poo

The first thing we noticed was the hiding to pee or poo. Which to begin with was a bit strange. Ordinarily Charlie is incredibly bad at hiding. These are his go-to places when we play hide-and-seek:

He either hides in the same place every time or just sits down wherever he is and places a shallow box on his head that he believes renders him invisible. Alternatively, sometimes when it's my turn to count he just stays at my side and counts with me. Then when it's my turn to hide he comes along and hides in the same place. When there's only two of us playing, it's shite.

Like I said, the kid – God love him – is absolutely terrible at hide-and-seek.

Yet suddenly, when he needed the toilet he started to disappear. He would nip behind the settee or behind a curtain without noise or disturbance, like a ninja. And if you weren't paying attention in the moment of his vanishment he could be difficult to locate. Not least because he would not respond to us shouting for him until he'd finished what he was doing. At times, the only way to find him was to listen for a faint grunting and straining that sounded like in the distance Hulk Hogan was trying to open a jar.

Interest in the potty

The second indicator, interest in the potty, was also evident. Charlie did indeed show interest. The slight problem with this was that he has **always** shown an interest in the potty. We bought one way too early and it has been in our bathroom, lying around, pretty much since he was born. So since he's been about ten months old this thing has been used as a hat, a drum, a receptacle to put his crisps in and as a 'boinker', which is something quite specific to our house and is the name for any object that you hit someone with whilst saying the word 'boinker'. (A 'boinker' can be literally anything, from a hammer to a muffin.) Probably not what the books had in mind . . . but let's give 'interest in the potty' a big tick.

Telling you that they're about to go

Charlie also started to tell us when he needed to go to the toilet. Sort of. The problem here is that toddlers don't really grasp the linear nature of time. The past, present and future are confusing ideas and so when they say 'I need a poo' it often means 'I've already done a poo. It was a while ago and it's everywhere. I mean this thing is in my socks.'

Interest in other people's toilet habits

Finally, Charlie began to show a toddler's classic 'interest in other people's toilet habits'. As we discovered in Chapter 1, intruding on a parent's attempts to use the bathroom becomes part of a toddler's day. (In fact, this fascination with bodily functions is characteristic of all children and continues long after toddlerhood. It is why between the ages of three and ten everything about this stuff is hilarious . . . you 'poopybumhead'.)

Charlie's interest in the smallest room in the house turned into a fun game. He started putting things into the toilet, blocking it with everything from Stickle Bricks to Lyns's phone to a small pot that contained the ashes of our first dog Pickle (rest in peace, P-dog).

He had another game too, which for a while he thought was the funniest thing ever. He would run into the bathroom whilst I was standing there taking a leak, close the toilet lid and then run away laughing. Leaving me to try desperately to stop mid-flow whilst peeing on to the closed lid, the splash-back soaking me with my own urine.

You'd be forgiven for thinking that being unable to unlock your phone because you have shit on your finger is **the** low point for any parent. Well, it isn't mine. Mine was once forgetting that Charlie had done this with the toilet seat, then wearing the same jeans for the following two days. I suddenly remembered I was wearing the same jeans whilst in a queue to buy a scone in a Marks & Spencer's café, my memory jogged by the couple in front of us discussing whether they could smell piss.

All in all, our toddler was showing plenty of signs that he was ready to try ditching the nappies. He was showing evidence of all of the four indicators laid out in *Seven Days to Success* and seemed ready to go. But at this point you can't just point to the toilet or your brand-new state-of-the-art potty and say, 'Okay, kiddo . . . you do it here now.' Now comes the hard bit.

Training Your Toddler

If you don't want to splash out on a party potty which is so goddamn exciting that your child will simply demand to go to the toilet, then you have to find other ways to encourage them to go. Apparently, the best way to do this is to communicate with your child about the whole process. Chat about it.

It is a pretty odd conversation to strike up and so a good way to broach the topic is through children's books. And just as there are books to teach adults about their role in toilet-training, there are plenty for kids too.

If a lot of the books to help parents are infuriating, the ones aimed at explaining the process to children are much better. Or at least some of them are. There are others that are just plain disturbed. Books that, after you've read them, make you want to pluck out your eyeballs and bleach your brain so that no memory of them remains.

For example, books like *Softy the Poop* and *Peter Poo* in which a sturdy shit is the protagonist. These are the friendly faces of faeces.

Charming characters that explain the process of toileting from the perspective of the bacteria-ridden waste that is the end result.

In the same way that I'm creeped out by the idea of anthropo-morphising a potty, I'm even more disturbed by the idea that you make a turd the cheerful hero of your story. Who the fuck thinks this sort of thing is a good idea? I mean, who goes to the toilet, turns around and thinks, *Ooh, that's cute, I'll draw it with some googly eyes, the kids'll love it.*

At best, these efforts are just picture books with excrement on every page and at worst, they are instructional books that encour-age your youngster to think of their waste as their best pal. Feel free to buy them if you think they'll help, but you've only yourself to blame if one day your kid scoops a shit out of the bowl to give it a cuddle, or insists on taking their new nutty-brown friend out for a ride on their scooter.

These aren't the worst nor the strangest books available. There are other books that, rather than a friendly crap, make a character out of the lavatory. I'm thinking of one particularly disconcerting book called (and this is real) *I Want to Eat Your Poo*.

The star of this particular adventure is a toilet (which for some reason has a moustache and looks a bit like eighties TV detective Magnum) who must persuade a child to shit in him.

In this charming tale, toilets are alive. Not only are they alive, they eat human poo to remain so. And if little Timmy doesn't learn how to use the toilet our hero will die of starvation.

Okay, I have many questions about this book. But my main one is . . . how did that publishing meeting go?

'Hey, Bob! We're super excited to hear about your new book. We know you've had to have some time off for personal reasons . . . But everybody here at the publishers can't wait

to find out more about the new project. So, yeah! What's it about? What's the title?'

'It's called I Want to Eat Your Poo *and it's about a dying toilet who eats shit.'*

[*nervous laughter*] 'Ohhkaaay . . . Er . . . Listen, Bob . . . Y'know, maybe you've come back to work a little too soon, huh? [*quietly lifts phone receiver to ear*] Security to floor fifteen. Let's . . . just see if we can get you a taxi home . . . Is your wife home, Bob, will Linda be at home, buddy? Security to floor fifteen.'

In fairness, not all children's books about potty-training are this demented. There are some great children's books that simplify and create a sense of fun around the process. We are a fan of *Pirate Pete's Potty*, for example, or *Potty Superhero!* These books take things that Charlie is already interested in (pirates and superheroes) and places them in a story that makes toilet-training an adventure. Something heroic. It's a simple and brilliant idea. These are the types of character that Charlie copies every day anyway as he wears a cape on his shoulders or makes his nannan walk the plank. These books expand that universe to say that these pirates and super-heroes use the toilet too, and why not emulate that as well. They certainly beat books that suggest that, by not learning to shit properly, he is brutally murdering a depressed toilet.

Training in Action

So Charlie's books were a great starting point. We chatted as best we could about the whole thing and, coupled with the advice we found online and from friends who had been through the process numerous times before, we got off to a pretty good beginning.

Charlie was soon peeing in his potty first thing in the morning and then again in the evening before his nightly bath. I think you're supposed to sit them down to begin with but he was insistent on copying me and standing up. Which meant that more often than not he missed the potty completely and peed on the floor. Actually, Lyns insisted that this was Charlie copying me with incredible accuracy.

[Lyndsay's note: Like most fully grown men, Matt has not mastered the art of not pissing on the floor. For some reason the harmless penis can become an uncontrollable fire hose when confronted by the simple domestic toilet.]

Thank you, Lyns.

It wasn't just a failing in Charlie's aim and accuracy. There were times when he'd turn around mid-pee to tell you something and happily just piss on your shoes. Or wave himself around whilst peeing, singing Andy and The Oddsocks. But we cheered every dribble we managed to collect and were happy to be heading in the right direction. We figured we were starting to crack it. We hadn't managed to collect anything solid but we were filled with optimism. It was time for phase two.

Nappy Free

Whether you follow a book's teachings to become trained in the art of the porcelain over twenty-four hours, a weekend or seven days, it is advised that at some point you allow your child to go 'nappy free'. Which feels like something of a leap into the unknown. One of our books likened it to taking the stabilisers off a bike. Which it is. A particularly unpredictable bike, that wheels itself around the house crapping wherever it wants.

For this particular step, it is suggested that you choose a period when you can take some time off work or when you don't need to go anywhere. A few days when you can stay at home and devote your time and attention to the task at hand. This is a good idea. Having a nappy-free toddler in your home is like sharing your living space with a small bomb, quietly ticking. And it is one thing to have a ticking bomb at home but quite another to be taking the thing out in public and risking collateral damage and casualties.

So the first time we tried going nappy free, it was for a weekend. We didn't leave the house and for three days we gave laser-focus to our task. We followed the instructions to take the nappy off and we observed our child keenly for signs that he was about to go to the toilet. In the event of any kind of sign, any disappearance behind a sofa, any strain, we endeavoured to get him to the potty immediately.

It's safe to say that, to begin with, this was not a great success. A chain is only as strong as its weakest link and I am our weakest link. The main problem with this phase is that it requires considerable observational skills.

'Keen observation of your little one is the key to successful nappy-free potty-training' our book insisted.

I'm not the most observant person in the world. My brother once removed a picture on our wall of my grandma Cath and replaced it with a photograph of Vin Diesel. A switch I failed to notice for about six months. In truth, I only really noticed then because my Grandma died and I went to get the photo to use for her obituary in the local paper.

(In my defence, I did at least notice it at this point, otherwise my grandma's death notice would've read: 'Catherine Lowry, much loved grandmother, mother and sister 1939–1998' but would have been accompanied by a 6 x 4 picture of Vin Diesel as Dominic Toretto in *Fast & Furious 6*.)

Besides my crappy observational skills I wasn't entirely sure what I was supposed to be looking out for. Lyns was brilliant at noticing a shift in our boy's body language or facial expression and getting him to the potty. But for me, the first indication that our son wanted to go to the toilet was after the event, when I picked up a smell from behind the TV that made all the hairs in my nostrils die.

Added to my lack of observational skills is the fact that I am incredibly easily distracted. Charlie can make whatever face he likes, if *Bake Off* is on I'm barely registering that he's in the house. And if it's the grand final, I can easily forget that we have a child at all.

So our first attempt at going nappy free was not great, with a success rate of about 15 per cent. But it is generally agreed that as you embark on this journey there will be many more 'misses' than 'catches'.

So we persevered and the following week we tried again with a slightly different method. A more proactive approach. Instead of just trying to guess when your little one wants to go to the bath-room, some theories suggest sitting your child on the potty every fifteen minutes. The thinking is that eventually lightning will strike and you will catch them in the act. At which point you shower them with praise. And like a puppy on newspaper, they learn that this is the correct way to behave.

Again we dedicated ourselves to our task. The logic of this approach seems utterly sound. Until you remember that trying to get a toddler to do something they don't want to do, let alone every fifteen minutes, is incredibly difficult. We can barely get Charlie to stay still long enough to eat a meal three times a day. Trying to get him to sit in a particular spot forty to fifty times a day is just impossible. Especially with all the distractions of modern-day life.

I always find it daft when people of older generations insist that potty-training children in their day was easy. Of course it was, everything was boring then. Toys were things like a stick and a hoop. Even as late as the eighties, all the kids were going mad over slinkies, some coiled wire that walked down the stairs . . . woohoo.

Modern-day kids face the distraction of remote-controlled cars, robotic toys, learning centres with computer chips and TVs with 3 million channels of cartoons.

Toddlers are just busier now. They've got much better things to do with their day than be dragged away to sit on a potty every few minutes. Especially one that doesn't have a built-in iPad, you cheapskate bastard.

Motivation

By the end of the weekend I think Charlie was just soiling the carpet in protest at being hassled every few minutes. But then we hit upon the missing component in our plan . . . motivation.

Over the next few days Charlie began to understand what was required of him, he just didn't want to do it. And so we introduced the simplest tried-and-tested method available to any parent: bribery. And when it comes to bribery, there is no more powerful weapon in the toddler-parent's arsenal than The Sticker.

All hail the sticker chart.

Children just love stickers. They are toddler currency. Every activity we do at the moment with Charlie (from baking to swimming) ends with the organiser handing out a sticker. And the kids fight for one as though it is the Victoria Cross or the Medal of Honor rather than a small piece of sticky paper with a cartoon thumbs-up on it and the words 'You Did It!'

(I always think that this 'You did it!' – or sometimes even 'You're the best!' – affirmation on these stickers is a bit overblown. It makes it sound like they've just run the London Marathon rather than spent half an hour sticking some glitter to a paper plate or drawing a face on a boiled egg.)

In my experience, though, there are very few things that toddlers will not do for a sticker. Make them choose between a sticker and the gift of immortality or riches beyond their wildest dreams, and they will go for a 'sticky stick' every single time.

So it made sense that having a chart blu-tacked to the fridge would be a great way of encouraging toilet time. And one of our many books recommended this as a sure-fire way to success.

For us, it did kind of work. We began to get into a rhythm and started to see a significant increase in our success rate. It wasn't perfect. Charlie's love for a sticker was so great that sometimes he was attempting to go to the potty when he didn't need to, and straining until he looked like his head was about to implode. Other times he would demand a sticker for just sitting on the potty, whether he had used it or not. And, of course, he was still occasionally disappearing behind the TV or an armchair. But generally speaking, we felt that we had turned a corner. The sticker chart was a revelation not just for us but for Charlie who no longer felt harassed and was delighted when he could celebrate his own achievement in a way that was tangible and on display.

It seems simple, but the chart just made the whole thing so much less confusing for everybody. (Apart from the dog who since the beginning of this process has been confused as to why when he successfully craps in the house he doesn't get stickers and a Kinder Egg, he just gets shouted at and put in the garden.)

As I write this we are still in the midst of potty-training but the chart is still going strong. We have many more catches than misses these days but we are not finished with this process yet. We still collect the occasional bags of shame from nursery and we still race Charlie to the toilet as though he's a grenade with the pin removed, shouting 'Just a minute! Hold it just a minute!' and praying that we make it before the point of no return.

So . . . to be continued.

Which I think is an appropriate way for me to bring to a close tales of our own path through toilet-training. Charlie is almost three and still not quite fully toilet-trained. We're getting there. But it's not something that we worry too much about or agonise over. For the simple reason that our son has something remarkable. A thing that makes a mockery of our scrambling to get toddlers trained in twenty-four hours or three or seven days. Charlie has the thing that literally defines **all** children. He has time.

And after listening to other parents' stories I'd say one thing is pretty clear: these programmes and books which suggest that a toddler can be fully toilet-trained in a matter of hours are largely nonsense peddled by snake-oil salesmen. They might be able to start them down the lavatorial path but for most of us there is no quick fix. There is no three-day solution or twenty-four-hour wonder method. No spell or incantation that makes them magically become a member of continent society overnight.

Even when you think you have achieved that big-boy or big-girl pants day when your little one is 'trained' there will still be problems. One dad told me about a time when he was proudly chatting about how his daughter was fully toilet-trained when, at that very moment, behind his back, that same daughter was sitting at the top of a playground slide, watching her own urine flow to the bottom, creating a kind of piss log flume for the kids further down the same chute.

And a mum, listening to this conversation, told me that her little boy had been out of nappies and using a potty for three months. And that her and her husband had been telling anyone who would listen how straightforward it had been and that they couldn't understand the fuss that surrounded toilet-training. They then realised how premature this self-congratulation was when they discovered that, on many days during those three months, their son had been disappearing into the kitchen, pulling open a drawer where they keep their best saucepans, and shitting in there instead.

So if you're in the midst of toilet-training, relieve some pressure on yourselves and scratch the idea of a two-minute fix to a complicated problem – whether its weaning, walking, talking or anything else. It's a hard lesson but parenting just doesn't work like that.

The Madness of Toilet-training Toddlers

Dog lovers always say the same thing about their pets. They always say (in a voice that is supposed to convey the wisdom of the ages), 'Y'know, they understand every word you say.' But they don't. Not really. Dogs understand almost nothing. Maybe 'walkies', 'dinner' and if you're really lucky 'Rex, stop licking your nuts in front of the telly.' But if a dog tilts its head when we speak, we assume it comprehends in some way, that it grasps the complexities of what we're trying to tell them.

This is all wishful thinking, of course. Even the brightest dog has no idea what you're talking about 99 per cent of the time. Don't get me wrong, I love dogs. Our Jack Russell Eddie was our baby before we had a baby, but his understanding of the English language is limited to 'sit', 'stay' and 'sausage'. Like most dogs, he's a fucking idiot.

It's the same with toddlers. We like to believe that they are absorbing everything we say. That they understand and can decipher this complex thing we call language. And whilst they are better than the average dog at understanding (and they are no doubt getting better every day), it's still safe to say that just like a dog, on the whole, they have no idea what we're talking about.

Also just like a dog, toddlers have an almost zero attention span. Try explaining anything to a dog when a squirrel walks by. Their brain interrupts both you and them to say 'Fucking squirrel!!' And there is nothing either of you can do about it. Physically and mentally, in that moment they're gone.

And, it's worse with toddlers because dogs are only interested in squirrels and other dogs' arses. Whereas toddlers are interested in **everything**. To the curious mind of a child, everything is a 'fucking squirrel!!'

So isn't it ridiculous that we choose this time, when they are unable to focus on one thing for more than a nanosecond, to begin teaching our young about going to the toilet? When they are barely verbal and only just starting to understand the basics like 'tree' and 'car'. Why on earth do we choose this particular time to take them to one side and try and get them to understand something so seemingly beyond their capabilities?

'Okay, junior, here's the thing . . . You know how since you've been born you've always shit your pants? Well, we don't want you to do that any more. We have this chair thing that we keep in the smallest room in the house. Except the chair is not really a chair, it is connected to a network of underground pipes . . . Anyway, that's not important . . . We sit on it and then thanks to an equi-balanced plumbing system the waste is taken awa—'

'Fucking squirrel!'

And they're gone.

You see my point. It would be far easier if they could compre-hend and we could just explain to them what on earth is going on, rather than this weird puppy-training approach we take: trying to catch them when they have an accident, looking for signs, interpret-ing facial expressions. It's madness. Why can't we just delay it until they are much older? Why can't we wait until they are like eighteen or something and have perfect grasp of English and a bit of focus?

But, of course, we can't. It's massively frowned upon by society to send your kid off to school still swinging a full nappy between their knees like a carrier bag full of apples. And it's even more so to send them off to college or their first job interview still pissing and crap-ping themselves. Nothing is more likely to scupper their chances of landing that dream job than pausing halfway through an interview to go momentarily beet-red in the face whilst straining. (Even if they do barely miss a beat before telling the interviewer how well they work 'both individually and as part of a team'.)

And so we do what we always do . . . our best. And for some of us that means that our children are toilet-trained by six months and for others it means still having to change wet bed sheets when their little ones are twelve years old. We have learned nothing by this point if we have not come to understand that our children aren't little clockwork toys to be adjusted and set. They do not obey cal-endars and timetables and charts . . . even if there **are** bloody stickers on it.

What I do know is this: if by the time your child is thirty-six months old they are not sticking the newspaper under one arm, announcing that they've got 'turtle-head' and disappearing into the bathroom for an hour, I wouldn't worry too much. They'll get it.

There is one other thing. As I finish this chapter I keep thinking about the story we started with, the story of a six-month-old fully toilet-trained baby. And her mum who felt that her child's ability to potty-train so early demonstrated some sort of intellectual superiority. Reading the news article about it again, I'm drawn to some of the mum's other comments, such as how she played Mozart to her little girl whilst she was still in the womb; her insistence on speaking to her daughter in the way that she speaks to other adults, and 'never in baby talk'; her clear pride in the fact that her child doesn't enjoy toys and refuses them in favour of books.

And I contrast this story with that of the dad whose much older little girl created chaos by peeing down the slide in the park. I laughed as he told me about it, and asked him if he was mortified, but the guy just shrugged and said: 'She's just having such a good time, she blocks out anything else. She puts off going to the toilet and we have these little accidents.'

It's interesting to compare these two parents and these two kids. I don't know whether one of these children is smarter than the other. I really don't. But I do think this: that nipper on the slide? That kid sounds happier.

7
Days Out

'Are we there yet?'
'No.'
'Are we there yet?'
'No.'
'Are we there yet?'
'No.'
'Are we there yet?'
'No.'
'Are we –'

'Actually? You know what? YES! We are there. We've clearly arrived! I mean, I know to any remotely rational human being it appears that we're still hurtling along on a motorway at seventy-odd miles a bloody hour in the same way that we have been doing for the last four pissing hours!? But fortunately our destination exists outside of the temporal nature of time and fucking space!? So YES!!? You know what?!! WE. ARE. THERE!!?! AAARRGH!'

. . .

'Are we there yet?'

[*applies brake, pulls car over, exits car and pours petrol over self before setting self on fire*]

DAYS OUT

I'm writing this in the car on the way back from a day out at the zoo. I think it's fair to say that we set off this morning in the highest of spirits. The zoo in question is one of Europe's largest. Charlie loves animals of all sorts, so do I, so does Lyns, and I imagined us walking through the different zones and enclosures 'oohing' and 'aahing' at all the exotic beasts. Occasionally, I would surreptitiously refer to the information plaque on the wall at the side of a cage and pronounce that this particular animal was a 'mountain bongo' which is 'a type of antelope'. And we'd all marvel at how clever daddy is and stroll onwards. Yes, this would be a fine day out. A day of family bonding, with moments of joy amongst the beauty of evolution and glory of nature's majesty.

Upon entering the zoo, the first thing we saw was an enclosure that contained two monkeys. One of whom was casually wanking on a tyre swing, whilst the other was shitting into its own hand and then throwing it at the one that was wanking.

In hindsight, I should have seen this as some sort of portent.

It is surprising how often a morning begun with such enthusiasm can turn into a day of misery. We imagine our trips out with our children will be filled with wonder, yet so often, metaphorically speaking, they are filled with wanking gibbons.

Our trip to the zoo is a good example of how expectations and reality seldom meet. In fact, they seldom find themselves in the same postcode. And yet each time we embark on these excursions we do so with blind optimism that this time, on this occasion, it will be a day so perfect that Lou Reed would piss fire with jealousy.

So, recognising that we have a kind of amnesia for how these days tend to go, I kept a diary of some that we 'enjoyed' this summer:

First of all, back to our zoo visit.

The Zoo

28th April

So today was marked by an unholy trinity of shitness. The zoo was busy, it was pissing it down and we had brought along a child who couldn't be arsed to be there. And all three of these issues were my fault.

For a start, the fact that it was busy is something I have to take the blame for. Because Charlie isn't of school age yet, we are not restricted to excursions during half-term holidays. So here's a question? What kind of nob chooses to go to these places when the schools are on a break and they don't have to?

Yes, we could have gone a couple of weeks before or after the holidays but why bother going when you've got the place to yourself? Why not time your visit for those few weeks of the year when every family on Earth is zoo-bound? When the car parks are so full that the distance from your parking spot to the entrance requires a fucking monorail. Why not wait until the place is packed with 40,000 screaming kids, all of whom wish to pet the same wallaby, so that by the time it's your turn to pet the wallaby it looks as though it is considering killing itself by throwing its body on the electrified fencing?

Why not wait until the queue for the ice cream van snakes so far into the distance that it disappears behind the curve of the Earth? And why not wait until the displays and shows are so packed that you're forced to stand at the back, so that when the bird of prey display is on, and the peregrine falcon comes swooping back into the arena, it nearly takes your fucking head off.

Yeah, we'll go at half term. Twonk.

In my defence, I was certain that it wouldn't be all that busy today, due to the fact that this morning's weather forecast had suggested showers. My mistake. I've since learned that parents are a hardy bunch when they can't stand another day trapped indoors with their kids ricocheting off the walls. A little rain is nothing to the desperate.

In any case, it wasn't a little rain. Can I just digress one second to say that if you're a weather forecaster, you suck balls at your job. I never noticed how terrible weather forecasters are at actually predicting weather until we had a child and I became forced to do outside stuff. Since we've had Charlie I have been caught in hail, sleet, torrential rain, thunder and two feet of snow. All because I have listened to these professional guessers who have all the weather-predicting accuracy of my auntie Pat's knees (which apparently creak when it's going to be damp).

Let's be clear. The weather man this morning said 'showers'. I remember him distinctly winking at the camera and suggesting an umbrella just to be on the safe side. 'There's a chance it could be brolly weather,' he said (before awkwardly chatting with the main newsreader woman about how one of them was doing a charity bed push that weekend or some bollocks like that).

Brolly weather? This was ark weather. It was like the end of days. There was a UK record amount of inches of rain in two hours. When they announced that the monorail had stopped working due to 'localised flooding' I even got scared. I thought I was going to have to kill and hollow out a rhino and fucking kayak in it back to the car.

The weather did slightly improve over the day but then it was just a constant drizzle, the miserable drip-drip off the end of your nose that says 'family fun day'.

A zoo is the worst place to be in this sort of weather. Because most animals are not as stupid as people. They go indoors when it's raining. Consequently when you go to a zoo in bad weather you spend most of your day shuffling along, peering into yet another empty field or cage optimistically, hoping to get a glimpse of an aardvark that is probably sat in a tiny shed in the corner of its enclosure with its feet up. (And peering out occasionally to see if those dopey humans are still standing there, soaking wet through and peering back gormlessly.)

Even when the morning deluge ended and the weather brightened the puddles remained. Obviously, we'd not bothered to bring Charlie's wellies and as the rain had flooded and cleaned out the enclosures, the puddles became part rain water and part animal excrement. So Charlie, wearing brand-new trainers, spent most of the day cheerfully splashing away in African mongoose shit.

Which brings us to the final reason why the day did not go as I envisioned. For Charlie, the zoo animals faded into insignificance. He had little interest in them. He was much more interested in the puddles. For him, there are just few things that are better. He genuinely prefers a puddle to an elephant. In fact, even if this zoo had a giraffe-tiger hybrid that breathed fire and shit peanut M&Ms, Charlie would still have derived more pleasure from two inches of bloody standing water.

And so I spent much of today vaguely annoyed, not because it had cost so much to get in (the best part of a hundred quid), not because it was busy and not even because of the rain. Although that's what I suggested to Lyns. No, privately I was just pissed off because I wasted half of yesterday learning the names of all these stupid animals in order to appear smart . . . and in the end no one gave a shit. I mean what am I supposed to do with the fact that I now know the difference between a capybara and a fucking wombat?

Actually, there was one moment when I thought my homework might come in handy. Towards the end of the day we went to a feeding session for koalas where all the kids got a chance to hold one and have a photograph with it. It was after the pictures were taken that the keeper asked if anybody had any questions and I realised I had a small piece of brilliant trivia about koalas stashed away in my brain. Here was my chance to appear knowledgeable and smart to my family and I seized the chance with both hands:

'Is it true that loads of Koalas have got chlamydia?'

. . .

Following a beat of silence the keeper awkwardly nodded as the crowd made horrified faces and began furiously pumping hand sanitiser on to their crying children's hands.

'You're an idiot,' Lyns muttered, shaking her head as she walked away pretending I was a stranger.

A Country Walk

18th June

Let's go for a walk. Let's sing as we go . . .

'We're going on a bear hunt! We're going to catch a big one! We're going on a . . . No, I'm not carrying you. We've only been going thirty seconds! Just watch where you're going, don't stand in that! They're nettles, they sting you. No, we can't go home. We're going for a nice family walk. Okay, you can go on my shoulders. Oh Jesus! What's that smell?! When did you stand in THAT??'

[*passes couple walking their dog coming the other way*]

'Morning! Yes, yes, it is a lovely day for it!'

[*couple disappears around the corner*]

'For God's sake! Oh Christ, it's in my hair! Have we got any wet wipes? NO! You can't get down I need to get this off your shoes . . . Bollocks to it, let's just go to the pub.'

And with that we walked the seven metres back to the car.

The Seaside

19th July

The comedian Bill Hicks used to say that he could never understand the attraction of going to the beach. 'What's the fucking deal? It's where dirt meets water.' But the seaside is so much more.

Where else can you ruin a perfectly good picnic by eating it on a bumpy field of damp powdered glass? Surrounded by pasty-looking white people you've never met before, trying to get their pants off under a towel?

Where else can you find yourself under constant aerial bombardment from psychopathic seagulls, so jacked up on discarded candy floss that they'll fuck you up for a chip?

Where else can you take leave of your senses so much that you feed thousands of pounds into a machine that allows you to take control of a rigged, grabbing hand for the remote chance of snaring a three-quid, fluffy, knock-off Wreck-It Ralph that no one really wants?

Where else can you wade into a sea the colour of Typhoo, so cold it sends your testicles shrivelling into your body, only to wade out of the crystal-brown waters again with a used johnny hanging off your big toe?

Yeah, there really is nothing quite like the charm and innocence of the Great British Seaside.

I don't find the seaside all that charming. Especially not the North Eastern coastal town we visited today. I'll not reveal the name of the place, but let's just say it was recently described on TripAdvisor as 'the place where fun went to die'. Which is not an unfair description. In fact, I think 'fun' went there in the late seventies, checked into a crappy B&B, filled a bath and climbed in holding a toaster.

You will recognise the place or you will know one similar. A seaside town so rundown it is twinned with Pripyat (the Ukrainian village still off limits after the Chernobyl nuclear power plant went tits up in 1986). A place where for most of the year it is a sleeping ghost, only for it to wake up for three months of the summer, flick on a switch for the dodgems, and pretend that it can be arsed.

In contrast to our trip to the zoo, today was the hottest day of the year. On the whole, the weather in Britain is drizzly and a bit shit. But the moment that there is a break in the clouds we embrace the sun like no other nation can, and on this occasion thousands of other families had the same idea to head to the coast.

For some reason, all seaside towns only have one road in and one road out. So we began our day, as all trips to the English coast do, by sitting in traffic, entirely stationary and hating everybody in the surrounding cars for being the kind of tossers who go to the seaside on the hottest day of the year.

After parking as close as we could get to the seafront (a parking space which was so far away it was a stone's throw from the house we'd left three hours before), we walked the several miles to the beach – a trip that the average Sherpa would have refused, as we were laden down with deckchairs, windbreak, bucket, spade, an ice box and a ten-foot blow-up crocodile that was already inflated because I figured it would save us carrying the pump.

Inevitably, the beach was crammed and so we searched for a gap. A spot that would be far enough away from those next to us that we could lay down a towel. And I could perhaps change into my trunks without bending over and wiping my arse on the flag of some kid's sandcastle.

Eventually, we found a space. Right next to a family of pissheads drinking Strongbow Dark Fruits and arguing about someone called Karen

The head of this family was a loud, aggressive gentleman with a Leeds United neck tattoo. He was wiry, pale and stripped to the waist, and one of those 'real men' who are really skinny but walk as though they have enormous biceps, and so look like they are carry-ing around an invisible pig under each arm. Apparently, as a 'real man', he believed himself to be impervious to the sun and refused all offers of sun cream. You could almost hear the sizzle as the sun cooked him to ham. And as I spent the next few hours listening to him describe how Karen was a 'complete bitch', I found myself root-ing for the sun and hoping that he would spontaneously combust.

Despite our new neighbours, we settled down to an afternoon of sandcastle building, interrupted only by the occasional frisbee to the face. (And, at one point, a red-faced woman chasing a wind-caught lilo who ran straight through the middle of our sarnies.) We'd head down to the sea to collect water and try not to stand on anybody or fall into one of the mineshafts that kids seem to dig instead of sandcastles these days. (It is strange, kids seem to get to about four or five and they have no interest in castles any more, they just want to dig a huge hole. It's like all children get to school age and suddenly feel the need to practise getting rid of a dead body.)

Then we'd wander back to our base, avoiding the six donkeys ploughing a furrow back and forth along the beach, looking so depressed that they were daydreaming about the day when they would be melted down for glue.

Ladies and Gentlemen, the Great British Seaside.

And Charlie absolutely loved it.

When I said that I've never found the Great British Seaside all that charming, that's a lie. I used to, and watching Charlie I was reminded why.

Paddling in the surf with him as he ran shrieking with delight as the waves touched his feet reminded me of when I once did the same. I remembered a time in my own life when a busy beach was somewhere that was alive with excitement. A time when building forts out of sand felt like creating art. Art that we knew the sea would claim but was no less vital or important for that fact. I was reminded of a time when swaying side to side on a miserable donkey was something thrilling. The first donkey I sat on was called Brandy. I don't remember the name of my first teacher, but I do remember that.

And so it's not that I don't understand the charm of the seaside, it's more like I've forgotten it. Maybe because I'm old and maybe as much as it pains me to say it, I have become something of a miserable dick about such things.

So we ate ice creams and fish and chips and Charlie rode on a donkey for the first time (Poppet). And we splashed each other and soaked Mummy and we dug holes and we made sand citadels, and as the tide came in and the sea took them we headed to the pier and arcades to feed two-pence pieces into slots to win more two-pence pieces. We spent twelve quid directing a grabby hand to win a two-quid cuddly Minion and made ourselves sick on donuts. And we laughed a lot and I remembered when the seaside was the greatest show on Earth and loved the fact that for Charlie it still is.

Update note: I hate sand. It clings to everything and it comes home with you on your child, on their clothes, in your shoes and socks, in ears and arseholes. It is three weeks since we went to the beach and I am still finding it. There was a report on the news this morning about how coastal erosion has got worse recently. It's little wonder . . . we've got most of it in the boot of my fucking car.

The Deep

13th September

Today we visited The Deep in Hull. The Deep is a world-renowned, multi-million-pound, award-winning aquarium. A huge complex of tanks, underwater tunnels and a glass elevator that ascends through a 10-metre-deep endless ocean exhibit. It has everything from penguins and bioluminescent creatures to sawfish and sharks. It 'tells the dramatic story of the world's oceans and brings that story to life'. Suffice to say, Charlie spent at least fifty minutes in the café just playing with this bloody pedal bin.

Actually, once I could tear Charlie away from the – admittedly impressive – 40-litre chrome Brabantia with foot-operated pedal opening and silent-closing lid, he was utterly mesmerised by this place. It is a sensory overload for a kid obsessed with *Finding Nemo* and 'Baby Shark' (doo doo doo doo doo) and he raced from exhibit to exhibit absolutely captivated.

Actually, this was one of those rare days without incident or accident so I have no more to say about The Deep other than that you should go. Oh, and . . . apologies if you were near the penguin exhibit at about 12.35pm.

To explain, for a while Charlie called birds 'dicks'. I think he picked it up from nursery rhymes and books in which birds are called 'dicky-birds'. This got shortened in Charlie's mind to 'dick-dicks' and eventually 'dicks'. This abbreviation could obviously present problems.

So today, as we enjoyed the penguin display, Charlie recognised these majestic creatures as birds, and every time he saw one, he would shout 'dick!' at the top of his voice. Most people just ignored him but a woman, stood at the side of us during feeding, clearly wasn't happy and kept glancing at us with a disgusted side-eye, as if to say, 'What kind of parent teaches their young child that all penguins are dicks?'

I tried to give her a look in return that said: 'He's not saying what it sounds like, he's not actually swearing at the bloody penguins,' but she didn't look convinced.

Especially when, just as she walked past us later on, Charlie pointed to a jellyfish in a tank and shouted 'cock!'

Mind you, let's face it, he's got a point about jellyfish, the stingy, see-through bastards.

CBeebies Land

24th May

Mecca. Santiago de Compostela. The Vatican. For centuries, devotees have travelled to these places of pilgrimage. For parents of toddlers, one such sacred place is CBeebies Land (or Legoland if you're scared of coming a bit north).

CBeebies Land is a small sectioned-off area of Alton Towers specifically designed for very young children. A place 'where all your favourite CBeebies characters are brought to life!'

I read this description whilst buying the tickets yesterday and my first thought was *Christ, I bloody hope not*. Could anything be more terrifying? It is one thing to find Iggle Piggle charming when he's safely trapped in your television but probably quite another to be confronted by a six-foot-tall, waving, blanket-obsessed, furry blue

phallus in real life. And even as an adult I would be unnerved to meet the inbred half-clown Tumble family in real life.

The good news is that upon arrival it becomes clear that these characters are not actually brought to life. They are just recreated in shit animatronics.

(Which, for your information, Alton Towers, is not the same as being 'brought to life'. If that were the case, when a loved one dies we could just insert some cogs and springs inside them that made them wave, and hey presto . . . back from the dead.)

There is something about these animatronics that lends a nightmarish quality to the whole place. Take the *In the Night Garden* experience, the ride that we headed for first. This is a 'magical' boat ride where you board a painfully slow boat which is then tugged through a recreation of the Night Garden. Your journey is accompanied by the possessed music-box soundtrack of the show. Along with a narration by the incredibly creepily voiced Derek Jacobi, who suggests that you try to spot the different characters like Upsy Daisy.

'Can you see her?' he asks menacingly. Yes, Derek, I can . . . There she is, looming out of the trees, dead-eyed and moving jerkily like something from *The* fucking *Ring*.

And so it goes for what seems like the next four hours. Stuck on a boat that's travelling through the water at the speed of a dead mussel. Trying to catch sight of a pinky ponk.

None of us, including Charlie, were particularly impressed by our boat ride through the nightmare garden and so we moved on to the Postman Pat Parcel Post ride. Which is a chance to ride alongside Greendale's finest as he goes about his deliveries.

I had some irrational concerns about this ride. Having watched *Postman Pat* for years I am well aware of how crap Pat is at his job but also how utterly useless he is at driving. So part of me thought that, if they are going to keep this ride true to the TV programme, there was a good chance we'd hit a cow and burst into flames.

The one thing that I didn't expect was that we would climb aboard Pat's van and then go around in a circle on a track without anything happening at all. And yet, that is exactly what happens on this ride. Nothing. None of Alf's sheep in the road. None of Ted Glen's old bangers broken down and in the way. Not even the unacknowledged sexual chemistry of a chat between Pat and Mrs Goggins. Literally nothing happens. You and Pat deliver the parcels without incident. What a disappointment.

And so painfully slow again. I mean, I understand that these rides are for young kids and you can't have toddlers achieving Mach speed to the point of blackout, like in a cosmonaut's centrifuge, but these rides move at less-than-walking pace. Even Charlie was dozing off by the time we got back to the bloody post office and were greeted by a big sign saying 'Mission Accomplished!'

Incidentally, what was the mission, Pat? To deliver parcels in the slowest time possible? This is supposed to be the Royal Mail, not fucking Yodel.

Never again.

Disappointed by the lack of excitement so far, we decided to head towards the *Go Jetters* ride. Charlie's favourite CBeebies programme, at the moment, is *Go Jetters* and this ride looked great. And standing in the queue we sang along to the tune:

♫ *'Xuli, she's the pilot with the power with the speed, Kyan's so fantastic when gymnastic's what you need, Lars can make and fix it super quickly with his –'* ♫

'Sorry, mate, he's too small.'

Apparently, to ride the *Go Jetters* ride you need to be 100cm tall. And Charlie, despite standing on my feet, was indeed too short. Tits. Disappointed, we decided to try the *Octonauts* ride, for which Charlie was also too small. So to avoid further disappointment we joined the queue for Justin's Pie-o-Matic Factory, which is advertised with the insistence that the kids 'Go wild, have fun, there's only one rule – there are no rules!' Well, there is one rule, Justin, you've got to be one metre bloody tall.

'Sorry, mate, he's too small.'

'What??'

'He's too small. You've got to be one metre tall to go in the Pie-o-Matic Factory, on the Numtums, the Octonauts ride and the Vroomster. Have you tried the Night Garden or the Postman Pat Parcel Post?'

Two minutes later . . .

'Yes, we're back again. Screw you, Pat, you smug prick.'

I don't want to be too harsh on CBeebies Land. The rides that Charlie was too small for do look great. So when he's a little taller I think we'll make the pilgrimage back to the land of Igglepiggle and Mr Tumble. After all, he really did enjoy the other stuff. He loved The Furchester Hotel show and was blown away to meet the big dog himself, Duggee, at a meet and greet. So not a bad day out. In the end he really enjoyed it.

Actually, so did I.

I mean, just because **short-arse** is too small for The Vroomster doesn't mean we should all miss out . . .

THE OPEN FARM

28th October

I don't know whether this is true in other parts of the country, but in Yorkshire we have a lot of open farms. Working farms that are open to the public. They are basically a poor man's zoo. Instead of jaguars and pandas they have pigs and cows and the occasional confused llama.

There's a very good reason why marketing experts choose to brand trainers, nightclubs and cars with names like Tiger, Puma and Gazelle. These names conjure a certain dynamism and excitement that you wouldn't get if you called the latest sports car 'cow' or 'goat'. And that's because these animals, through no fault of their own, are really fucking boring.

This was a thought that occurred to me as we wandered around yet another open farm today. The sixth or seventh of this summer. (I've lost count, and after a while they all tend to blend into one another.)

Look, maybe you disagree and you're the sort of person who loves these places. The sort of person who is fascinated by farm animals. Maybe your idea of a killer day out is shuffling through a shed with a few cows in it. And then wandering into another shed containing a few other cows that look marginally different from the first ones. I don't want to come across as anti-cow. But, for me, when you've see one you've seem 'em all.

I think that's true for most people. At today's open farm I was split up from Lyns and Charlie for twenty minutes and had to wait for them to catch me up. And so I stood in the viewing area of an enclosure that contained a single highland bull. Every person who came into the area commented on the size of this thing's bollocks. And this is my point. I mean, how bored are we all if we are noticing and pointing out to one another the size of a bovine's testicles?

It's no wonder there is a slight buzz of excitement amongst the crowd when one of the animals does a massive piss or the cows start banging each other. It's because we are all bored to tears.

And this is not just me being a dick. Today, Charlie wasn't any more interested in this stuff than I was. Once he had seen a sheep and fed a goat he was far more interested in an ice cream or the small adventure playground than he was in seeing yet another cow or some bull's pendulous gonads.

But to feel like this had been an educational outing, and to get our money's worth, we spent another hour or so looking at more cows and then some sheep and then some pigs.

And during that hour I began to cheer up a bit. Because, observing other parents and their children, I realised that we were the lucky ones. The one positive thing about wandering around this open farm with a toddler was that, for now at least, Charlie was too young to understand that all these animals would probably be dead and on the shelves of Aldi next week.

I kept catching awkward snippets of such conversations between parents and older children. Parents attempting to explain to an inquisitive child that they were basically wandering through a kind of animal death row. And these kids were discovering that zoos are fundamentally better than open farms, not just because the animals are more exciting but because when you're staring at a giraffe you know that the chances are next week it won't be a sausage.

I also caught similarly awkward discussions about what was going on when one animal mounted another.

Little boy: What are they doing, Daddy?

Dad: Erm ... y'know, I think they're just playing and hugging.

Older brother: Really, Dad? Cos it looks like they're fucking to me.

Dad: Ethan!

So yeah, it occurred to me that we might as well enjoy it because there is no way we are going to these places when Charlie is older.

It's true that today's open farm was a bit shit. Maybe I'm a city person by heart. I love nature and views of rolling countryside and all that, but I can take or leave the horse flies and cow manure and the oddball countryfolk with tombstone teeth and three fingers. And all that stuff about invigorating country air, I've never understood either. If you genuinely love that smell, you could recreate it at home by shitting in a bucket and sitting there with a towel over your head breathing it in like its Olbas Oil. So these glimpses of the real countryside are not really my thing.

That said, some open farms are better than others. We have a great one near us that Charlie loves called Cannon Hall. It has sweeping grounds, a stately home, a collection of priceless antiq— okay, it has a bar. But it also has other cool stuff like meerkats, a huge adventure playground, even ferret racing (which has to be the most Yorkshire thing since Geoff Boycott punched a whippet for looking at his gravy). It has a collection of snakes and spiders and lizards. And a petting area with rabbits and guinea pigs. This place is great.

The worst one I have ever been to was called Roy's Farm and it was just one big barn with two cows in it and a man called Roy with an apparent udder fixation. Roy and his son Billy manned the ticket booth (a deckchair), did the milking demonstrations and even popped up behind the counter in the makeshift giftshop. Our visit to Roy's Farm was the one and only time that I have wished I'd gone to a place when it was busier. Because being the only people in there when Roy is doing the milking demonstration – whilst eyeballing you – is the stuff of nightmares. I swear to God, I turned around for a couple of minutes, then turned back to find Roy had milk froth on his moustache.

The whole place was like the film *Deliverance* set on the outskirts of Wakefield – and we are never, ever going back.

Santa's Grotto

1st–23rd December

After visiting every Santa's grotto in the UK in the past three weeks I'd just like to confirm that 98 per cent of them are taking the piss.

You can't just stick a shed outside TK Maxx and call it a 'Winter Wonderland'. You can blu-tack a laminated A4 sign to the door saying 'The North Pole' and staple as much cotton wool to the pissing roof as you like . . . it's still a fucking shed. It doesn't become Lapland just because you put a fence around it and put two bored, pissed-off 'elves' outside.

You want to make it a winter wonderland? Try not employing the least enthusiastic people on the planet.

It's not just Santa who is often a miserable shit. We went to one today with a teenage lad as an elf. A teenage lad?! Yeah, they're always full of the joys of the festive season, aren't they? Nothing screams Christmas like a surly elf, stinking of weed and Lynx Africa, welcoming you to Lapland with such thick sarcasm he might as well be doing the 'wanker' sign in your face.

I don't blame him. He knows it's shit, he's on minimum wage and he lives in fear that his mates will come out of Argos and see him standing about in unconvincing pointy ears and stripey tights from Claire's Accessories.

The only thing worse than the standard surly, pissed-off elf is the other elf who is reeeally into it, and prances about doing the voice and asking questions about your favourite reindeer and all that. And because you've got a two-year-old kid whose vocabulary is virtually non-existent, you, as the adult, have to answer and you have to answer in your own sing-songy voice.

'Are you looking forward to seeing Santa?'

[*Charlie silent and distracted*]

'Er, yes, you are, aren't you, Charlie?'

'Have you got a chimney?' . . .

'Er, no, but we've got a magic key, haven't we, Charlie?'

'And what abou—'

'Look, er . . . I don't suppose there's any mulled wine in there is there? Anything really . . . It doesn't have to be mulled . . . or wine . . . Y'know, just any kind of alcohol that makes this whole conversation more bearable.'

Of course, if you're really lucky, the winter wonderland you're visiting will have a real-life reindeer and you can avoid queue chit-chat with Tinkerbell Snufflebottoms the elf by keeping yours and your little one's attention on that.

But then the reindeer is probably the most depressing member of the whole bunch. A reindeer's natural environment is the plains of Siberia, so it's no wonder Prancer looks pretty fucked off to find himself in a shopping centre in Doncaster. This magnificent beast is accustomed to looking at Arctic vistas not two blokes vaping outside Wilko.

No great surprise, then, that it's just stood there wishing for a last sleigh ride to the knackers yard. If I were stuck in a shopping centre in Doncaster for seven hours at Christmas I'd want a bolt gun to the head as well.

And this is all just in the bloody queue. That's before you even get inside and meet Santa, a prospect that is terrifying to about one in three kids, who are waiting in line like it's a queue for vaccinations or the dentist. Which is again not surprising, when every other kid is being carted out of the winter wonderland shed in meltdown.

Santa is terrifying to a lot of kids. Of course he is.

'Hey, kids! You know that thousand-year-old supernatural being that survives all year round in sub-zero temperatures and keeps short people as slaves? You know, the one that's always watching you to see whether you live up to his standards of niceness. And then one day a year, he bypasses all our home security and gets into the house in the middle of the night and creeps about chuckling to himself? Yeah? Well, that creepy, fat, judgey shit is in this wooden hut and you're going to sit on his knee.'

'Am I fuck' is not a strange response, it is absolutely the rational one.

And so eventually you're inside and confronted by the big man himself.

Except he's not big, is he? Since when did Santas get so thin? There's an obesity crisis in this country and half the Father Christmases I've seen this month look like they need a good meal. I've seen more meat on an Ikea pencil.

I'm not being funny but it can't be that hard to find a fat guy to stick in a red suit. Just go along to the local type 2 diabetes clinic with a big net.

And if they've got to be skinny, at least put them in a half-decent costume. Not this homemade crap or one of those shite Santa suits from Chinese Ebay that are comprised of so much polyester that if Santa rubs his legs together too fast he'll set the place on fire.

And the beards? The fucking beards?! Have you ever seen less convincing facial hair than a shopping-centre-Santa's beard? If you think that beard is fooling anybody, try it as a disguise. Try sneaking out of Nazi Germany with that beard as a disguise, you'd have been caught before you could say 'Ho Ho Ho, fuck! I've been shot.'

They're just wrong. It's the mouth bit up around their nose or below the chin. The visible elastic they're constantly pulling at like it's an awkward pair of pants that are disappearing up their arsehole. And it's all made out of that crap you stuff duvets with. I could make a more convincing beard by Pritt-sticking my face and gluing on a handful of goat pubes.

Obviously, the costume may be part of the problem but there's no way that I can get Charlie to sit on Santa's knee without him screaming the shed into pieces. (And I'm quite glad about this . . . Charlie not sitting on his knee makes it a bit easier to ignore Santa's prison tattoos and the whiff of White Lightning.) So again it is you, the adult, who has to engage in the small talk with 'Santa'.

'And has Charlie been good this year?'

'. . . Oh for fuck's sake. Not this again!? Look, he's not going to answer you. At best he might sing the theme tune to *Peter Rabbit* or jump up and down on one leg making fart noises. So can we just get to the present and get out of here? Otherwise, let's face it, it's just two fully grown men standing about in a shed talking about magic flying deer, with a child nearby. It's weird.

And so, after less than thirty seconds and a photograph of two middle-aged men (one in costume) with a two-year-old kid in the background trying to destroy a Christmas tree . . . it's over.

So we leave the 'magical and wondrous winter wonderland' (as described on the flyer), say goodbye to thin, malnourished, dead-beat, flammable Santa and goodbye to the elves Flutterbottom and young Miseryshit and, clutching a wrapped gift (that looks suspiciously exactly the same shape as every other kid's gift who exited in the hour we were queuing), we depart, griping about the tenner and hour lost.

And we walk away to the nearest café.

And then . . . something odd happened.

As Charlie tore into his present and 'oohed' and 'aahed' at the plastic piece of crap he found inside, it became clear that he had enjoyed the previous hour. He remembered the reindeer's name. He told me that Santa was nice and that his favourite elf was the teenage kid because he was funny (pretending that the other elf was crazy and making faces). Charlie didn't see the elastic on Santa's beard, or the cotton wool on the roof. Because it wasn't a shed in a shopping centre, it was what it said on the laminate, it was the North Pole. Of course it was. Because when you're two years old, magic isn't sleight of hand . . . it's just magic.

So Charlie did what all kids do, he invited me into his version of the day. Kids invite you to do this all the time. All you have to do is wipe your feet and step inside. And as he chatted nonsensically, I was caught by his jingling excitement and his electric-lights enthusiasm and I realised that I have absolutely nothing to teach this kid about Christmas and everything to learn. Or maybe it's more accurate to say that, just like with the seaside, I have everything to remember.

And what a Christmas gift that is from this amazing little human I now share my life with. A reminder to wipe over that grimy window that looks into our own childhood, into something lost in adulthood and the shit that goes with it. A peer into a world of magical people and astonishment and impossibility, a world where a winter wonderland is just that. No more out of place in a crappy shopping precinct than it is in the Polar North.

And, of course, the whole thing is ridiculous and, of course, it's impossible. But fuck it. If you're too old, cynical and stupid to understand that that's how magic works . . . then Christmas will always be a shed.

A Posh Meal

17th February

Quick question. Let's say you're out for a pub lunch and your toddler is arguing with you about their ability to use a 'big fork'. And let's say you try to wrestle that big fork away from him, and in doing so your child catapult-fires a piece of sausage and it lands, oh, let's say twelve feet away in some bloke's pint with a plop.

Do you tell the guy?

Supplementary information:

a) The guy is in the toilet so has not seen the sausage land in his pint.
b) The piece of sausage has been regurgitated at least twice because it was 'hot'.

No. Of course you don't tell the guy. Neither did I. He came back from the toilet, necked his pint and was none the wiser. Apart from a slightly confused chew at the end of his drink. Besides, this is the least of the crimes that can be committed by a toddler out for a meal.

Is there anything more stressful than taking a toddler out to a restaurant? When we do dine out we ordinarily choose somewhere to eat that is 'family friendly'. Which I think is restaurant speak for 'we don't care how much disruption you cause, our food is shite anyway'.

We go to these places so that we can surround ourselves with like-minded and like-destructive other families who expect a certain amount of chaos. It's just a lot less stressful to be in the company of people with standards as low as our own.

But today, we chanced our luck and ventured outside our comfort zone. We went to somewhere without a playground, without crayons and tear-off colouring sheets. A place with tablecloths, for Christ's sake. Oooooohh, fancy.

It wasn't on purpose, we're not complete morons. It was getting late, everywhere for families seemed to be busy and we needed to find somewhere quickly before Charlie reached that point of hunger when he turns into Thanos and wants to destroy half the universe.

I knew it was a mistake the moment we set foot inside, when I heard the low agreeable hum of adults chatting, punctuated occasionally by the clink of wine glass on crockery. Rather than the shrieking, clattering, apocalyptic noises of a riot in a prison canteen that we had become accustomed to when enjoying kid-friendly dining.

A waitress approached and asked us where we would like to sit and, looking around, my immediate thought was to say, 'Just as far away from civilised people as humanly possible, please. In fact, if you have a hut in the car park we'll happily sit in that and you can push the food to us under the door.'

Instead, we were escorted to a table and seated next to a couple apparently enjoying their thirtieth wedding anniversary. They predictably looked over at our arrival as though we'd just come from being filmed for *Benefits Britain* and I was wearing a string vest and had no teeth. We requested a high chair and one was conjured from somewhere, and the upmarket nature of the establishment was confirmed . . . Ladies and gentlemen, THIS HIGH CHAIR WAS CLEAN.

Almost every high chair I have come across when dining out looks as though the waiting staff have just fished it out of a skip or a nearby canal. The crevices hold debris and bits of food like you might find in the oven door hinges of a student house and the straps look like a tramp's belt. And they are always delivered to your table without acknowledging the horror of them. 'I'll just give that a quick wipe.' Yeah, awesome! A quick wipe with a tea towel should kill the 7,090 undiscovered viruses currently partying on the fucking thing. Great!

But no. This high chair was spotless. And if that wasn't enough evidence of this place's poshness, we took a look at the menu . . . No Turkey Dinos.

We were in enemy territory.

We ordered Charlie fish fingers (goujons) and I asked if they came with beans, to which the waiter looked at me as though I'd ordered something wildly exotic and insisted he'd need to check with the kitchen.

(To give you an idea of the pretentiousness of the place, me and Lyns both ordered 'Rock Cod, Chipped potatoes and pureed petit pois'. Fish, chips and mushy peas to you and me.)

As we waited for our food, the server appeared again with our drinks and the appropriate knives and forks.

Which brings me to an important public service announcement, for all serving staff all over the world.

Dear waiters/waitresses, just a heads-up. If you place a knife and fork within easy reach of a toddler, they will stab you, or me, or themselves with it. This is not a threat. I'm just saying that if you put cutlery within twelve inches of a toddler, someone is going to get shanked.

On this occasion, no one was hurt. I was able to wrestle the cutlery away from Charlie without too much damage. But for fuck's sake, don't present a toddler with a steak knife. It's bad. The same goes for placing a plate that is the same temperature as the Earth's core in front of a two year old and announcing: 'Careful with that, it's hot'. Toddlers don't see that as a warning, if they understand what the fuck you're talking about at all. They see it as a challenge.

The food took a while to arrive. And when this happens Charlie has a tendency to shout 'Where's my dinner! Where's my dinner!' whilst banging on the table like a hungry Viking. This is cute and funny at home but can come across as a little impolite whilst enjoying the à la carte menu at Le Bistro.

That said, on this occasion Charlie's shouting proved quite effective and we seemed to get served rather quicker than the surrounding tables. We began to tuck in.

Charlie ate the way he always does, as though the purpose of food is to fling it around and decorate your surroundings, like the Swedish chef from The Muppets. His philosophy seems to be that if some gets in your mouth then that's a bonus. So, as usual, before long our table and the surrounding area began to resemble our driveway when the cats have been at the bins.

To make matters more uncomfortable, Charlie's lack of manners was compounded by the waiter coming over to ask if everything was to our satisfaction. Usually when a waiter asks if everything is okay with our meal I do the usual British thing of replying 'Yes, it's lovely, thank you' even when the food is inedible and tastes like a foot. But Charlie has no such social grace or respect for etiquette and he barely waited for the question to finish passing the waiter's lips before he announced to the restaurant that his meal was 'gusting', 'orrible' and that he didn't like it before spitting a mouthful of fish into his own hand and then dumping it on to the waiter's shoes. As restaurant critics go, toddlers can be pretty harsh.

The worst thing about eating in proper restaurants isn't the lack of a toddler's manners or the disapproval of other tables, nor is it the noise and mess your child makes. It is that you are dining against the clock. Toddlers have no patience for the whole culinary experience. Grown-ups like to spend two hours savouring their food whereas for toddlers two hours is an age. They don't want to rest between courses and have a chat about politics or how it's going at work, they want to eat, get down from their chair and explore. Life is passing us by, you boring twats.

And so all meals are curtailed, and rarely savoured. The point at which your kid demands to GET OUT of their high chair is the time to order the bill and sod off. Especially in a proper restaurant where it can be frowned upon to go chasing each other around the tables until one of you needs a poo.

So toddlers have none of the airs and graces of posh-restaurant goers and, to be honest, you have to love them for it. The social niceties, the order of cutlery use, the wait for the bill, the hand-wringing about whether to have a dessert or a starter . . . To a toddler these conventions seem utterly ridiculous, because they **are** ridiculous. Who is the more daft, the toddler enjoying his food noisily or the adult who is sniffing their wine and ensuring they use the correct spoon?

And I thought about this as we ate our dinner. The only thing spoiling our meal was our perception that other people were annoyed. Maybe they were and maybe they weren't, but I decided not to give a shit. After all, Charlie certainly didn't.

Besides, having worked as a waiter, I can tell you that there are far bigger arseholes in restaurants than the average toddler: the non-tippers, the diners who are rude and obnoxious to staff to demonstrate their virility to their date. The ones who complain loudly about bugger-all to get a free starter. The romantic couples who feed each other as foreplay. The teeth-pickers. Those who chat too loudly about how important their job is. And, yes, the wine sniffers. Restaurants, especially expensive ones, are full of annoying shit-heads. There is nothing that marks my son as being any more annoying than any of these people, he's just a bit shorter in height and less full of bullshit.

So, eventually, we finished our dinner and requested the bill. And we left a hefty tip to compensate for the fact that where we had been sitting looked like a table had been placed on a landfill site.

And we left, like the closing credits of an action movie, striding into the horizon and never looking back at the devastation behind us.

And went to McDonald's for dessert.

It was like coming home.

Expectations

Sometimes a day will live up to expectations. Sometimes it will even exceed those expectations. I have found myself at the seaside this summer ankle-deep in the surf, tossing Charlie high into the sky and catching him again. And I will always remember his laughter drowning out his mum's giggly fear that I'm throwing him too high. Since writing this chapter, we have wandered around zoos and farms in glorious sunshine, fed alpacas by hand and eaten picnics overlooking rolling hills as the sun sets. And we have been to music festivals and huddled together beneath stars and spent those moments more acutely aware than ever that we will love this boy until the very last of them go dark.

And all of these days out have conjured entirely unforgettable memories. But we laugh more about the days that go tits-up. The day when I slipped and fell into the river as I was pursued by a duck. The day when we made a hasty exit from a café because Charlie had spooned his yoghurt into the hood of a woman's coat. The day when it rained so badly that we squelched back to the car and drove home with the heaters on full blast and steam rising from our hair.

These are some of my favourite memories of our days with Charlie. Because our love for him is the same as our love for each other. It is the same as the love we have for the very best of friends. Yes, it is moulded in enjoyment of each other's company but it is fired and set in days that can be challenging, tough and grinding. Being able to laugh at those times, being able to be pissed off without being angry, being able to say 'fuck it, tomorrow is a fresh start' and plan another day out with the blind optimism that no part of it will be a disaster. This is how a family is made. And maybe beyond DNA and blood it is how a family become friends.

And what's a couple of wanking gibbons amongst friends?

8
Days In

Productive morning with the boy so far. Spent half of it on the phone to Nannan and the other half buying a massive egg.

Days In

As magical as days out can be, on the whole the British aren't really an outdoorsy kind of people. In fact, according to research, we don't get out of the house anywhere near enough. We are about thirtieth in the world rankings for healthiness, and in the World Health Organisation's own 2018 report it specifically states that the British 'excel at drinking, stopping in and doing fuck all'. Or something like that.

These health rankings are always dominated by countries like Australia. Countries populated by people with tanned skin and white teeth, rather than the other way round. Countries that live their lives outdoors.

Obviously, we are encouraged to be more like our Antipodean cousins. But there are good reasons why Brits don't live in the same way. Australians enjoy glorious sunshine all year round. They also have mad stuff like spiders the size of a car hiding in their toilets and if there was any chance of that shit in my house I'd be outside all the time too.

Also, more importantly, there are times when we just can't be arsed to go out. Can't be bothered to put on pants, spritz our arm-pits, flannel our bits or pick the morning's weetabix out of our hair. Some days all that feels a bit 'la-di-da'.

And so, as parents, much of our lives are spent indoors.

Babies are incredibly easy to entertain indoors. Pull a face or hide behind your hands and 'peekaboo' . . . These simple routines repeated over and over again can occupy a baby for hours. Babies are like the viewing audience for UK Gold, their threshold for being entertained is just phenomenally low. Not so toddlers. They demand distraction and stimulation or they begin to use their powers for evil. And entertaining a toddler indoors can be a real challenge. Strategies must be developed to keep your child occupied and busy, so that they don't spend their days inside reducing your home to rubble. Or following you around like a soul-sucking shadow that constantly asks stupid questions whilst wiping its nose on your jeans.

Thankfully, there are many ways of occupying tiny minds indoors and just maybe keeping your own mind intact at the same time.

In theory.

Baking

Whilst scrolling through social media, I often come across parents and children enjoying quality time and bonding over a shared love of baking. These pictures are usually incredibly sweet. A toddler, with a little apron tied at the waist, perhaps a smear of chocolate on one cheek, smiles happily at the camera, as they and their mum cheerfully show off a tray of perfectly crafted brownies. Beneath which appears a caption that reads: 'Look at what little Katie made ♥ x.'

Often I'll click to 'like' that picture. I'll 'like' it for what it represents: something simple and pure, a moment of bonding over the simplest of creations and a metaphor for family: different ingredients mixed together to create something wholesome and good.

And then I'll scroll onwards thinking, *Fuck off, Donna. Your kid did not make those buns in a million years. You can tell a mile off. For a start, they're not completely shit.*

Because toddlers are not good bakers. If they're not dropping eggshell into the mix, they are sneezing into the batter. Ingredients find their way into the bowl by accident and not by design. And the end result, at best, resembles something the neighbour's cat might hack up on your doorstep and, at worst, something decidedly poisonous.

So when I see pictures online of parents and children joyously baking, I more than suspect the 'smoke and mirrors' of social media at work. It's not just the perfectly formed end-product that looks like perfectly baked bullshit. I also look at the settings of some of these photos and my suspicions are further aroused. These surroundings look ordered, clean and tidy. It is as though, during the baking process, these parents and their kids have managed to measure ingredients, keep everything in the bowl and, with a final lick of a spoon, returned the place to neat order. Just in time to remove their perfect brownies from a preheated oven, gas mark 6, 200°C, after 20 minutes. Ding!

After a morning spent baking in our house, our surroundings do not look like this. Our kitchen looks rather more like one of The Four Horsemen of the Apocalypse has ridden through . . . whilst fucking a cake.

Clouds of flour and caster sugar settle on the kitchen counters like dust after the eruption of Pompeii. Chocolate adorns the walls like blood spatter and the inside of the microwave is a horror film. The sink is blocked. There is a ceiling-high Jenga stack of pots and pans and food-mixer parts. And we discover that 'hundreds and thousands' are named 'hundreds and thousands' because they get fucking everywhere and trying to clean them up makes you want to punch yourself in the face hundreds and thousands of times.

And this is just after making one of those Aunt Bessie's ready-made packet things which only require you to add an egg.

Never mind the state of Charlie after all this. Whereas in other bakers' posts there is a picture of a clean kid with a cute wisp of icing sugar on the tip of their nose, Charlie is head-to-foot in cake mix and looks like he's motor-boated a chocolate trifle.

And your reward for the fact that your kitchen looks like Prue Leith has sampled a showstopper laced with PCP and smashed up the *Bake Off* tent?

Three shitty cornflake buns. Buns that have been moulded by toddler fingers that haven't paused in their constant rummaging up nose and arse since you started. These things are not just visually unappealing, they are also about as appetising as Novichok.

Put it this way: there's no way **I'd** eat them. I usually save mine and Charlie's efforts for visiting relatives or send them off to the bake sale at nursery and then keep an eye on the news for word of unexplained deaths in the area.

So despite its popularity, baking is not an ideal pastime for a day indoors with a toddler. It always seems like a good idea but the clean-up is industrial-level and the end result is rarely worth it, if edible at all.

Arts and Crafts

We are a nation of hobbyists apparently. Arts and crafts are in our blood. We love to make things that look a bit amateurish and crap rather than buy something professionally made. My own family is full of people who enjoy making their own Christmas cards and people who like to crochet and knit. I even have an uncle who is really into glass-blowing. (Something he's unaccountably proud of.) Which means whenever we go round to his house, we stand around drinking out of surrealist, wonky glasses. Which in a strange way makes sense given that we are drinking his homemade beer that gives everyone the shits.

I am not one of these people.

I think my hatred of arts and crafts goes all the way back to 1987. St Ann's Primary School. Mrs Wilson's class. When in the run-up to Mother's Day, Mrs Wilson announced an impromptu craft hour in which we would be making a jewellery box by taking an old margarine tub and gluing some dried pasta and seashells on to it.

Because, obviously, that's what all mums want for Mother's Day: something in which to keep their most precious possessions. And more specifically, a plastic tub that smells vaguely of Cleethorpes and I Can't Believe It's Not Butter.

I remember my own efforts very well. I painted my box bright red and adorned it with the shells and the pasta provided. I also decided to etch the word 'jewellery' into the top of it using a compass.

As I began, I was convinced it would be a masterpiece.

Unfortunately, my enthusiasm betrayed my ability. I ran out of time and failed to finish etching the word 'jewellery'. Also on the way home all the shells and pasta fell off. In the end, what I presented to my mum on Mother's Day that year was just a blood-red tub with the word 'JEW' scratched into it.

Of course, it goes without saying that my mum pretended to love my creation. She then used this sinister anti-Semitic horror box for years. Because that's what mums do.

Since this inauspicious entrance into the world of homemade art, I have avoided making things like this at every opportunity. When you become a parent, though, this is not allowed. When you are the parent to a toddler, you must be patient and kind and tolerant and organised. Oh, by the way, you also have to be Kirstie fucking Allsopp.

I don't think I'm the only parent who hates 'crafting'. I think most do. Because there are only two types of parent when it comes to this sort of pastime. You are either like me, in that you hate it because it all seems a bit pointless and crap. Or you hate it because you actually enjoy crafting and you like things to be done correctly. In which case, you find the whole experience of making things with your child infuriating because THEY. KEEP. DOING. IT. WRONG. Lyns is the latter type. She enjoys arts and crafts and likes the idea of Charlie engaging in hands-on, creative activities. Right up to the point when he's putting a gingerbread man's eyes where it's balls should go.

As with baking, my main problem is the mess. The effort and the clear-up is, again, rarely worth it. Glitter, for example, even in minuscule amounts is never good. It's like house herpes and impossible to get rid of once your home is infected. We made a glittery angel for a Christmas tree almost two years ago and our sofa, the dog and Charlie's nannan still shimmer if the light catches them right.

Now, you may be reading all this and thinking: *Well, actually, Matt, it's not about whether **you** enjoy doing crafty stuff. The important thing is whether **Charlie** enjoys it.* And that's a fair point. But the question of whether Charlie enjoys hobbycrafting is complicated and the answer is: sometimes and briefly.

The issue with toddlers making things is one of attention span. For example, here is a series of pictures, taken over a twenty-minute period, in which you can actually chart the deterioration in Charlie giving a fuck about making card Easter bunnies.

1st Bunny!	Interest Waning Bunny	Not Arsed Bunny	Peak 'Fuck-it' Bunny

At Christmas too, our attempts to make a festive wreath degenerated as Charlie's interest faded. Soon into the task he was bored of attaching the more traditional elements of holly and ivy to his project and insisted on making it 'better'. Which is why our wreath (that hung on our front door for the whole of Christmas 2017) had Iron Man and a balloon gaffer-taped to it. As well as bits of crap Charlie found in our cardboard bin. If you look closely you will notice a wrapper for a Bounty and the packaging for a Bloo disinfectant toilet block.

(The one positive about this creation was that it kept away the carol singers, who were understandably concerned as to who might live inside this particular house and how long they'd been off their meds.)

Halloween also throws up the spectre of arts and crafts, when pumpkin-carving becomes the thing all parents must do. (Because what is missing from the joy of crafting with a toddler is the jeopardy of a massive knife.)

Actually our creative attempts this Halloween weren't too bad. Admittedly, our pumpkin turned out so shit I didn't even take a picture of it before throwing it over our back fence, but that's not to say all our Halloween creations were crap. I forgot to buy all the bits we needed to make spiders' webs and witches' fingers so we had to improvise with stuff we already had around the house, but I was particularly pleased with this Tampax ghost.

(For those interested in making their own I have included instructions below.)

Step 1: Stick some googley eyes on a Tampax.
So arts and crafts shouldn't be ruled out as a pastime when trapped indoors. As you can see from Casper the friendly sanitary product, sometimes it's worth it.

In our house, paintings by Charlie adorn our fridge door like it's a wall in the Louvre. An autumn picture that Charlie made at nursery – a collage of leaves stuck to paper – hangs on our hallway wall as the first thing you see when you walk in. And a sad, indiscernible clay sculpture sits on our mantelpiece with Charlie's thumb and fingerprints frozen in it like a proud signature. All these things that Charlie has made sit in pride of place in our home and for good reason.

There is something connective to the past and the passage of time about things made by tiny hands. And this makes these objects and pictures beautiful without being anything close to perfect. Just like that jewellery box I made for my own mum. And this, thirty-odd years later, that Charlie made for Lyns for Mother's Day:

Lyns adores this masterpiece. She thinks it's art.

Objectively speaking, is it a bit shit? Maybe. But tell that to Lyns – a mother, like my own, who loves her little boy so much that her eyes have stopped working.

Other Activities

Of course, looking after a toddler indoors whilst also nursing a hangover has roughly the same fun-rating as ball surgery. And on these occasions the standard toddler pastimes of baking a cake, painting a picture or making homemade Christmas cards can seem like a truly horrifying prospect. I recently found myself in this situation, my head clanging, desperate to occupy Charlie for a while. So I quickly searched online for activities that might help us successfully kill an hour or two rather than one another.

Straight away I was delighted to discover the 'top things to do with a toddler indoors'. It was an interesting list to consider. And consider it I did:

Make slime!

Nope.

Face-painting!

Nope.

. . . Okay, before we go any further . . . any ideas that don't involve slime, paint, having to redecorate afterwards, that sort of thing?

Make an obstacle course!

Nope.

Empty the recycling bins and get building!

So go fishing in our bins? I don't think so.

Chat!

Chat? . . . Chat?!!

Toddler yoga!

. . . What?

Make your own musical instruments!

Okay . . . are you actually fucking high?

Exasperated, I thought: *There **must** be one good, effective, indoor activity to pass the time on days in. One that won't destroy our home in a cataclysm of glitter and baking powder and one that doesn't require all this faffing about and, well, effort.*

And, of course, there is.

In fact, there's an absolute belter.

Television

Obviously, TV is one of the trappings of modern life that poisons tiny brains. It's why none of our kids spend more than fifteen minutes watching television a day. Fifteen minutes and no more. We enjoy the rest of our time with our children chatting, making scones, teaching them Mandarin and creating dream-catchers out of recycled pipe cleaners and twine.

No. We don't.

There is a reason why parenting experts call the TV the 'electronic babysitter'. What confuses me is that they say it like it's a bad thing.

The television can be a saviour when you want your toddler to stay in just one place for more than five minutes. It can be the secret to a warm cup of tea and a piss spent alone. Yet we are told that it is dangerous and harmful and that allowing your child to watch television is evidence that you are a bad parent, slovenly and uninterested in developing your child's brain. Popping the telly on? You might as well be driving a railway spike through their skull.

So most parents deal with this thorny issue in the simplest of ways. They take all the professional opinion and critical research into account, consider it thoughtfully . . . and then they ignore it and lie about how much telly they allow their kids to watch, so that no one judges them.

Sometimes I lie about it too. Especially when I'm speaking to somebody who is vehemently anti-telly. I was talking to one dad at a barbecue who kept banging on about how much he hated the 'mind-numbing' effects of television on kids. So much so, in fact, that he claimed to have got rid of their TV as soon as their youngest was born. Elliot would not be exposed to such nonsense. (*Whoopee fucking doo for Elliot*, I thought, as I nodded earnestly.)

The guy was clearly a weirdo but during this conversation I felt pressured to insist that Charlie watched very little TV too. Although I suspect this fella was less than convinced. My insistence was slightly undermined by the fact that Charlie was behind me at the time running around in a *Blaze and the Monster Machines* T-shirt and belting out the theme tune to *Shimmer and Shine* word-perfectly, and with actions.

I shook my head. 'Where **do** they get it from?'

To be honest, I don't know whether this dad was telling the truth about not owning a TV. I do know that some parents make wild claims like this, and many more insist that they radically restrict their kids' TV access. And yet, whenever they post a picture on social media, there in the background is a two-foot-tall Octonaut being beamed into their living room via a 55-inch plasma screen, a hypnotised child staring into it like it's the face of God. I'm going to go out on a limb and suggest that most kids watch TV quite a bit.

So, putting this debate to one side, let's assume that your children do catch the occasional glimpse of a telly. For a parent it becomes a question of what they watch, which are the shows we hate, which are the shows we love. Which are the ones that make us want to take our television, rip the plug from the wall, strap it to our backs and walk up the highest mountain in Christendom, just so we can throw it from the top.

Toddler Telly

When I was a kid there were only three TV channels. Three. (Yes, I am older than Methuselah's balls.) And I don't really remember too many kids' shows. In the seventies and early eighties, TV seemed to be a constant cycle of news, snooker and various sitcoms complaining about the fact that Asians had moved in next door. Now, though, there are forty-odd channels just for kids, some broadcasting twenty-four hours a day. With hundreds of different programmes, an entire book could be written about this subject alone. So here's just a snapshot of some of Charlie's favourites over the past couple of years. Shows that, in some ways, also represent the three stages of toddler TV viewing.

The utterly baffling world of very early toddler TV: *In the Night Garden* and *Teletubbies*.

The marginally less confusing stage of mid-toddler TV: *Bing* and *Postman Pat*.

And the wild west of pre-school TV: *PAW Patrol* and *Peppa Bloody Pig*.

In the Night Garden

Man vs. Baby – 14th July 2018

A while ago I got into an online debate about In the Night Garden *with a mum who's a massive fan of it. She'd seen an earlier post when I'd suggested that Iggle Piggle and Upsy Daisy were Nazis and 'Jen' wasn't at all happy.*

At one point she argued that 'The Night Garden is sweet, is about fun and friendship and at the end of the day wouldn't the Night Garden be just a lovely place to live?'

To which I replied: 'Really? Okay, but in whose house?'

And it's an important point. If you had to live in the Night Garden, whose house would you live in? Because they're all crap.

The Tombliboo house looks nice from the outside but the interior looks like it's been built out of twiglets and varnished dog shit.

Makka Pakka's cave is basically a f**king tomb. And it's also built in a dry river bed on a flood plain . . . which means if there's a flash flood he's f**ked it. (And in a flood the first thing that goes is the sewage drains, so any prolonged rainfall and he's going to be either dead or knee-deep in Haahoo shit.)

On the face of it, the Pontipines have the best house but you've got to bear in mind that it's a semi-detached and the Wottingers next door have got eight bloody kids.

Obviously, the Wottingers have exactly the same problem, living next door to the Pontipines and their eight kids. But for them it's even worse because they've got to live next door to Mr Pontipine . . . who I've always thought was a bit of a smug prick with his dopey moustache that he obviously thinks makes him look like Burt Reynolds but actually just looks like a hippy's bush has been stuck to his stupid ball-shaped face.

Upsy Daisy and Iggle Piggle don't even have a house. Upsy Daisy's got a bed on wheels that she drags around like some lost mental patient after a f**king apocalypse . . . and Iggle is apparently homeless. He's just got an old crusty blanket. I don't even know where he sleeps, but if the Night Garden has a branch of Greggs he's probably curled up in the doorway every night freezing his bollocks off and drinking lighter fluid.

So like I said to Jennifer, the Night Garden would not be a lovely place to live at all.

> Me: 'And you saying it is, is just papering over the cracks of the fact that it's in the grip of a severe housing crisis.'
>
> . . .
>
> Jennifer: 'Matt, you have thought about this way too much.'
>
> Yeah, that's a fair point.

Jennifer's point that I'd maybe spent too much time thinking about *In the Night Garden* is a fair one. But for Charlie, as for most kids in the past ten or so years, *ITNG* was his first real exposure to television (it's like a gateway drug to the harder stuff like *Sarah and Duck*), so for months we lived in the world of Iggle Piggle. And, of course, we spent a lot of time thinking about it, talking about it and debating it. Because TV targeted at the very young makes absolutely no sense whatsoever.

Each episode begins in exactly the same way, in the 'real world' with a child being lulled to sleep by an adult and a haunting voiceover. Before we are transported to a dream/nightmare garden populated by a blue fluffy cock, a huge-headed skirt-lifting doll, two families of clothes pegs, a thing that lives in a cave and looks a lot like the shit emoji, a load of massive inflatable faces and three weird man-babies who can't keep their trousers on for two minutes and sleep together in a massive bush. Oh, and everybody gets around by Ninky Nonk, which is a runaway train. Or an airship with flapping wings and a big fake tit glued to the front of it, called the Pinky Ponk.

Objectively, the whole thing is weird and creepy. There is no discernible story. Or even an explanation for what these things are. The scale of everything also keeps changing. (And so parents spend a lot of the time shouting at the TV that the whole thing is bullshit because Iggle Piggle is clearly bigger than the Pinky Ponk, so how the bloody hell can he fit inside? How?!)

If all this isn't terrifying enough, it is made all the more so by the endless repetition. Every episode begins in the same way, but also ends in the same way too, with an unnerving dance in which all the main characters sway side to side as though it's the end of the film *The Wicker Man* and just out of shot they've got Edward Woodward burning to death in a hundred-foot-tall wooden effigy.

Well, isn't that a pip.

So this sort of TV, the television aimed at the very young, is the most baffling stage in a child's viewership. There is no grounding in reality, just a shock of primary colours and nonsense. *Teletubbies* is another good example, if your toddler prefers that. A programme named after the four main characters who have televisions surgically implanted in their abdomens and, in strikingly similar style to the characters in *ITNG*, constantly repeat the same actions, can't string a sentence together and won't stop fucking waving.

It's difficult to assess the effects that these shows have on a child's mind but I can comment on the effects they have on the adult. With regular viewing it begins to feel like the televisual equivalent of 'trepanning', the ancient custom of drilling into someone's skull to release demons.

Thankfully, whether your toddler is first introduced to TV through *In the Night Garden*, the *Teletubbies* or even the *Twirlywoos*, this is a temporary kind of hell and they do move on.

Bing

Eventually, toddlers are ready for something more sophisticated. Ready for shows with more of a storyline. This is not to be celebrated too hard though, especially if the show your child moves on to is *Bing*.

The main character in *Bing* is a massive-headed rabbit in dungarees, who constantly fucks everything up and then whinges about it as though it wasn't his fault in the first place. (That's the entire premise.)

The other main character is Flop, Bing's guardian. It is not clear whether he is Bing's father, nanny, babysitter, social worker, parole officer or lodger*, but basically it is Flop's responsibility to be Bing's guide as he ballses up pouring a drink or colouring inside lines and then moans about it for the rest of the episode.

If parents hate *In the Night Garden*, they **really** hate *Bing*.

I do completely understand why parents can't stand Bing Bunny. I do find him incredibly annoying but if I'm honest it is Flop who I consider **the** most infuriating character on kids' TV. I think he's supposed to represent the perfect parent or guardian. Always patient, always understanding. Flop never gets irritated and never ever raises his voice. But his response to Bing's overall shitness is so incredibly calm and measured that it is just odd. He has the unnatural calmness, in fact, of somebody who is taking the edge off things by quietly drinking all day:

'Oh no, look, Flop, I've set fire to the curtains!'

'Oh, never mind, Bing Bunny, I've been drinking sambuca since half eight. I couldn't really give a fuck.'

---

* Due to the fact that no one really knows what the relationship is between Flop and Bing, dark theories about this abound online, the most popular being that:

'Flop is a figment of Bing's imagination, created in his mind as a coping mechanism after all the grown-ups died from The Virus.' Or that: 'Bing and the other animals are clones being looked after by Carers until their organs are needed for harvesting.'

If Flop isn't a drinker then that's even more concerning. Because, in that case, maintaining the same unnervingly calm tone of voice – regardless of the circumstances – suggests he may be a dangerous sociopath.

There's a bit in *The Silence of the Lambs* when Lecter bites a guard's nose off and the entire time his heart rate never goes above 'resting'. And Flop has that same weird freakish calm about him, regardless of what Bing has done. Admittedly, the things that Bing does aren't that bad but I can easily imagine an episode in which Bing goes on a murderous rampage, stacking up the bodies on the coffee table, and Flop moseying in with a cup of tea in one hand: 'Never mind, Bing Bunny, it's just a little mess, let's get cleaned up, shall we?'

Murder: it's a Bing thing.

Whereas *Night Garden* is aimed at kids as young as eighteen months, *Bing* is aimed at two to four year olds and so there is a narrative, it does make some sense. But even at this secondary stage of toddler viewing there are many unanswered questions.

I have no idea what Flop is. Bing is a rabbit but Flop is some sort of cross between a sock-puppet, a door stop and a knitted ball-sack. In fact, all the adults in *Bing* are the same – like freakish misshapen cuddly toys – whereas all the kids are recognisable animals like elephants and pandas.

And the adults are all so much smaller than the children. Which gives the impression that Bing isn't a child at all but actually a huge, dumb, hulking adult like Lennie from *Of Mice and Men*.

And why does no one mention the fact that Bing's mate Pando the panda takes his trousers off at every opportunity? My uncle Martin used to do the same, but that's only because in the late seventies he hit a tree on his moped and had a metal plate put in his head, he did all kinds of mad shit.

I think the main problem with *Bing*, and the reason why so many parents hate it, has nothing to do with Flop or these unanswered questions but back where we started, with Bing's incessant whining. The fact is that, if you're a mum or dad, you already have your own little person in your house, in real life, wandering about making a mess of stuff and moaning about it. The last thing you need is another one broadcast into your living room every day as bloody entertainment.

Postman Pat

Eventually, Charlie moved on from *Bing* too. And, like most older toddlers, his TV watching preferences became more diverse and the shows themselves less confusing, with actual stories and characters that make sense. Shows like *Fireman Sam* and *Postman Pat*, animations set in a real world.

I don't actually mind *Postman Pat*. It's a classic and has been a kids' favourite for over forty years. It does concern me, however, what this programme may be teaching our children about work ethic and capability. Pat is, after all, the shittest postman in history. The kind of postie who might hold the occasional birthday-card envelope up to the light, looking for cash or vouchers (and then pocketing it before chucking little Jimmy's card from Grandma over a wall).

The kind of postie who sticks a card under your door saying that you weren't in, when you've waited in all day and are stood on the other side of that same door waiting for the bastard.

There are even theories/rumours that Pat is shagging half of Greendale whilst on his rounds. It is definitely suspicious that Pat is the only red-headed adult in the village and yet all the kids seem to be ginger. (They also all seem to share his unusually penissy nose.) Certainly, when the theme tune at the end asks, 'Can you guess what's in his sack?' it is tempting to think: *Well, some particularly potent baby-gravy for a start.*

In fairness to Pat Clifton, the truth is that he's probably not a thief or a womaniser. What he is, though, is incredibly bad at his job. He opens other people's post (which is mail fraud, by the way, with a custodial sentence of up to two years). He also loses or breaks parcels all the time and is constantly delayed by being lost, confused, forgetful or taking back roads and getting stuck behind one of Alf Thompson's sheep.

Pat is a postman who has a helicopter, a speedboat, a snowmobile, quad bike and other phenomenal resources the average local sorting office can only dream of, and he still can't seem to get Mrs Goggins' new vibrator, or whatever, to her before 12.30pm.

Special Delivery my arse.

And really, what sort of grown man takes his cat everywhere anyway? To be honest, the more I watch *Postman Pat* the more I'm convinced that he's just the local idiot that everyone has a soft spot for. And so he wanders around pretending to be a postman and everyone just plays along.

'I've got a parcel for you, Ted Glen!'

'Course you have, Pat! Just pop it on the table.'

And then as soon as Pat's back is turned, Ted is twirling his finger at his own temple, muttering 'Mad twat'.

CBeebies

So these are some of the shows that Charlie has enjoyed in his first three years. There have been others too that are not quite as annoying and some that are even brilliant. Shows like the *Go Jetters*, *Octonauts*, *Andy's Prehistoric Adventures* and the televisual brilliance that is *Hey Duggee*. These are educational and smart and funny. Yes, there is still the high weirdness of kids' TV: the leader of the Octonauts is a polar bear and on his team he has a pirate cat and, inexplicably, some walking, talking vegetables; in the *Go*

Jetters, the creators couldn't help but inject oddness – they created a group of fairly standard superheroes but then made their mentor a disco-obsessed unicorn. Safe to say, recreational drug use is alive and well in the production of kids' TV.

But all of these shows are more than bearable. And all of these shows have something in common: they are part of the programming schedule of CBeebies, the BBC's kids' channel that has saved our day and sanity on more occasions than I could ever count. I shall always be grateful for its existence.

There is one major issue with CBeebies though.

I sent them a letter about it:

RE: BEDTIME HOUR
Dear CBeebies,

I am writing to complain about Bedtime Hour.

Since becoming a parent I have very much enjoyed your programming. I love almost everything about it, from Hey Duggee to Andy's Prehistoric Adventures.

Yes, Abney & Teal's a bit shit, Bing's a whiny dick and the Tumble family can be a bit unsettling (I'm just going to say it: Mr Tumble, Grandpa Tumble, Polly Tumble, there's not a single member of that family that doesn't look like they keep body parts in the freezer), but generally speaking CBeebies is pretty awesome.

That said, Bedtime Hour . . .

6 o'clock?

6 o'f**king clock?!

In what parallel universe does CBeebies exist where kids are settling down for bed at 6 o'clock??!! Most kids are still crayoning cocks on the radiators at half 7!? And that's the really well-behaved ones.

Have you ever tried to get a kid anywhere near their bed between 6 and 7? They'll have your bloody eyes out. It's like trying to get a pissed and f**ked-off badger into a carrier bag. (It doesn't want to go and someone's gonna get hurt.)

Far from being bedtime, between 6 and 7 is the time when most kids' piss-taking abilities are at their most powerful. For them, it is the perfect time to go mad, face-plant off the settee, smash the place up, get out every toy they've ever owned and party like Charlie Sheen on a bender.

6–7pm is go-f**king-nuts time.

It's not just our house. I've done extensive research on this and I can categorically say that 6 o'clock is not bedtime hour in anyone's house that contains young children.

In fact, if you're interested, the hours preceding bedtime are actually as follows:

6–7pm: Negotiation Hour

7–8pm: For-f*ck's-sake Hour

8–9: 'No, how many more times, you're not watching the bloody Incredibles, it's bedtime!' Hour

9–10: 'It was your idea to have kids in the first place' Hour

10–11: Losing-the-last-dying-embers-of-your-will-to-live Hour

11–12: Bedtime Hour

12–?: 'How are you up again? What are you, a f*cking vampire?' Hour

With all due respect, I know it must seem like you've got Bedtime Hour correct because it gets massive viewing figures, but that's only because Tom Hardy sometimes does the bedtime story and half the mums in the UK are licking the screen.

In truth, four hours after you lot have knocked off – to go on the piss with Dr Ranj, Mister Maker and the cast of Biggleton – most parents are still negotiating with their mini terrorists to find out what they want in return for just going upstairs.

And the worst thing is that, without CBeebies, parents are then forced to stumble over to Nick Jr to endure American cartoons about talking cars and 'being buddies' and an endless cycle of adverts for plastic unicorns and dolls that piss and shit themselves.

Look, I'm sure there's a Topsy and Tim-type family somewhere in the Home Counties where the kids adhere to this 6–7pm bedtime hour. I'm sure these kids are tucked up beneath hemp blankets, that mommy weaved just that morning, gently dozing as daddy plays 'Let it Be' on an acoustic guitar. But not in our house, where if we can get our child to bed without a major fire or anybody dying that's a pretty good evening.

So, please, for the sake of the threadlike sanity that every parent in this nation clings to at the end of each day, do the right thing. Move Bedtime Hour to . . . let's say . . . reality.

Matt x

P.S. Oh, and not to be a dick about it, but to make matters worse you lot don't start the programmes again until 6 in the morning. This morning my son got up at 4am. He couldn't have got up any earlier if he'd invented time travel. I was that tired I couldn't feel my face . . . and where were you? Nowhere!!

If I hadn't had a couple of Go Jetters stacked up on the Sky planner I'd have thrown myself under the bin lorry at 8.

P.P.S. and thanks for 'The Stick Song' by the way, you utter barstards.

P.P.P.S . . . love you really.

So, as much as we love CBeebies, there comes a time when we have no choice but to stray from the righteous path. Away from the state broadcaster's educational programmes that teach our children about colours and numbers and the world at large. And into the wild west of channels like Cartoon Network and Nickelodeon. Channels that seem to give less of a fuck about that sort of thing.

It is here that we first gain sight of proper pre-school TV. Shows like *PJ Masks* and the two big hitters: *Peppa Pig* and *PAW Patrol*.

As a family we have somehow managed to avoid the phenomenon that is *Peppa Pig*. After watching a few episodes we'd quickly flip the channel whenever it appeared and so Charlie never got lured in. I know that there are many parents who actively try to avoid the programme too, parents whose problem with Peppa is that she, supposedly, encourages bad behaviour, naughtiness and bullying. I don't know whether that's true. My objections were more to do with it being shit.

The whole thing looks as though it is animated in Microsoft Paint and as far as I can tell every episode involves Peppa moaning about losing a game, being a dick to her mates or fat-shaming her morbidly obese father. At which point everyone stands around snorting, as presumably Daddy Pig dies a little more inside and takes himself off to comfort-eat his way to that inevitable heart attack.

Don't get me wrong, not everyone has a problem with *Peppa*. Far from it. It is broadcast in over 40 languages and in over 180 territories. Everywhere, apparently, except in our house. Where it is subject to a soft ban. A ban that will only be lifted for the very last episode, they eventually make, in which hopefully this happens:

Peppa may not be part of the background to our days in. *PAW Patrol*, on the other hand, is our fucking wallpaper. I was so pre-occupied by avoiding *Peppa Pig*, that Ryder and his team of pups sneaked in like we'd left a backdoor open during The Purge.

PAW Patrol

> ♫ *PAW Patrol, PAW Patrol, whenever you're in trouble!*
> *PAW Patrol, PAW Patrol, we'll be there on the double!*
> *Whenever there's a problem, round Adventure Bay,*
> *Ryder and his team of pups will come and save the day.*
> *Marshall! Rubble! Chase! er . . . Skye! . . . the one with the*
> *boat . . . the other brown one . . . kill me . . . kill me now . . .* ♫

It is difficult to sum up exactly how much my heart fills with leaden dread at the sound of the theme tune to this bloody programme. Because, as catchy as this tune is, it also means that we are about to go on another 'mission' in Adventure Bay. And by mission, I mean Captain Turbot has fallen off his fucking boat again.

For the blissfully ignorant, the PAW Patrol are basically five dogs who provide all emergency services for a place called Adventure Bay. It's unclear how puppies got these roles (my experience of puppies is that they don't do a great deal more than chew every-thing and piss everywhere). But in the event of a crisis, these super pups are called into action, when they assemble just like The

Avengers! (If The Avengers sniffed each other's arses and were susceptible to worms.)

Their leader is a Tony Stark-type figure called Ryder – a young
boy who apparently has no parents, lives in a state-of-the-art
surveillance tower and has access to millions and millions of dollars.
Which he wastes on kitting out dogs with military-grade hardware so
that they can fly, speedboat and drive to the rescue of whichever Bay
resident has clumsily ballsed up the simplest of tasks that day.

And that is pretty much it.

There are way too many annoying elements to *PAW Patrol* so
here are just my top five:

1. **The Pointlessness of Rocky**

   Each pup has their own speciality. There's Chase who is law
   enforcement. Marshall who provides the fire service. Rubble is a
   disaster relief engineer. Skye is air force, Zuma is coastguard,
   and then there's Rocky. Who is in charge of . . . er . . . recycling?

   Of all the pups, Rocky is the shittest and rarely involved in a
   mission. As Ryder assembles the pups and allocates tasks it
   becomes abundantly clear why:

   'Chase, I'll need you to set up a perimeter; Rubble, I need
   you to clear up the damage, Skye, I need you to provide air
   support. Er . . . sit this one out, Rocky, eh? We don't need
   anyone to sort the plastic from the fucking cardboard on this
   mission.'

   Rocky is basically a bin man.

2. **Chase's Brown-nosing**

   There is a pecking order in the PAW Patrol and if Rocky is at
   the bottom then the self-appointed leader, Chase, is at the top.
   Chase is Charlie's favourite. Apparently, he is every toddler's

241

favourite as they are too young to understand that Rubble is actually the best and Chase has brown-nosed his way to the top and is there without merit.

Unlike the others, Chase is involved in every mission. And is always the first to report for duty, standing to attention and sucking up to Ryder. 'Ready for action, Ryder, Sir!' Ugh. Just once I wish Rubble would turn around and say, 'Oh, fuck off, Chase, why don't you just climb up his backside, you arse-licking twat.'

3. Mayor Goodway

The question of where multi-millionaire playboy Ryder gets his money is a topic of some debate but the chances are it is given to him by local government, given that the town's elected mayor, Mayor Goodway, is clearly insane. Of course, she's not going to see the problem in having dogs as first-responders, the woman carries around a fucking chicken in her handbag. (She even calls it her 'purse chicken', as though that is a thing.) Mayor Goodway is inept, incapable of solving the most basic issues and has a ridiculous aristocratic accent. And just imagine the amount of chicken shit in that bag.

4. The Fake Laughter

Sporadically during the mission, one of the characters will say something that is about as funny as eczema. And, when this occurs, the pups do these horrendous fake laughs that are so cringeworthy it makes my teeth hurt. It is particularly pained and unnatural when Ryder cracks the joke. All the pups fall over themselves to fake chuckle like Ryder is their supreme leader and unless they force out a laugh they will be taken out to the back of the lookout tower and shot.

5. The Fact That It Never Stops

Eventually, by the end of each episode, the mission has played out successfully. They rescue Captain Turbot from the water or save a pterodactyl's egg, or whatever, and Ryder gathers them all together to tell them that they are 'such good pups'. They then have one last fake laughing fit and the screen fades.

And that is that . . .

Or maybe not.

♫ *PAW Patrol, PAW Patrol, whenever you're in trouble!*
PAW Patrol, PAW Patrol will be there on the double! ♫

Because it's fucking on again, isn't it. It's always on. Back-to-back episodes like a recurrent nightmare. This programme keeps coming like a T-1000 and it never ever stops.

The one saving grace is when an episode starts and you realise you've not seen this one before.

. . . Just kidding, you've **always** seen this one before.

So television, the 'electronic babysitter', is not always the key to sanity on days spent at home with your toddler. And, actually, I don't think any of us really want to park our kids in front of the TV all the time anyway. It might not be the poison we are constantly told it is, but, on the other hand, it doesn't seem the best idea to allow our kids' main social interaction to be with a body-shaming pig, a wank postman and a bunch of delusional dogs.

Maybe human interaction is preferable. And maybe on days in, if the worst should come to the worst, you could always try playing with your toddler?

Playtime

When it comes to spending a day at home playing with Charlie we have more than we need.

In one corner of our living room is a play kitchen. In another, on a shelf, Iron Man, Thor and The Hulk sit assembled and in a line, ready to save the Earth. In another corner is a seven-foot inflatable dinosaur that looks on nonplussed as a foil Minion balloon floats by like a ghost. And this is just the stuff that is visible. There are also toy boxes stacked against the wall that groan with train tracks and jigsaws and blocks and cars that transform into robots (and robots that transform into cars).

The fact that Charlie has so many toys isn't entirely our own doing. Do we buy Charlie too many toys? Absolutely. But the problem is exacerbated by the fact that all the parents we know have kids who are older. So our house is the perfect place to offload all their old toys too. And so friends and acquaintances pull up outside our house periodically with bin liners full of more robots that transform into cars (and cars that transform into robots) which they hand over with glee and then drive off at speed to return to their own house which is now wonderfully less cluttered with this shit. Cheers.

I know this sounds ungrateful but add to this the new influx of toys from friends and relatives that occurs on each special occasion and I worry that we are one Christmas or birthday away from the sheer weight of all this crap causing a sinkhole beneath our house and our home falling through the Earth's crust.

The obvious answer to this problem is to do as our friends do and pass our own unloved toys on to other families. But as I said, most of our friends have children who are much older than Charlie. (I mean some of these kids are at university. So I somehow doubt

244

that they would appreciate a Rusty Rivets robo-tiger, even if it does come with the flashing eyes.)

The other alternative is to send unused toys to the charity shop. But have you ever tried to put a toddler's possession into a charity-shop bag? That long-forgotten toy suddenly becomes precious treasure and they react like you are donating their spleen.

So from exciting electronic playthings to educative and expensive games, Charlie has a LOT of toys.

And Charlie's favourite toy at the moment? This spatula.

A spatula. Despite the incredible volume of sophisticated toys in our home that are designed to engage and entertain our child, my son prefers to play with a plastic kitchen utensil that can literally do no more than turn over an egg.

It's not even a good spatula.

And this is not the weirdest thing he has ever enjoyed playing with. A while ago, his favourite thing to play with was a carrot. A fucking carrot. One Sunday, Charlie's granddad, whilst making dinner, showed him a particularly misshapen carrot which looked like it had a nose. This then became Charlie's new best friend. It was called Nobby and he carried it around for a whole month, playing with it like it was an Action Man. To make matters worse, this was around Christmas and so Nobby was involved in the countdown to

Santa. Whilst every normal parent was spending their evenings moving around Elf on the Shelf, I was moving around Nobby, a slightly deformed, slowly rotting vegetable that by Christmas Eve was turning black and beginning to smell like a vegan's arsehole.

At this point, I was beginning to think that Charlie was taking the piss, making a mockery of the small fortune we spend on things for him to play with. But, apparently, this is quite normal. I have spoken to many parents whose kids also make toys of the oddest things. Toilet roll, sandpaper, a cheese grater, an unopened tin of chopped pork, a frying pan, and one mum whose little girl wouldn't go anywhere without her favourite toy: a potato in a discarded envelope.

One thing is clear, when it comes to playing with your toddler: filling your house with the latest toys and gadgets is not the answer. Most toys are unable to hold their interest for long. One day it's a Power Ranger or a Hatchimal, the next it's a spatula or a root vegetable. The vast majority of a kid's toys are disposable and transient.

But there is an exception, one constant toy, their very favourite toy:

You.

The pain of play

Play time is such a magical time for bonding and interacting with your child, I thought this morning, as we entered the second hour of me and Charlie playing 'wrestling' – a game that follows none of the rules of any particular wrestling federation but actually just involves Charlie climbing to the highest point on our living room furniture and then hurling himself off to piledrive into my testicles.

It is surprising the number of games we play that include this kind of infliction of pain. 'Playing pirates' is another good example. Far from a game that evokes the swashbuckling age of buccaneering adventure, it is more likely to be an hour or so of Charlie just twatting me with a plastic sword, whilst occasionally squinting and shouting 'Aaarrgh'. To mix things up he will, every now and again, demand that I stand on the arm of our sofa and then insist that I 'walk the plank' whilst jabbing me in the arse with the same sword.

Even playing at being a doctor is not a safe zone. Charlie has his own play medical set and he uses it like a torture kit. Taking my temperature means opening wide and then being forced to deep-throat a thermometer. And I made the mistake of showing him that the little plastic hammer in his kit was used to test reflexes by tapping the patient gently on the knee. He has more of a tendency to try and hobble me with it like Kathy Bates in the film *Misery*. I find myself playing this game having to constantly remind my son of the Hippocratic oath to 'first do no harm'.

It isn't just this random violence that is the problem with playtime. It's the dictatorial way in which children order you around and the abstract rules to games that make no sense. And let's not forget the cheating. Kids **really are** cheating little shits.

For example, whenever Charlie picks two toys to have a scrap with each other, he always picks something for himself that's dead hard. He then gives me something proper shit that doesn't stand a chance. I've spent many afternoons begrudgingly playing 'Dinosaur versus Noah's wife'.

I'm sick of it, it's complete bullshit.

It's the same sort of scam when we play our version of 'cops and robbers' using Buzz Lightyear and Evil Emperor Zurg action figures.

It's not simply the fact that I am always forced to be the weakling or the baddie, it is also that the rules change halfway through the game. Charlie can shoot me from the other side of the room and demand that I die theatrically. But I retaliate from point-blank range with my own imaginary laser and he insists: 'You missed.''. . . How did I miss, you little shit?! I'm seven centimetres away!?' I've been heard to shout, before Lyns pops her head around the door to remind me that I'm in my forties.

The thing is, people talk about playing **with** toddlers but often that's not really what is happening. A lot of the time you are just a prop in their play or an actor for them to direct. And God forbid you ad-lib or go off-script.

'You HAVE to be Evil Emperor Zurg and I'll be Buzz Lightyear.'

'Okay, I'm Zurg!'

'No! Do the voice.'

'Okay, I'm Zurg!' [*in character*]

'No, it's not Zurg! It's Evil Emperor Zurg. You have to say "I'm Evil Emperor Zurg and I will destroy you!"'

'Okay, I'm Evil Emperor Zurg and I will destr—'

'NO YOU WON'T! I'M BUZZ LIGHTYEAR! BASH BASH BASH. You're dead now . . . Do you want to play again?'

'Yeah, why not?'

In these ways, playtime is not always as enjoyable as it is depicted on the box. But other times it is. There are days I spend with Charlie when we make elaborate dens from blankets and pillows. There are days when we treasure hunt or hide from rampaging T-Rexes in the cupboard under the stairs. This sort of playtime is weirdly wonderful and – that strangely non-adult word – fun. And it is not hard to see what the difference is between days when playing can be a grind and days when it is something wondrous. The difference is me.

On days when I invest in the game, no matter how ridiculous, those are the times when play is at its most enjoyable for both of us. Toddlers sense when you're half-arsing it and when you can't be bothered they treat you with the disdain you deserve. But if you release your inner idiot and buy into their nonsense with enthusiasm, they open up their world to you. And it's quite a world to get lost in.

Imagination

In 1991, a scientist called Harris carried out an experiment that involved forty-eight toddlers. Half of the toddlers were individually presented with an empty box and told to imagine that inside was a lovely, cuddly puppy. The rest of the toddlers, when shown their box, were told that they should imagine that inside was a monster. The experimenters would continue to reaffirm that the box was in fact empty, and the kids would agree that this was true and all this was just pretend and make-believe.

When the scientists made some excuse, exited the room and observed the child left alone with their empty box, they discovered something interesting. The toddlers who had been told to imagine a puppy would approach the box and peer excitedly inside. The toddlers asked to imagine a monster would shy away from the box and not go near it at all.

Imagination is never more powerful than at this age, when the line between fantasy and reality is so thin as to make an empty box a magical doorway.

Charlie might prefer a spatula or a carrot, but how many times have you said or heard a parent joke that having bought their kid an expensive present they prefer to play with the empty box? Watching Charlie play, the reason for this is pretty obvious. It isn't an empty box. It's a doorway, a pirate ship, a castle or a dinosaur's belly. It's a racing car and a cave. And it's also a place where a monster or a puppy can spontaneously come to exist simply by the power of believing that such a thing is possible.

vs Reality

I think this is the key to surviving and maybe even enjoying playtime. Enjoying not toys but the universe-sized toy box of your child's imagination. Not going through the motions but embracing and submitting to the foolishness and absurdity of it all and doing so without distraction.

Playing without distraction, though, is not always possible. I'll be the first to admit that there are days when playing can feel like a bit of a chore. Sometimes I'm just tired. Sometimes I'm preoccupied by the everyday. Sometimes the house is too much of a tip to ignore the things that need to be done. There are times when I'm just too busy to hide from dinosaurs.

I can't always do much about that. For Charlie it is always playtime but not for me. But I have learned on those days when I can't be part of Charlie's universe that I should be careful not to tread on it. Because universes can be fragile things.

I remember one day being at home with Charlie and being stressed with the amount that I needed to get done, the seemingly insurmountable number of boring chores that had accumulated. And Charlie, desperate to play, was sat in our laundry basket and refusing to get out. It was, he said, a spaceship.

Tired and exasperated I told him that it **wasn't** a spaceship. I told him that it was, in fact, a laundry basket. A basket that we used to put the washing in, to hang out on the washing line, and that I needed it.

It took some persuasion but eventually Charlie conceded. He reluctantly stepped out of his space rocket and I was able to carry on with what I was doing.

A couple of hours later, and with things less fractious and busy, we were playing in the living room and I suggested that we might use his spaceship in the game. Without a moment's hesitation he replied that we couldn't do that for a very simple reason, because it wasn't a spaceship. It was, he said, a laundry basket.

A basket that we used to put the washing in.

In that moment I felt like an arsehole, monumentally pathetic and petty. That I could take something otherworldly and make it so ordinary, without even thinking, felt shameful. Only the worst kind of bonfire-pisser would shoot down a spacecraft like it is nothing.

It was a hard lesson, and I promised myself that in the future I would try to make sure that I never say something quite so stupidly grown-up in his presence again.

It took a while for Charlie to be convinced that the wash basket was, in fact, a spaceship after all. It required a convoluted story about how it was in disguise. About how it may appear to be a plastic basket but this was merely its camouflage. We had to add bits of cardboard and tinsel for him to be absolutely convinced, but it was worth it.

Playtime can so often seem pointless. We are conditioned by adulthood to think of play as a waste of valuable time, when we could be doing other super-important adult stuff. But this one incident taught me something incredibly valuable about playtime, about our days in and about this spell – in every sense of the word – of time we have with our kids:

The ironing pile, the mess, the bills and the stress of unanswered emails, all of it, in one form or another, will always be there.

The opportunity to go to space in a laundry basket? That won't be.

SO, DAYS IN

As a parent, days in have their advantages. A day indoors means a day not having to face the judgements of others when your toddler has a nuclear tantrum. A day in means not having to worry about other parents and their awful, germ-ridden, unruly kid coming into contact with your own awful, germ-ridden, unruly kid. It means not having to deal with dragging your child from a park or soft play, or having to fold them kicking and screaming into a car seat when they find themselves too tired to go home. It means not having to fight to get your toddler to wear gloves or a hat, or any clothes for that matter. And not having to worry about running into a soft-play Berzerker or a chlamydia-riddled koala or worry about your little companion shitting themselves in the queue in Argos.

Let's face it, being a parent to a toddler in the outside world is no picnic. Even if it is a picnic.

But days in are not straightforward either. Toddlers are like forest fires, they are not easily contained and within four walls it can feel relentless and exhausting in the attempt.

The worst of these days can feel like the clock on the wall that ticks, then takes an eternity to tock. There are days when sneaking off to the toilet is the only chance for a break or enjoying a secret biscuit eaten over a sink is the only treat. And like an animal in a trap who chews off their own foot to get free you would do anything to escape half-arsing your way through yet another game of 'dinosaur versus Noah's wife'.

It is not all ordered playtime, baking and arts and crafts. If only the Instagram lies were true. If only all days at home were so simple, so sweet, so harmonious, so ordered and calm.

Nah, fuck that.

Our days in with Charlie are rarely calm. They can be harum-scarum and anarchic, annoying and amusing in equal measure. And sometimes unreasonably long. But that's because home isn't just where the heart is, it's where the whole nervous system is. It's where we live, argue, be human, be stressed, bored and make mistakes.

Whether we're trashing the living room by building a den, baking inedible cookies, arguing about socks, sword fighting to the death or lying under a duvet on our sofa watching *Toy Story* for the thousandth time, I can look out at the world as it passes our window and do so with some contentment.

Because I know that should the world look back, it may well see and hear the sounds of exasperation, of temper and frustration, but it will also see and hear the rhythm of our family. The sounds of beautiful chaos, an honest love, music and, more often than not, laughter.

. . . Punctuated, only occasionally, by the anguished cry of a man having his testes body-slammed by a relentless three-foot-tall lunatic.

Oof.

9
What is a Dad?

Here's a weird thing: when you're a man on your own, some people assume that you can't possibly be in charge of a baby or toddler. Twice now someone's had a go at me for parking in parent/child spaces when I've actually got Charlie in the back seat. They see a man pull in and assume that I am just another childless dickhead taking advantage of the space.

I was in Asda car park just last month when, upon arrival, a woman knocked on my window before I could even turn the engine off.

'Excuse me! You know these spaces are for people with children?' she demanded.

I literally had to point my thumb in to the back of the car and say: 'What's that? A fucking cat?'

What is a Dad?

It is odd that in 2019 so many people struggle to comprehend the idea of dads being in sole charge of their own kids.

As a man who often has Charlie on my own I come across this attitude all the time. It's usually not malicious, just ingrained. And so I might be asked things like: 'Ooh, is it daddy and son day today?' or 'Ah, bless, are you giving Mummy a break?' These questions are normally asked with a patronising nod – as though I am being humoured – like I'm the local fuckwit taking his pet brick for a walk.

When Charlie was very little, I was even asked a couple of times if I was 'being mummy for the day'. To which I was tempted to respond, 'Yes, apologies for the damp circles on my Def Leppard T-shirt, I'm currently lactating.'

This last example I find one of the strangest. It speaks volumes that there are people, in this very century, who would describe a man parenting as 'being mummy for the day'. As though dads are not really parents but temporarily assuming the role and just putting on a costume like Mrs Doubtfire.

One thing is certain, Lyns would never be asked the same questions: 'Is it mummy and son day today?' or 'Aww, bless, are you giving Daddy a break?' It just wouldn't happen. There is a sense that this is the correct order of things.

Another variation on these questions I'm asked is: 'So, where's Mummy today?' This seems like a pretty innocent enquiry. But again, I doubt Lyns would ever be asked the same thing, just because she is out with Charlie alone. In truth, the subtext to this is obvious: 'Where's the **real** parent today, numbnuts?'

I remember that the first time I was asked this particular question was by a cashier in Home Bargains and it confused me completely. When she casually inquired 'Where's Mum today?' I genuinely thought she must know my **own** mother and was actually asking about **her**. It's no wonder she looked so confused when I answered that she was at home and that she'd just phoned me to say that her arthritis was acting up, the neighbours were still acting suspicious and she couldn't find her teeth.

(It is only in hindsight that I understand the cashier's horror. Particularly when from her point of view I went on to mention that we'd just celebrated my wife's seventieth.)

Babysitting?

Interestingly, Lyndsay is also asked questions that I would never hear if the positions were reversed. So if she is out alone and without Charlie she will often be asked: 'Is Dad/Matt **babysitting** today?'

Okay, I object to being called a 'babysitter' for a few reasons. Not least because I'm a forty-odd-year-old man and not a fifteen-year-old girl with braces, twirling her hair and covering her school books with pictures of Zayn from One Direction because he's super dreamy (although, in fairness, he is super dreamy).

But my main problem with being called a babysitter is that it is to be considered something less than a parent. When I have Charlie I have exactly the same responsibilities that Lyndsay does. Important stuff like feeding him, watering him, changing him, making sure he doesn't jump off a motorway bridge chasing a fucking bee, that sort of thing. And yet whereas Lyndsay is parenting, I can be described as 'babysitting'.

And these are not my only objections. I also object because, and forgive me if I'm wrong, but one of the defining characteristics of a 'babysitter' is that they get paid. I do not get paid for looking after Charlie. Fair enough, I could write something touching here about how every moment with Charlie is priceless and I am paid in the glowing love of my child. But, yesterday I was 'paid' by being shat on in Debenhams and by Charlie pouring his Ribena down the arse of my jeans as I was trying to retrieve a plastic stegosaurus from under the settee.

And this is the point: it's hard this dad-babysitting lark, almost as hard as parenting. In fact, it **is** as hard as parenting because guess what? When I'm being shat on in Debenhams or lying on the floor having pissing Ribena poured down my arse-crack . . . it's exactly the same fucking thing.

For me, a father is not a babysitter any more than a mother is. And there is a growing movement, that includes mums and dads, who agree that it is impossible to 'babysit' your own children. I'm not particularly militant about this sort of thing but they've got a point. Their slogan is 'Dads don't babysit, they parent' and this is not just semantics. There is a problem with reducing a father to the role of babysitter and it's not just that it might hurt a dad's feelings (we can handle that shit, we're men and into car engines and stuff . . . grr).

The real problem is that it suggests that a dad's role is something lesser. That it is a novelty for a dad to look after his own kid. It is something outside the natural order. And those who suffer most from this attitude? Mums. It reinforces the idea that dads are a backup plan rather than 50/50 partners in parenting, the secondary alternative for when mums, like Lyns, want to go off and do something really selfish like be ill or work. Dads are the spare.

Well, Lyndsay isn't selfish. I'm not the spare. And I don't babysit.

Women's Work

It's not hard to see why the idea persists that parenting is more of a mum thing than a dad thing. There are signposts directing this traffic wherever you look. Whether it's the baby-changing facilities that are only available in the ladies' toilets or the fact that parenting brands are almost exclusively aimed at women. (I mean I don't expect Pampers to have a picture of a bearded brickie on the front, but you know what I mean.)

And think about almost every support network available to new parents: Mumsnet, netmums, madeformums, these are forums that discuss parenting issues but encourage (if by name alone) the idea that nappy changing, weaning, potty-training and all that . . . Well, that's mum stuff and not dad stuff.

When I first became a dad and searched online for advice I was constantly referred to these sites. And yet upon arrival it often felt like I was intruding. There was barely another dad in sight and when I logged on that very first time I noticed subtle hints that, as a man, maybe it wasn't the place for me.

Trending on that day was the thread:

'AIBU to put Bonjela on my fanjo.'*

and a post simply entitled:

---

* These forums are a bit daunting anyway, partly because they have their own language. AIBU means 'Am I being unreasonable' (the answer is always 'yes'); FWIW: 'For what it's worth'; DH: 'Dear Husband', etc., etc. So for example comments read stuff like: 'FWIW I had exactly the same problem with DH when I was EBK with my DD! IKWYM!' Basically, you need to be a Navajo code-breaker to work out what the fuck is going on. (It's not always worth the effort, by the way. I spent ages working out one thread and it turned out to be a woman complaining that next door's cat was pissing on her bins.)

'Fanny Condensation'.

These are the largest parenting communities in the world but being a dad in there, stumbling around, it can feel like being a stranger in a strange land.

Don't get me wrong, I get it. Mums deserve these support networks. Mothers deal with the lionesses' share of the hard bits of being a parent, not least pregnancy and giving birth (no one should ever complain about the amount of support provided for a human who has done the equivalent of shit a pineapple). But, again, it's not hard to see how, even in the modern online world, the idea that parenting is not for men is unavoidable.

It's not any of these organisations' fault, they are a reflection of society and there are still large numbers of people who believe that child-rearing is very much a woman's role, that women are just naturally inclined to be more loving and nurturing than men, who struggle with this sort of thing because our hairy balls, beards and love of sports get in the way.

WMs and SAHDs and WTF?

Nothing stirs these attitudes like discussions about 'Working Mums', 'Full Time Mums' and 'Stay at Home Dads'. Whenever this subject crops up in comments and forums it doesn't take long before someone chimes in with the opinion that mums should always stay at home. That mothers should take primary responsibility for raising their children and not because they want to, but because they are supposed to. The very fabric of society depends upon it. Goddammit, women! Mums not staying at home any more is the reason why our children are all eating Ariel Liquitabs and don't know where France is!? . . . or something.

When these comments slide into the discussion with the apparently innocuous words 'In my opinion . . .' or 'To be honest . . .' or my personal favourite 'I'm not being funny, but . . .' you know the sort of attitude that is to follow. (And no, you're not being funny SheilaMom68, you're kind of being a prick.)

> 'I am a firm believer that if a family can afford to keep the mom at home, then that is her role in the home. I do know that some moms still need to get out and do something part time, and that's fine. But again, a mother's role is to put her husband first, then her children and her home and lastly her job.' – MommaBear2

> 'Why have a kid if you just hand them off to someone else to raise them? There are occasional circumstances where a mom has to go out to work, husband becomes disabled for example, but those are rare. Most women do not need to work so they make up stupid excuses about working making them better moms (like not being with your kids makes you a better mom) or daycare socializing their infants but it doesn't change the fact that they're terrible excuses for mothers. If you love your child you will stay home and raise them. If you don't care then feel free to fob the poor innocent child off on someone else.' – BCMember

> 'The problem with children today is that so many mothers put their so-called careers before their children!' – SheilaMom68

Blimey.

Hang on, SheilaMom68. For a start, not everyone has the option of not working. Some mums have to work if they wish to provide their children with wacky and fun things like food and a roof.

261

Also, believe it or not, some women **like** to work. They gain fulfil-ment and purpose from it in the same way that some men do. For what it's worth, I personally think these people are crazy. I would happily never work another day in my life and sit around in my pants watching *Bargain Hunt* and eating Space Raiders all day, every day, until I die. But you know what, SheilaMom68? We have something in common: it's none of our fucking business. Just saying, to be honest, in my opinion, not being funny, lol, #nooffence.

Stay-at-home Dads

Of course, if circumstances allow and you choose to be a full-time stay-at-home mum, then all power to you. Christ knows, it is a job and a half. (And without all the perks associated with a regular job like pay, lunch breaks, holidays and being able to photocopy your arse at the Christmas party.) But judgements about whether mums should or shouldn't work ignore the realities of modern life. And I dunno, maybe we should be guided by our own views of family and our own personal situations, rather than what the likes of SheilaMom68 thinks is best from her viewpoint in the 1950s.

Outdated and judgemental attitudes like this no doubt contrib-ute to the fact that there are so few households in which men are the ones who stay at home. But there are other reasons too.

Cash is a major factor. Men statistically find themselves in higher positions at work and on average are still paid more. So it's just less of a blow to the bank balance for dad to return to work. And a lot of families cite this as the main reason why they do.

But times are, of course, changing . . . a bit.

Over the past few decades, slowly and very unsurely, society has started to realise that it may be wrong that men do earn more than women and that this shouldn't automatically be the case. That maybe, just maybe, men shouldn't necessarily rise to power and earn more just because they can piss standing up. And that maybe this whole system is a bit like taxing vaginas.

So as we head blindly into this brave new world (in which more and more women are being allowed to have a crack at dead-important manjobs), an admittedly small but increasing number of men **have** begun to assume the traditional role of stay-at-home parent. In fact, tiny though that total amount may be, the number of stay-at-home dads has nearly doubled in the past twenty-five years.

There's now about seven of us.

For my own family, it was a fairly straightforward decision. At the time that we decided Lyns would go back to work full time I was a struggling graphic designer doing a job that I hated. There was none of the glamour I'd imagined when I took up the role. I thought I would be creating clever marketing campaigns for big brands. But, as it turned out, my last job – before I quit – was for a company called KleenerDrive. Which was a man called Ian who power-washed driveways and wanted me to photoshop the weeds and cat shit out of twenty-four photos of block paving.

Before   ***After***

(Smashed it.)

Lyns, on the other hand, had/has a job that has a profound effect on people's lives. I am proud of what she does for a living in a way that I've never told her. She doesn't take compliments easily and would no doubt wrinkle her nose and say 'Shut up, nobhead' (such things are the reasons why we are made for one other). But she works for an organisation that gives people a second chance. Sometimes those people have had their lives destroyed by addiction, homelessness and even war. And through the power and impossible energy of education their lives can be transformed.

So Lyns went back to work. Because, here's the thing: when it comes down to a couple's choice between who should return to work full time and who shouldn't, maybe that's not a decision to be made based on who has the bigger tits?

Manhood/Dadhood

There is yet another reason why there are not that many stay-at-home dads around. There's no doubt that mums suffer judgement for stepping outside the home but men can receive the same treatment for stepping in.

When you speak to stay-at-home dads they talk about something called the 'Mr Mom' effect. They often complain that they are seen as 'girly' and effeminate for taking on the 'role of mum' as though it is somehow to be less of a man and unnatural.

Obviously, this is nonsense. There are plenty of men who rise to the challenge of parenting, sometimes alone and for all kinds of reasons. And the idea that it is somehow unnatural is not borne out by nature. Lots of animals from marmosets to wolves are involved dads and some are even stay-at-home types like the penguin. The male emperor penguin is solely responsible for protecting their chick's egg during the Arctic winter. And not only does he do a great job, he does the whole thing in formal eveningwear, looking sharp as fuck.

But there remain those who believe that women are just better designed to look after children, they are soft and squidgy whereas men are better suited to eating red meat, urinating on toilet seats and reverse-parking efficiently.

I talked about how ridiculous all this is on a blog post and I received a message from a guy who described me as 'pathetic'. He went on to suggest that it was my kind of politically correct, leftie attitude that was responsible for the breakdown of society and for men 'going soft'. He was of the opinion that women naturally belonged in the home and that men should 'hunt and gather' as this was in **our** nature. (I clicked on David's profile to see what this particular hunter/gatherer did for a living. He works in IT.)

It's an understatement to say that some people are extraordinarily confused by all this 'being a real man whilst being a dad' stuff. And not just with regard to SAHDs but 'hands-on'* dads, generally. If you think that David is a little befuddled, how about the guy in October 2016 who found himself in the news because he had announced to his wife that he would not be changing his son's nappies because – and I quote – 'it's gay'?†

These are extreme examples of attitudes you sometimes come across when living a life online. You need no licence to use the internet and that means that even those amongst us with brains that don't get quite enough oxygen are allowed to drag their knuckles along a keyboard in expression of a dim opinion.

But in more mainstream media, this confusion between manhood and dadhood rears its head all the time too.

Piers Morgan caused some controversy earlier this year when he suggested that it was 'emasculating' for a man to wear a baby carrier. He mocked James Bond himself, Daniel Craig, and suggested that he was less of a man for choosing to carry his own little girl in this way.

Don't get me wrong, I completely understand why Piers has a terrible fear of being emasculated himself. Emasculation means the removal of the male sex organ and the man is about 98.9 per cent dick. If you removed everything of Piers Morgan that could be considered 'penis' you'd be left with just his fucking socks.

But this is a weirdly outdated opinion to hold about men in 2019.

---

* Another weird term that only ever refers to dads. 'He's a real hands-on dad' as opposed to what? A dad who parents his kids by levitating them around the house using the power of his fucking mind?

† I mean, in a way he's right. Same-sex parents are statistically much more likely to share the burden of looking after children equally, but I don't think that's what he meant.

Pleasingly, there was a fair old backlash. Celebrity dads shared pictures of themselves 'baby-wearing', including Captain America, Chris Evans. And I myself received lots of pictures from mums of their husbands and partners happily carrying their little ones in slings and baby carriers.

Look at these big girl's blouses:

(Incidentally, I was asked to go on *Good Morning Britain* to talk about this and politely declined, but I'm now thinking that I should've sent the 'unmanly' fella in the middle on in my place. It would've made great telly to see him rip out Piers Morgan's spine on live TV and hold it aloft like *Predator*.)

The sad thing is that Piers and our weird IT guy David are not alone in holding these strange, outdated and dusty ideas about manhood and dadhood, and when they manifest in real life it can be pretty depressing.

One of the most disheartening things I've seen recently was when I was wandering down our high street, and I saw a dad batting away his son's hand as he reached out to hold his, saying, 'You're a big boy now, you don't need to hold hands.' The kid was about ten and clearly saddened by this. But this guy thought that it was somehow less than manly to even hold hands with his boy, he thought it embarrassing. What complete and utter crap.

In the end, I know very little about this leaking, mutinous and wayward parenting boat that we find ourselves on. But I do know this: if your ten-year-old kid wants to hold your hand, hold his hand. The days when he wants to are disappearing, the days when he will find **you** embarrassing are due any time. And not to get all 'Cat's in the Cradle' but if you don't take his hand now, the day will come when he doesn't reach out at all. Hold his hand, dipshit.

Father's Day/Man Day

One of the institutions that encourages this misguided, gruff, tough-guy masculinity about what it is to be a dad is that supposed celebration of fatherhood, Father's Day. (A day so wrapped up in traditional ideas of what it means to be a man, it might as well have a brand logo of a bloke with a pint of bitter in one hand, fucking a bear.)

I remember my second Father's Day as a dad. I don't really remember the first one. Charlie was just six months old at that time so we were still in the daze of early parenthood, when bewilderment and lack of sleep turns you into dribbling wreckage.

So my second Father's Day actually felt like my first. It was certainly the first when I felt something like a parent. Strange, then, that it was this day that made me question my dad credentials all over again.

In the run-up to Father's Day almost every 'what to buy dad' list includes a 'day at the track' or a cordless screwdriver. It's a day for which the marketing and thinking is stuck in the seventies, when all blokes wanted was power tools and a go in a sports car. It's a miracle that these lists don't still include a 'big norks' calendar and a VHS video boxset of *The Sweeney*.

And when these tired old lists come under headings like 'What every man wants for Father's Day' it pisses me off. 'Every man' is no more a thing than 'every woman' is. And the fact that I have no interest in half of the stuff that I'm supposed to seems designed to make me feel like Father's Day is actually a celebration of manliness to which I'm not really invited.

I'm not particularly interested in sports cars, not that bothered about cultivating a beard or brewing my own ale. And I'm certainly not interested in power tools and DIY.

Here is a picture of my last attempt at flat-pack furniture, for Christ's sake.

I'm still not entirely sure what it was supposed to be.

If you want an even clearer example of how I am not **that** guy, a few months ago I got chatting to two blokes who were welding some railings across the road from our house. I stupidly tried to pretend I knew what they were talking about, and when it became obvious I didn't have a clue, I came clean and joked that, to be honest, the only stuff I actually knew about welding came from watching the 1983 film *Flashdance*. To make matters worse they hadn't seen the bloody film. So I then spent the next twenty minutes explaining to two hairy-arsed welders the plot to *Flashdance*: a tear-jerking romance in which talented dancer (and welder) Jennifer Beals dreams of a career in ballet but must overcome . . .

. . . Oh for fuck's sake, I'm not explaining it again.

Anyway, the point I'm trying to make is I'm not what anyone would describe as a man's man. I enjoy a Pornstar Martini, I struggle to grow a moustache, I once cried watching *Pitch Perfect 2*. And all these things are no good reason why I should feel an outsider to the tradition of Father's Day.

Even greetings cards are stuck in some sort of time-warped idea of what a father should be. I came across one the other day that had this verse in it, a poem simply called 'DAD'.

'DAD'.

"God took the strength of a mountain,
The majesty of a tree,
The warmth of a summer sun,
The calm of a quiet sea,
Then God combined these qualities,
And then there was nothing more to add,
He knew His masterpiece was complete,
And so, He called it - Dad".

And this is what I mean. That doesn't sound like me at all. I may have the warmth of a summer sun and the calm of a quiet sea but the strength of a mountain? I once dislocated a finger opening a jar of pickled onions.

To be honest, this caveman manliness crap is just not me. And it's time Piers Morgan, IT Dave and Father's Day caught up with a world in which men don't have to be defined by their love of contact sports and machinery.

Because you can ask my little boy. I may not be a real man, but I am a real dad.

Stick that in your fucking greetings card.

The Crappy Daddy

In the end, it's not hard to see how dads can get a bit confused about what it means to be a father. We are told that it is a woman's job, that it's okay to be a hands-on dad as long as you do it in a manly way and when you do take care of the kids you're basically just babysitting. It's no surprise that some men begin to feel like an outsider to this whole parenting thing. Especially when we are also told repeatedly how crap we are at it.

The media is filled with examples of dads being portrayed as inept and clueless, and before you say, 'Christ on a bike, Matt! You're making a career out of doing that shit,' I'd like to acknowledge that this is true. I hold my hands up. These books are about me and Charlie and not about **all** dads but I take the point.

The following is what I posted on the day that Lyns went back to work. It's hard to deny.

Man vs Baby
16th April

Tough week. Charlie's mum's maternity leave ended. So the person in our house who prevents fires etc. returned to work.. Whilst I found myself looking after our little boy properly on my own..

Its true to say that as Lyns walked out the door that first morning there was quite a few tears, sobbing, and protest-soiling.. but, in my defence, by lunchtime I had calmed down a bit.

Anyway, to alleviate Lyns' concerns about leaving Charlie in the care of a f*ckwit, I promised to keep in touch...

Obviously, I'm not the only one contributing to this idea of the clueless dad. Portrayals of fathers that are bumbling and inept are everywhere. TV and film are full of them and can be traced through screen history, from the likes of Fred Flintstone through Homer Simpson to Peppa Pig's old man, the very 'silly' Daddy Pig. And it's not just TV and film, the internet buzzes with hashtags of #dadfails and #daddydisasters. Video and photographic meme upon meme of dads retching at the sight of a soupy poo or ballsing up the most basic of tasks, from nappy changing to dressing. As though for most dads parenthood comes with a free lobotomy.

So maybe dads should be up in arms. Maybe it's about time there was a backlash against this idea of the crappy daddy in the same way that there was against all that yummy mummy bullshit. Maybe it's time that dads tackled these portrayals and assumptions that we're all clueless dickheads. In fact, maybe I should lead that charge. Maybe it's time to take a stand, to say 'No more'. Maybe I'm the hero that Gotham needs! After all, I hate this clueless dad stereotype . . .

Or at least I *would* hate this clueless stereotype if, in my case at least, that stereotype wasn't entirely accurate.

I've spent this whole chapter suggesting that dads should be treated as equal and just as capable as mums. But here's the twist . . . maybe they're not?

Don't get me wrong, there are dads out there who excel at the practicalities of parenting. Some incredible fathers who are forced to excel by circumstance. And there are, of course, the pain-in-the-arse fathers who take the whole thing super seriously and are organised and well researched – and they are just as annoying as 'perfect' mums are. They are dads who know how to swaddle, and boil quinoa, and, no doubt, if they hear a baby cry in the next village milk shoots out of their nipples.

But from what I've seen, most dads aren't like that. Sorry, but a lot of dads, perhaps even most, can be a bit shit. Let's be clear, I'm not talking about the deadbeat dads ('deadbeats' are off up the road at the whiff of the first nappy without leaving a forwarding address).

No, I'm talking about Mr Average, keen to be a modern involved parent. Good, decent men. But when it comes to dadding they are fundamentally heart-in-the-right-place muddlers.

Dads like me.

So, I really can't challenge the crap-dad stereotype . . . because I am one. And I also can't challenge it because it's not just me. We exist, and exist in numbers.

That said, don't judge us too harshly.

After all, this is all a bit new to us.

Mums, in the west at least, have long been responsible for child-rearing. For millennia, knowledge and wisdom about all this stuff has been passed down the female line. From grandmas to mums to daughters like a secret code.

My own dad's generation didn't set foot in the delivery room. Instead, they paced up and down in the waiting area with an unlit cigar. What advice could our grandfathers give us about changing a nappy when often the closest they ever got was shouting for their wife when they could smell something bad?

For years, dads have gone along to antenatal appointments and baby health checks, not as parents but as the person who holds the coats. In school, when talk of pregnancy and all that stuff cropped up, the girls were taken to the school hall to be informed whilst the boys were taken outside for a game of rounders. Even the idea of shared parental leave is less than a decade old. Of course we can be a bit crap. For most men this is a whole and brave new world for us.

Here's the thing, though: yes we're crap but we're getting better. We really are. Modern fathers are part of a transitional generation. There is no doubt that we are an improvement on the often absent fathers of yesteryear. And maybe, just maybe, we are the forerunners to the great dads of the future.

We are frontiersmen. And so I'm okay with being a bit inept and clueless. I'm okay with sharing the truth of that. And I'm okay with being tagged in photos with #daddyfails and #daddydisasters. Because I'm happy to be a forerunner to something better. And will continue trying to do my best even when my best falls well short.

And if I do nothing else right as a parent, I will at least raise my own little boy to be better at all this stuff than I am and maybe then the bungling, inept-dad stereotype can be confined to the rank nappy bin of history, where it belongs.

What is a Mum?

Okay, being a 'modern' dad has its own unique challenges and we are stumbling our way through the darkness with a torch that is brand new. A torch with a beam that gets wider and wider as we become more experienced in what it means to be a parent. But it is difficult to complain too much about the trials and tribulations of being a dad when to be a mum is that much harder.

It is no coincidence that 'to keep mum' also means to keep quiet, to shut up. Because that is so often what is expected of mothers. Shut up and keep mum about that promotion you missed out on by being on maternity leave. Shut up and keep mum about the loneliness of being at home. Shut up and keep mum about being made to feel like a pariah because you bottle-feed or breastfeed in public. Shut up and keep mum about PND or struggling to cope.

If you type into Google 'being a mum' it autocompletes as follows: 'being a mum . . . is hard'. Actually, it does the same when you type in 'being a dad . . .' but, in reality, no one really gives two shits whether I return to work soon after becoming a parent. No one is telling me to snap back my body three weeks after giving birth. I might get chuckled at for making a mess of the practicalities of being a parent, but mums face an onslaught of comments and opinions and each one offers a different reason why they are failing their children and hopelessly fucking up as a parent. In contrast, more often than not I just get a thumbs up for giving it a bash.

So being called a babysitter is irritating. Being portrayed as an idiot, inept and clueless, is maybe a little harsh and unfair on a lot of dads. And having to change a toddler on the backseat of a car because the baby changing room is in the ladies toilets is a piss-take for everybody. But all this will change. Pathetically, I doubt attitudes to mums will change quite so quickly. In the meantime, I'd suggest that mums avoid the websites and magazines that peddle this nonsense and if cornered by SheilaMom68, politely advise that she go suck a bag of dicks.

So, What is a Dad?

Okay, so what is a dad? I don't know. What is a good dad? I haven't got the faintest idea. I suspect that it's a bit like good mums. Good dads come in all different guises and flavours: working dads, stay-at-home dads, single dads, dads who strip car engines and dads who enjoy nothing more than a *Frozen* singalong.

What defines them, though, is that they want what is best for their kids. They want to protect them and teach them to be better.

And sometimes just teach them how funny it is when the ketchup bottle makes a farting noise.

I can't help thinking that what good dads have in common is that they give a fuck. Sometimes they show that in obvious ways, and sometimes not so much, but in the good dads it is always there if you know where to look.

Take my own dad, for example. He was the opposite of what the modern-day parenting professionals suggest is vital to be a good father. He wasn't a great communicator, he belonged to a generation that was reserved and hugged rarely. He was shy and wasn't just out of touch with his emotions, sometimes it felt like they orbited a different planet. But he probably taught me more about what it means to be a dad than anybody with a PhD ever could. And so I'll conclude this chapter with something I wrote about him for Father's Day.

Because, what is a dad? For me, it was this fella.

ME, MY DAD AND THE PHANTOM FLYER

When it was suggested that I write an article about my dad, and what he taught me about being a father, it seemed like a good, neat and tidy idea. Especially since he died a few years ago. When someone's died it makes the wise things they said seem a bit wiser. Yeah, this would be a good article.

But when I sat down to actually write the thing I had no idea where to start. I tried to remember all those conversations in which my old man had imparted a father's wisdom. Those times when we'd share a beer, sat beneath a starry sky as he shared some pearl of truth: 'Son, always remember that . . .' etc. (before we chinked our bottles and stared off into the distance).

277

But that never happened. We didn't talk like that. In fact, my dad? He barely talked at all.

He just didn't say a lot. He never did. He hated small talk and hated big talk even more. And the idea that we could ever have had a long father/son conversation about feelings, and all that, is such a weird idea that it makes me shift uncomfortably just thinking about it. We just didn't share that language.

So, after scratching my head and staring at a blank screen for an hour I was starting to think that what my dad taught me about being a father was . . . well, not a lot.

That afternoon I took Charlie out on his trike and (over and above the fact that I had 1200 words to write and nothing to say) it started to bother me that those father/son conversations didn't and never would exist for me and my old man. And I resolved to make sure that it wouldn't be the case for me and Charlie. I'd make sure that we shared the language that me and my dad didn't. After all, I'd read the parenting books, this being open and talking is vital stuff. It's the cornerstone of being a good dad and in turn making your own son a good father. Communication is key.

Well, maybe not.

The thing is, despite the wisdom of parenting manuals, my dad was a great dad, he was kind and generous and I never doubted for a second how much he loved me and my brother and sister . . . He just wasn't a talker. And in thinking about that, I remembered something from when I was a kid. Something that, once remembered, made me realise that my father was teaching me what it was to be a dad all the time. And he was teaching me without saying a word. And, in actual fact, words would have cheapened the lesson.

Here's a story about a bike.

In 1985 it was the height of the BMX bike craze. Every kid on our estate was doing tricks off of drop kerbs on their BMX Burner. Every kid that is apart from two: Me and Martin Ogley.

Martin Ogley was the owner of a purple Raleigh Chopper and, whilst these may be considered retro-cool now, in 1985 to be seen riding one was proper embarrassing. The kids on the estate would mercilessly rip into Martin about his shit bike at every opportunity. And despite the fact that I didn't own any kind of bike at all, I would join in. In fact, I did more than join in, I was the ringleader. I knew that by keeping the focus on Martin, I was less likely to be a target and so I harangued him cruelly. Especially when I discovered he had added a sticker to the handlebars that read 'The Phantom Flyer'. What a fucking loser.

When anyone asked where my own bike was I would lie and say that my BMX was so top-of-the-range that I didn't ride it on the street and used it only in competition. I had been telling this lie for nearly a year and whilst I knew it wouldn't hold up to scrutiny forever I wasn't too worried. Because it was coming up to Christmas and, after months of whining and badgering my dad, I was confident that a BMX would appear on the big day.

On Christmas Day 1985, my family bundled into the back of our old Morris Minor and headed off to church. (Whilst other kids got to tear into the presents first thing in the morning we could only have access to ours once we had been to morning service.) On the drive back home I was disappointed to notice Martin Ogley playing on the end of our street on what was clearly a brand new BMX. Tits.

I had been hoping for a little Christmas Day Martin-bashing whilst showing off my new wheels to the estate that afternoon. Never mind.

On returning home me, my brother and my little sister lined up outside the living room door in age-order and, as we entered, my eyes were drawn to the armchair where my own presents were piled up neatly. There, leaning against that armchair was a bike bedecked with ribbon and tinsel. And not just any bike . . .

A Raleigh Chopper. And not just any Raleigh Chopper. A purple Raleigh Chopper. And not just any purple Raleigh Chopper. You see, in the week before Christmas my dad just happened to be drinking in the local Working Men's Club with Martin Ogley's dad. A dad keen to get shot of an old bike after buying his son a new one.

Yeah. I was now the proud owner of The Phantom pissing Flyer.

For years I felt scarred by this experience. I knew we were broke, I knew we had to make do . . . but how the fuck did I end up with Martin Ogley's Chopper?

To begin with I only took the Phantom Flyer out after dark, I hid in the shadows from the other kids on the estate. Unwilling to brave the verbal slings and arrows and peculiar cruelties that form the skillset of nine-year-old boys. But soon enough the BMX craze passed and I survived.

Although it seemed catastrophic to my nine-year-old self, over the years this incident just became an amusing anecdote, and the butt of the joke became my dad. He was just out of touch. To him a bike was a bike. He was clueless. He didn't understand the back and forth of kids and the pressure of the latest trends.

Except, he did.

It wasn't until I was in my thirties that we were having a Sunday afternoon drink in that same Working Men's Club and I reminded my dad of that year, the year of Martin Ogley's Chopper. My dad listened to the story, the way that I told it, and the way I gently chided him for his complete obliviousness. I honestly thought he wouldn't remember the whole thing but he did. And so I asked him the question: How the fuck did I end up with Martin Ogley's Chopper? And my dad smiled simply, took a sip of his pint and said as though it was the most obvious thing in the world:

'Well . . . Because you were mean to Martin.'

10

Lessons

In the past couple of years I have come to realise that the learning curve of a parent is a straight vertical line. To be a parent is to be always learning, always understanding a little more. Parenting wisdom and truths reveal themselves constantly in beautifully profound lessons.

For me, today's lesson? Never challenge a three year old to a fart-off, someone WILL shit themselves.

Lessons

It's strange when you think about it, but there are no classes teaching parents how to deal with their toddler. When you are pregnant with your baby, antenatal classes are not just encouraged, it is expected that you attend. After all, you are about to take delivery of an actual live human being, you should really know which end is which, and what sort of thing will make it break.

But these classes stop there. School is out. And you are expected to make your own way in the mum and dad world as though there is nothing more the Yodas of parenting can teach you.

It is as Charlie moved from baby to toddler that this really struck me as completely mental. Baby classes are great, but abandoning you at this point is like being trained to pilot a 747, only for the instructor to parachute out of the plane just after take-off, wishing you all the best and reminding you that the toilet in Economy is blocked.

Like that trainee pilot, the parent of a newborn tries to use their slender knowledge to keep things steady, safe and at roughly the right altitude. But always looming in the distance is toddlerhood, like a mountain just waiting to be smashed into.

And smash into it we do. At about one year into being a parent, confusing lights start blinking in the cockpit, lights marked *tantrums* and *independence* and *potty-training*, and everybody on board begins to scream, says their prayers, puts their heads between their legs, and hopes for the best.

It **is** crazy then that – despite the fact that the difference between a baby and a toddler is similar to the difference between a loaf of bread and a badger – there really are no follow-up classes to get you up to speed.

There should be. A toddler class would have a thousand useful things to teach. From anger management and terrorist negotiation tactics to the appropriate response when your child first sits on a potty and does a crap that looks like a proper man-shit. Apparently, it is not 'Lyns, come and have a look at this! It looks like a dead otter.'

But the main thing that these classes could teach are simple lessons. Truths that parents of toddlers learn in the hardest of ways.

1. Being a parent to a toddler is really quite hard

One Sunday afternoon many years ago I had to get a box out of our loft. I opened the loft hatch, lowered the ladders, went up into the roof space and found the box I was after. It was full of comic books and it was heavy. Really heavy. And so the sensible thing to do was to wait until Lyndsay came home so that she could help retrieve it. But, for some reason, I thought screw that. I came into this loft to get this box and get this box I shall. So I dragged it to the opening and started to descend the ladder pulling the thing after me.

It was at this point, halfway down the ladder and with a tonne-weight in my arms, that my pyjama trousers fell down.

I know. Comedy gold.

I don't just mean they crept low on my waist or revealed a seductive glimpse of arse cleft. I mean my pyjamas, with no underwear beneath, literally fell down around my ankles.

In that instant I was living in a seventies sitcom. '*Matt* is filmed in front of a live studio audience' etc. But, instead of this amusing bit of slapstick generating canned laughter, it generated something close to horror. You have to understand, I now found myself halfway up a ladder, holding a massive weight in my arms and because of my ankle-trousers I was completely unable to move. No more able to go up the ladder as I was down.

I couldn't pull my trousers up because my arms were holding the box and if I let go of **that** it would come crashing down on me, probably crush me to death under its weight and I would be discovered on our first-floor landing hours later, assumed to have died whilst apparently having sex with a cardboard box.

I ran a gamut of emotions. There was a moment in which I found it funny, then a moment when I found it ridiculous and finally I settled on an emotion that is best described as terror. I thought, *I'm stuck here, I can't move, no one knows I'm in this situation.*

This is how it ends.

I stayed like this for what seemed like hours (it was probably minutes), in a situation that, as far as I could see, could not get any worse.

It was at this precise moment that the situation got worse. As our window cleaner appeared four feet away, cleaning the landing window with a cheerful whistle. He peered in and, seeing me standing there, gave an uncomfortable thumbs up.

Now, a normal person would have seen this as an opportunity for rescue, but not me. I simply spent the next five minutes pretending I couldn't see him. I just stood there, facing forward, on my ladder, holding a large box and naked from the waist down, whispering to myself through gritted teeth, 'Christ, Kevin, how long does it take to clean a fucking window?'

Eventually, Kevin finished cleaning the landing window, made a mockery of my attempts to seem invisible by shouting, 'Alright, mate, see you later,' and then descended his own ladder.

Somehow, after a while, I managed to shuffle my feet out of my pyjamas, kick them to one side and slowly made my way to safety with some relief. Just as Lyns arrived home early.

'Why have you got no trousers on?'

'Well, I was getting the box out of the loft and –'

'Never mind. I do. Not. Want. To. Know.'

When it comes to the past couple of years, I keep thinking about this incident. It is perhaps the closest I ever came to feeling like a parent before becoming one. Being a parent is funny and ridiculous and embarrassing and sometimes absolutely terrifying. Some days it is like being in the middle of a task that has a higher purpose but on other days it feels like carrying a huge weight and being stood halfway up and halfway down a loft ladder with your trousers around your ankles, praying that no one can see how badly you're fucking the whole thing up.

Becoming a parent **is** hard. And it comes as something of a surprise to discover that it doesn't get any easier when your baby becomes a toddler.

The thing is, as tough as the first year can be for parents, during that time we all tell ourselves the same lie. A lie that sustains us. A very simple lie: that there will come a point in the future when everything will settle down and get easier. That in a few months, we can all relax, have a nice cup of tea and get back to the normality that existed before we introduced this tiny ball of chaos into our lives. Yup . . . it'll get easier. We just have to wait for the whole baby thing to blow over.

But that isn't how it works. When the toddler years arrive they bring a whole new set of challenges. Large challenges like keeping your child safe and alive when they have no sense of danger. And smaller challenges like trying to cling to your own sanity whilst they try to put gloves on, or they are screaming the Earth in two because some other kid pressed the button to call a lift.

And then there is the greatest challenge of all, dealing with the advent of personality, attitude and defiance. Because, in case it's not clear from the rest of this book, toddlers are egomaniacs.

2. Toddlers are egomaniacs

At the beginning of this book I described toddlers as little drunk-ards. And they are, they are drunk on power. They are like little celebrities with egos to match.

Not convinced? Here is a list of requests. See if you can guess which of these things are demands from Charlie and which are genuine demands from celebrities ahead of a show:

- A fish pond
- A rainbow on wheels
- Jelly
- Cauliflower and broccoli, to be cut up and then thrown in the bin
- A ham Dairylea Lunchable
- Felt-tip pens
- A square melon
- A shark
- Plastic drinking straw
- An inflatable animal over five feet tall
- Vitamins but only the Flintstones ones
- A banana

The answers can be found below, but if you correctly guessed that Charlie requested a banana and that all the rest are the demands of celebrities, then congratulations.*

* A fish pond – Eminem. A rainbow on wheels – Will Ferrell. Jelly – Jay-Z. Cau-liflower and broccoli, to be cut up and then thrown in the bin – Iggy Pop. A ham Dairylea Lunchable – Eminem. Felt-tip pens – Slayer. A square melon – Axl Rose. A shark – Hank Williams III. Plastic drinking straw – Mariah Carey. An inflatable animal over five feet tall – DeadMau5. Vitamins, but only the Flint-stones ones – Christina Aguilera. A banana – Charlie.

Eminem loves a Dairylea Lunchable apparently. He also requested the fish pond. Christina Aguilera adores Flintstones vitamins, Will Ferrell requested the rainbow on wheels. And it was Iggy Pop who demanded cauliflower and broccoli to be cut up and then thrown straight in the bin.

You see what I mean about the similarities between ego-mad celebrities and a toddler? I mean, any of this crap could make Charlie's request list on any given day.

So toddlers are like the famous: demanding and expectant. On good days they are Lorraine Kelly and on bad days they are Mariah Carey.

And it's unsurprising that toddlers can have days when they are the worst kind of diva. They are made that way by the same process that A-listers are. For the super-famous, everything is applauded. Everything is a triumph. Every lame joke is piss-funny, every dopey piece of tea-towel wisdom they spout is profound. Celebrities break wind and the people who surround them applaud. Of course they end up with whale-sized egos.

And toddlers' egos are inflated in the same way. Toddlers announce that they've crapped and we congratulate them. We enthuse about paintings and drawings that, let's face it, are terrible. They are driven everywhere, carried everywhere, their food is placed in front of them and they can dismiss it with a wave of a hand and without a taste. We laugh at them constantly and everything they achieve is a triumph. Not only that but our mini-celebs have an entourage of mum, dad, grandpas and grandmas, aunties and uncles who worship them. And it's an entourage that also doubles as paparazzi, capturing every moment from every angle. Remember that time when he dropped his hat down the toilet? Yeah you do, here's nineteen photographs of it from twelve different angles.

And herein lies the lesson. When you treat any human being like this you risk creating a monster. One day they are requesting a banana, the next a square melon and before you know it they want a rainbow on wheels. And this is the really hard thing about being a parent to a toddler. Finding that balance between keeping them happy whilst not indulging their egos so much that they become an arsehole. That's pretty much the whole mission.

And it is hard.

3. So, it's okay to moan and bitch about stuff
Because being the parent of a toddler **is** hard it is okay to moan and bitch about it sometimes.

People may make you feel like this is not allowed. They will make comments like, 'We just got on with it in my day.' (Thanks, Brenda, I'm sure burying all your emotions was super healthy, you fucking fossil.) Or they will make comments about how you should feel nothing but #blessed to be a parent. Occasionally, they might suggest that you have no right to complain because you've got 'just the one' or 'just the two' or 'just the three' kids. This is a fairer point. I imagine the more kids you've got the harder it gets, but just because you're lifting a truck doesn't make someone else's attempts to lift a car any easier.

Besides, all this somewhat misses the point. Moaning is really good for you.

Don't believe all that bullshit about warm summer's days and a love of puppy dogs being the things that unite us. Nothing unites us like complaint. All that nonsense about 'If you can't say anything nice don't say anything at all'? That's just an invitation to be banal. Nothing bonds two spirits like the ability to agree on something being a bit shit. Whether that's the weather or your boss being a bellend.

And being united by moaning and griping about stuff is nothing new, it is part of being human. Christopher Marlowe banged on about it in 1592. He said, 'It is a comfort to the wretched to have companions in misery.' And Spanish philosopher Unamuno said pretty much the same in the 1800s: 'Whenever I have felt a pain I have shouted and I have done it publicly' in order to 'start the grieving chords of others' hearts playing.'

Now, maybe these great minds weren't talking about the pain and misery of finding your toddler has shit in a drawer of your best pans, but the principle is the same.

The beauty of moaning about what time you were woken up this morning, or that your toddler is crying about stuff that makes no sense, is that you are sharing experience, sharing a connection. And a problem shared is a problem . . . if not halved, then at least with its edges polished off.

Ironically, it is exactly what toddlers do themselves. When they are upset they vent, they rant, they cry and sometimes scream . . . and they feel better.

When parents complain, though, we feel compelled to excuse our complaints by opening every sentence with, 'I love them to bits BUT . . .' as though that qualifying precursor is necessary. It isn't. Complain. It'll make you feel better and has absolutely no bearing on the way that you feel about your child and anybody who makes you feel like it does is an insufferable cock.

I was once asked at a book event/signing whether or not I thought Fireman Sam waxed his balls. This is not, however, the strangest question I have ever been asked. The oddest question I have ever been asked was this: 'Do you even like kids?' (It was a snarky question asked by a woman who, as it turned out, had a problem with something I'd written recently.) I asked her to repeat the question and she said that I sounded forever ungrateful to be a dad, and it was unclear whether or not I even liked being a parent on account of how much time I seemed to spend complaining about it.

I gave some inane response that she had wandered into the wrong room. And did anyone else have a question that wasn't quite so bat-shit?

What I wish I'd said is this:

'Love is not a word that can hold in its pathetic consonants and vowels the way that I feel about my son. He is the only perfect thing I will ever create. But just because this is true, that does not mean he can't be a dick when it comes to putting his shoes on. It's not a contradiction to moan about the annoying stuff that children do. This does not cast shade on the way that you feel about them, they are just the details of that love: the brush strokes on a masterpiece.

'So fuck off.'

4. It's also okay to say 'fuck it' sometimes

We entertain odd ideas about ourselves as mums and dads that don't withstand the reality of parenthood. Before Charlie was a toddler I thought that maybe I could be the sort of parent who wouldn't 'spoil' their child. I would draw lines in the sand about eating vegetables and watching too much TV. We would ensure that all experiences were **educational**. And that Charlie didn't stay up beyond his bedtime and that he never slept in our bed. These were all things that we had been told were crucial.

But when your child becomes a toddler, it becomes clear that an awful lot of this stuff is what us non-academics like to call 'wishful thinking' or 'optimistic horseshit'. It's impossible to maintain this approach and, even if you do manage it, it requires a parenting plan so draconian that you take all the fun out of it.

The sheer force of will that exists in a toddler brings to a crashing halt any grand ideas we have about parenting 'by the book'.

And there **is** a book. As a new mum or dad it can feel like you are given no instructions. But you are definitely given a rulebook. It is a book full of do's and don'ts about bottle-feeding, breastfeeding, sleep-coaching, swaddling and a thousand and one ways that you can mess up. And these rules are enforced by judgemental eyes and ears and magazine articles and pushy relatives.

To begin with we try to follow these rules. But just as your child changes into a toddler, you change too. Into a parent who has had enough of this crap.

You realise that the rules cannot always be followed. That the rules are bendy. (They have to be otherwise everybody snaps.) And one day you toss aside the rulebook and you embrace a new philosophy, the philosophy of 'fuck it'.

This is the one thing that I really wish I'd been taught about the toddler years in advance. Your liberating ability and right to say, without guilt or afterthought, 'never mind', 'so what?', 'don't worry about it', 'it'll be fine' and 'y'know what? Fuck it.'

No one tells you that this is okay. We kind of have to work it out for ourselves.

I remember the exact moment that I began to embrace this philosophy. I hesitate to tell the story for fear that parenting experts will arrive in Black Hawk helicopters over my house, rappel through the windows and take my child to a place of safety. But here goes:

[*deep breath*]

Charlie . . . had a Happy Meal.

That's right. A McDonald's Happy Meal. And, in the interests of full disclosure, he didn't even have the vegetable/fruit pack thing, he had a donut instead. And before you judge me too brutally, there are some mitigating circumstances: I couldn't be arsed to cook and so I thought 'fuck it'.

Astonishingly (and this is only anecdotal evidence, obviously), it was okay. It turned out that, despite what we'd been led to believe by the great and good, giving your child a Happy Meal won't make them bleed from their eyes or make their arse fall off. In fact, Charlie actually enjoyed it. It was fine. Phew.

But this is the point. The world didn't end, and Charlie wasn't harmed, just because we did something that some over-enthusiastic types might see as 'poor parenting'.

It sounds daft but this was a moment of epiphany for me. It was like the clouds parted and we had been granted access to a world in which everything was possible and easier and better and not so guilt-ridden. And so we now say 'fuck it' to other things too. Terrible things that would send parenting gurus convulsing in horror.

We sometimes let Charlie stay up way too late. We maybe let him watch too much TV. We sometimes (every day) let him sleep in our bed in the morning. And sometimes he has a chicken nugget. Sometimes.

So what?

As a brand-new mum or dad you concede to what everybody else thinks (the books, the professionals, and everyone else) because you are afraid. But as you start to get the hang of this parenting stuff, that changes. As your child becomes a toddler they get stronger and more resilient, but so do you.

And a quiet revolution takes place. We begin to do things our own way. We lay down the books, command the experts down from their pedestals and begin to trust ourselves to parent how we see fit, in a way that works for our child, for our lives. And when the cry goes up that we are doing it wrong (that a Happy Meal is bad, that you shouldn't give in when your child wants to go on a coin-operated Thomas), that in all these ways you are 'making a rod for your own back', we start to respond, quietly at first, with: 'No. It is our rod. It is our back.'

And whilst it is easy to feel guilty about this change and easy to think that we have lowered our standards, that simply isn't true. We've just come to the conclusion that they were never our standards in the first place.

For me personally it was as Charlie began to flourish as a toddler that I found I no longer felt guilty about the way that we choose to raise him. The opinions of others have been sacrificed on the altar of a simple truth:

I am the greatest parent in the world.

Ever.

(Well, I'm in the top two.)

Yes, okay, fair enough, I am the greatest parent in the world from the point of view of only one single human being. But that's good, it's the way it should be.

And it's the same for you.

If my kid thinks that I am the best dad who has ever lived, who cares whether a Mumsnet forum disagrees, who gives a shit if the *Daily Mail*, or Carol from work, has an opinion on it.

Charlie thinks I am.

So, yeah . . .

'Fuck it.'

5. You are the most important teacher they will ever have

Schools are an incredible thing. Centres dedicated to learning, powerhouses of knowledge where your child will learn how to make a battery out of a potato and how to spell *boobs* on a calculator. But for the first four years of their existence, home is where the school is and you, the parent, are the only teacher.

And teachers inspire the smallest hearts to grow big enough to change the world. (These aren't my words, by the way, I remember it from my own school. It was on a poster on the wall of our biology classroom right next to a diagram of how to put a rubber johnny on a banana.)

Yes, it is your job to teach your child the basics: to walk and talk and dress themselves and use a spoon and not pull and stretch their penis in the bath like it's a bungee cord. And all that stuff is undeniably important but anyone can teach them that.

When it comes to being **the** most important teacher they will **ever** have, I'm talking about teaching them the really important stuff like 'don't be an arse', 'try not to be sad'.

Because that sort of stuff is more important now than ever.

Whether it's the divisiveness of Brexit, terrorism or the most powerful nation on the planet electing a man-child with all the charm and intelligence of a fucking bollard, it feels like we live in an era in which civilisation has taken a step backwards into the dogshit of stupidity, intolerance and aggression.

Throw in a new cold war, global warming and the renewal of *Mrs Brown's Boys* for a Christmas special and, yes, the portents of doom are all around. And all this makes it easy to fear for our children's future and feel pretty helpless about it all.

But one of the greatest things about being a mum or dad is that helplessness is no longer a thing. Parents are never helpless, they wield a simple but mighty power: to make our kids the best of us.

We don't despatch our children into the future, it is something that they create themselves. They're not bystanders to the future, they are its fabric. And no one has a greater impact on the motivations, the values and the ideals that a child will take into that future than a parent.

When Charlie was about sixteen months, we took him to a wildlife park and while we were there we taught him the noise that a lion makes . . . and he hasn't stopped 'rahhrrrrriinng' ever since.

And every time he 'rraaaahhhrrrrs' it occurs to me that we could just as easily have taught him that a lion 'moos' or 'quacks' and he would have accepted that as truth, as concrete fact. And it further occurs to me that there is real power in that and a responsibility that comes with it.

We could so easily teach Charlie to be ignorant and aggressive and pessimistic and fearful. But, like so many of you with your kids, we intend to teach him the opposite: to be smart and kind and funny and tolerant.

And doing this will change the world forever. It will make it better. Maybe in a grand way and maybe in a tiny sliver that no one will ever notice but it will change it and that is a fact.

And you know what? Even if it doesn't, Charlie will thank me for it because at least he won't grow up afraid and a complete dick.

For me, since becoming a dad I have never felt more optimistic about the future. I understand parents' fears for the next generation, but I refuse to accept the shit, hatred and sometimes apocalyptic pessimism that seems to have festered in the past few years.

And I will never accept that I don't have the ability to change things for the better . . . because I have Charlie, I am the greatest teacher he will ever have and this kid will not be one that quacks, this kid will be one that 'rraaahhhhrrrrrsss'.

Toddler vs Man

So, three years ago this happened.

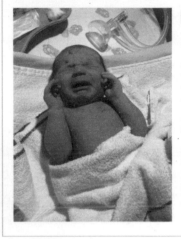

Man vs Baby
26th September

Charlie. World. World. Charlie.

Arriving this morning at 1.15am, at a fighting weight of seven pounds seven ounces and looking like an angry red potato.. 'Charlie Joseph Coyne'.

Mum and baby exhausted but doing champion, I'm beyond proud of them both.

Mark this date. If he has my looks, intelligence, charm... and Lyndsay's organisational skills and personal hygiene.. This kid could be a game-changer.

Welcome to Earth, baby boy. You could not be more welcome. x

Three years. Just thirty-six months. Say it fast and it doesn't feel like the last time I had a warm cup of tea or a piss in peace. But this also seems like a lifetime ago, because it was.

There is the me that existed before Charlie and the me after and those two versions would not recognise one another if they passed in the street. I am a different person now. Yes, I look older, tired and sometimes vaguely harassed. And if you had told me four years ago that in the future my favourite person would be under three feet tall and obsessed with farts I would have considered this quite unlikely. But I am changed much more fundamentally than that too. Because being in the presence of these weird, wild little creatures, as they go about discovering the world, how could you not be?

In this book I've written about toddlers as tyrants, drunks, petty celebrities, terrorists, infuriating and odd. And they are all of these things and more. But when you spend every day in their presence it becomes clear that what they really are is something much more impressive. They are lightning in a glass jar. They are humanity in a spark. They are a revelation. And they are the best of us.

How often do we, as adults, use our imaginations only to imagine the worst? How often do we waste our passion on things that we don't really feel passionate about? How often do we just play for play's sake? As adults we cast aside and misuse so many of humanity's finest attributes. But toddlers celebrate these things that make us human, these things that make us phenomenal and unique, and in doing so they remind us every day that when we grow up, in so many ways we shrink too.

This will probably be the last book I write about me and Charlie. I think there comes a time when this is less our story and more his own. And that seems about now. And so, as I write these last few words, I'm drawn to contemplate the future and what it is that I might want for him in that expanse. What I'd like him to know if I'm not around.

And I think that is simple: to be more toddler.

Dear Charlie,

I love you very much. This is a fact. Not like the Earth goes round the sun is a fact. Because one day it won't. Not like something written in stone is a fact because wind and rain can make the past of a fact like that. No, this is a fact like up is up and down is down. And this truth is an immovable object, a law. Like gravity or the speed of light.

And if you think that sounds unlikely, well, everything about our family is.

Let's look at the maths. We are hurtling through space on a rock travelling at 67,000 miles per hour. The chances of me and your mum meeting each other on that rock are about 1 in 20,000. Us liking each other enough to have a baby then multiplies that by about 2,000. The chances of the right egg meeting the right sperm – to make you – is about 1 in 400 quadrillion. And so on and so on, until we arrive at the statistical probability of you being born with us as your parents: $10^{2,685,000}$ to 1. That's a ten followed by 2,685,000 zeroes. More than the entire number of atoms in the known universe – 33,000 times more, in fact . . .

To 1.

To cut a long story short, our family is a cosmic impossibility, you are a miracle in a very real way. And yet . . . here we are. Mad, eh? Love is the least of it.

As I write this you have just turned three years old, and at times, I'll be honest, you can be a real pain in the arse. That's nothing personal, literally all toddlers carry this trait. (I hope one day that you will find this out for yourself and that when you do I'm stood nearby to see it.)

But you are also kind and funny and imaginative, and toddlers carry these traits too. And these are traits that a lot of people tend to lose as they get older. Which is a shame. Toddlers are better than adults in every possible way that matters.

So here it is. The purpose of this note. Here is what I hope for you . . .

I don't wish for you to be rich or famous or super smart, or that you marry into royalty or that yours is the first footprint on Mars. I wish only that you keep as much of who you are right now as possible, and carry it into the person you will become. Because who you are right now, as a toddler, is something remarkable . . .

You have no self-doubt. No shame, embarrassment or awkwardness. You think love is not something to pursue but something to share. You think rain is an opportunity and snow a wonder. Weather isn't good or bad, it's just the backdrop to the greatest show on Earth in which you are the star. You think the garden is a jungle, pebbles are treasure, a washing basket a pirate ship. You think farting is hilarious. Always. Your religion isn't something to fight over, your religion is a fat guy in a red suit, a bunny or a fairy that pays you for your teeth. You laugh without a hand to cover your mouth. Your jokes make absolutely no sense, but they are never at someone else's expense. You think peas are shit and you are not scared to say so, loudly. And you don't care if cereal is rich in fibre, only whether it comes with a free toy or is shaped like space rockets. You think money is just paper and metal. You think of home as a castle, but the nursery you go to every Wednesday and Friday? That is a place where you can fall in love between breakfast and lunchtime. Your only experience of sadness or a broken heart is a ball over a fence or a cuddly toy left on a bus. And more than anything, me and your mum wish this could always be the case . . . it hurts to know that it won't be.

We may be the greatest teachers you will ever have but you are most certainly ours.

We may have taught you how to crawl but you have taught us how to dance like complete dickheads. We may have taught you to talk but you have taught us the language of monsters. And we may have taught you how to make Rice Krispie buns, but you have taught us how to dig in our heels and be dragged through the passage of time, rather than go hurtling through it obsessed with work and money and things.

Sunshine, as much time as you have spent in the last couple of years sitting on my shoulders, the truth is that, in so many ways, it is me who has sat on yours.

I may make you a giant but you make me one too.

Be good,

Dad x

Acknowledgements

Writing a book is a weird thing. For months you sit at a desk and bash words into a computer. Words that you hope, one day in the future, someone will enjoy reading.

You are on your own most of the time. You don't get on a bus or a train or go anywhere like a normal human. You basically just sit around in your pants, unshaven, rarely escaping your dressing-gown all day, and call it work.

Thankfully, during those months there are people who stop you from going entirely insane. Individuals who stop you from going full Jack Nicholson in *The Shining*, typing 'all work and no play' – over and over again – and then chasing your wife through the snow with an axe.

These are my individuals.

Firstly, the Maverick to my Goose. The Mr Incredible to my Frozone. My agent at A. M. Heath, Euan Thorneycroft. Thank you for being a champion for my nonsense.

I'm incredibly proud to be publishing a book in A. M. Heath's centenary year. In those one hundred years they have represented Booker Prize winners such as Hilary Mantel and literary luminaries like George Orwell. And, though they wouldn't say it themselves,

I think it's understood that those ten decades have been merely building to the publication of the book you now hold in your hands. A book in which a sweary man from Sheffield describes 'shitmaggeddon' and having to be cut free from a soft-play ball pool. (Orwell must be spinning in his grave so fast he is currently drilling his way to the Earth's core.)

Thank you too to the family Wildfire. My uber-editor Alex Clarke, a man who keeps me motivated, honest and less libellous and is never afraid to give me editorial notes like 'maybe change this, it makes you sound like a proper weirdo'. And then giving me the thumbs up when I say 'naah, Alex, it'll be fine'. And to the other wildlings, Kate Stephenson and Ella Gordon who has the true patience of a saint. (Not one of the dead good saints like St Francis or Anthony. But y'know, one of the middling saints like St Bede.)

My thanks, too, to all at Headline. In particular, the marketing power-duo Jenni Leech and Jo Liddiard.

And as always, a behemoth-sized thank you to the followers of Man vs. Baby. It has been three years since I first posted about this stuff and in that time I have been given opportunities that I thought may have passed me by. And every single opportunity has come my way because you made a path for it. You are the bees' pyjamas. And should any of you need a kidney or anything you know where I am.

Thank you once again to my family. Charlie's best friend: my sister, Jo. And his second-best friend, her husband Pauly-face. To my Ma, Ron, Lorraine, I could not have written this thing without your support. (Well, I could have but it would've taken seventeen years and been **proper** shit.)

And finally, to my housemates, Lyns and Charlie. I have no idea what I did in a previous life to deserve you, but if karma is a reality

I must have been Jesus. 'Love is not a word that can hold in its pathetic consonants and vowels . . .' but I love you nonetheless.

Matt x

Sheffield, England.

*

Oh, and P.S. . . . finally, of course, thank you to God:

> ME: Hi God, I just wanted to say a massive thank-you for getting us through the baby months and now through the Terrible Twos, it's just really great to know that we're through the worst of it and that . . .

> GOD: BAHAHAHAHAHAHAHAHAHAHA!!

> ME: . . .

> GOD: . . .HAHAHAHAHAHAHAHAHAHAH . . . HAHAHAHA-HAHAHAHA . . . HAHAHAHAHAHAHA!!?? Oh fuck . . . ! You're serious! (*Wipes tear*) . . . HAHAHAHAHAHAHAHA . . .

> ME: OKAY . . . WHAT?

Matt Coyne is 44 years old and a writer from Sheffield, South York-shire. In September 2015, Matt's life was turned upside down by the arrival of his son Charlie. After three months of fatherhood, he logged on to Facebook and wrote about his experience of having to live with 'a furious, sleep-murdering, unstable and incontinent, breasts-obsessed midget lodger'. Within days, his post about sur-viving the first few months of parenthood became a viral sensation and was shared all over the world.

Following this, Matt created his popular blog Man vs. Baby, which now has over 200,000 followers. This inspired him to write *Dummy*, a book about his first year of parental triumphs and disasters, which was a *Sunday Times* Top Ten Bestseller.

Matt lives in Sheffield with his son Charlie, his partner Lyndsay and a Jack Russell terrier with 'issues' called Eddie.

Facebook: /manversusbaby
Twitter: @mattcoyney